THE KING
WITHIN

Other Books by
Robert Moore and Douglas Gillette
Coming Soon from Avon Books

THE WARRIOR WITHIN
THE MAGICIAN WITHIN

THE KING WITHIN

◆

ACCESSING THE
KING IN THE
MALE PSYCHE

Robert Moore and Douglas Gillette

AVON BOOKS ◆ NEW YORK

Permissions are listed on page 5, which constitutes an extension of this copyright page.

AVON BOOKS
A division of
The Hearst Corporation
1350 Avenue of the Americas
New York, New York 10019

Copyright © 1992 by Robert L. Moore and Douglas Gillette
Cover photo courtesy of Victoria and Albert Museum, London / Art Resource, New York
Published by arrangement with William Morrow and Company, Inc.
Library of Congress Catalog Card Number: 91-33794
ISBN: 0-380-72068-X

The William Morrow and Company edition contains the following Library of Congress Cataloging in Publication Data:

Moore, Robert L.
   The king within : accessing the king in the male psyche / by Robert Moore and Douglas Gillette.
      p.   cm.
   Includes bibliographical references and index.
   1. Masculinity (Psychology) 2. Sex differences (Psychology)   3. Archetype (Psychology)   4.   Kings   and   rulers—Miscellanea.   5.   Men—Psychology.
I. Gillette, Douglas.   II. Title.
BF175.5.M37M67   1992
155.3′32—dc20   91-33794
                                                                              CIP

Grateful acknowledgment is made to the following individuals and publishers for permission to reproduce material used in creating the figures in this book. Every effort has been made to locate the copyright holders of material used here. Omissions brought to our attention will be corrected in future editions.

Random House for permission to use the photos on pages 65 (bottom), 66 (top), 92, and 131.

William Morrow for the photos on pages 69 and 90, which were reproduced from L. Schele and D. Freidel, *A Forest of Kings*, 1991.

Metropolitan Museum of Art for insert photo 5.

Wheelright Museum of the American Indian for the photo on page 64.

Martin Sheridan for the photo on page 122.

University of Michigan for the photo on page 81, which was reproduced from Joseph Campbell, *The Power of Myth*.

Life Picture Sales for the photo on page 108.

University of Chicago Press for the photos on pages 64 (top), 48 (bottom), and 144.

Baron Hugo Von Lawick for insert photo 1 and the photos on pages 54 and 55.

J. B. Pritchard for the photos on pages 31, 66 (bottom), and 135, which were reproduced from *The Ancient Near East*, Vol. I: *An Anthology of Texts and Pictures*, 1958.

Bishop Museum, Honolulu, for the photo on page 48 (top), which was reproduced from Joseph Campbell, *The Mythic Image*.

Austrian National Library, Vienna, for the photo on page 67 (left), which was reproduced from Joseph Campbell, *The Mythic Image*.

British Museum, London, for use of the stone carving used in the photo on page 225, which was reproduced from Joseph Campbell, *The Mythic Image*.

Macmillan U.K. Publishers for the photo on page 70, which was reproduced from *History of Africa*.

Dr. Pedro Rojas for the photo on page 47 (top), which was reproduced from *The Art and Architecture of Mexico from 10,000 B.C. to the Present Day*.

Princeton University Press for the photo on page 128.

Random House for the photos on pages 16, 120, 127, and 212, which were reproduced from *Axis of Eros*.

Ferguson Publishing Co. for insert photo 2.

Western Publishing Co. for insert photo 12.

Time-Life Books for insert photos 9 and 11, which were reproduced from *Epic of Man*.

Nettie Debille of Stanford University Press for the photo on page 89.

Braziller Publishing for the photos on pages 68 and 119, which were reproduced from J. W. Perry, *Lord of the Four Quarters*, 1966.

Jung foundation for the photo on page 46, which was reproduced from E. Edinger, *Ego and Archetype*, 1973.

Viking Penguin for insert photo 4, and the photos on pages 78 and 172.

Harper and Row Publishers for insert photos 6 and 10.

To David, the King, to *all* the kings who have sought to steward their realms with justice and blessing; and to Carl Jung, Mircea Eliade, Erik Erikson, and John Weir Perry—four magician-kings who have cleared a space for generative men to make a stand and visioned a new world for all of us to create.

THE RETURN
OF THE KING
AND HIS BLESSINGWAY:
A HUMAN LONGING

OF ALL HUMANKIND'S PRIMORDIAL LONGINGS, PROBably the most widespread—within all times and cultures—is for the return of the "True King." Many people think messianic expectations are limited to fundamentalist Jews and Christians. But there is a hope common among many peoples for a ruler who will come to liberate us from oppression. Few of us are aware how prevalent the theme of a liberating king's return is in world mythology.

J.R.R. Tolkien's *The Return of the King*[1] and Frank Herbert's *Dune*[2] are two popular contemporary works built around this theme. Neil Forsyth's recent book *The Old Enemy* demonstrates the theme's worldwide historical ubiquity.[3] Striking parallels can be noted in accounts of the story from widely divergent cultures. Many stories begin by telling of monsters who reign over a chaotic world in the absence of the king. When the king arrives, first he defeats the monsters; then he reestablishes a cosmos wherein justice and peace can flourish.

This motif has the same mythic structure we find underlying the messianic traditions of Jewish, Christian, and other religions. Many adherents of Islam look forward to the return of the Madhi. Zoroastrians await Saoshyant. Buddhists expect Maitreya. What are we to make of this persistent fantasy of our species? Do these fantasies simply reflect vestiges of the dependency needs we associate with regressive—even "primitive"—premodern religions? Many contemporary interpreters of psychology and myth would answer yes.

We have a different view. We believe these recurrent fantasies reflect a human intuition that our species is capable of far more caring and generativity than the holocausts of recorded history would indicate. Encoded within our genetic inheritance, we believe, are what we call King and Queen "programs." If we can learn to access them adequately, they will enable men and women to cooperate in building a viable postmodern planetary civilization—a historical realization of mythic images of the cosmos. The King we await is within, a psychological potential every man carries with him. In order to free us from the monsters of chaos, this Liberator King will have to be embodied not in one but in millions of men who learn to access their inner sources of inclusive caring and generativity.

Is there any hope that men might learn to use their power for liberation and blessing rather than oppression and injustice? Could contemporary men find within themselves the vision and power necessary to confront the reign of monster boys on Earth? Many agree with the late, great Reinhold Niebuhr that power and goodness cannot reside together within our species. Many believe men to be inherently abusive of power. We disagree. *We believe both men and women have encoded deep inside an understanding of how to use their power for blessing and liberation. With the Navajo, we have faith that human beings can once again find the "Blessingway."*

Much is being written today about the "men's movement." Around the United States, and increasingly in other countries, men are gathering to explore what it might be like to become consciously masculine. Groups of men are seeking to understand how the masculine archetypes of the King, Warrior, Magician, and Lover can be accessed in a mature and generative way.

It is much too early to say where this contemporary ferment among men will take us. Perhaps one day it will seem as silly, reactive, and shallow as its eager detractors represent it to be. We will continue though to indulge our hopes that this will not be the case. Cynicism will never bring us the power we need to face our planetary challenges. Our hope is that more and more men will respond to the inner urge to maturity, and in so doing make themselves available to serve the world.

We offer this book as an aid to those men who think with Blake that "Earth might be fair" that we could realize a "universal brotherhood of Eden."[4] Many of us remember the Kennedy years and our fantasies of Camelot. We thrilled to JFK's admonition that "we can do better." Certainly we know politicians deceive us when they try to present themselves as the "expected one." *But we believe the voice these men are echoing is a real voice, resonating within each of us—and one which, if properly heeded, will begin to lead us in the Blessingway.*

ACKNOWLEDGMENTS

THE AUTHORS WISH TO THANK GRACIELA INFANTE FOR her careful reading of the manuscript, Margaret Shanahan and Graciela Infante for their many helpful suggestions, Patrick Nugent for his transcription of Robert Moore's lecture tapes, Noel Kaufmann for his location of research sources, Carolyn Dame, Daniel Meckel, and Angela Smith for their work on photo permissions, Angela Smith for her work on tape transcriptions, Max Havlick for his work on the Bibliography, Forrest Craver for his contribution to the Servant Leadership section of the manuscript and the inspiration he has provided us on this issue, Don Bowden at Wide World Photos, Inc. for his facilitation of the cover image, David Robinson and Rudy Vetter for their excellent photography, Maria Guarnaschelli (Vice-President and Senior Editor at William Morrow) for her intensive and superlative editorial work aimed at making the manuscript accessible to a wide range of readers, Elizabeth Portland for her tireless liaison work, Emily Ann May for her diligent and thorough work on securing permissions, and Joan Amico for her patient collating of our ideas (all at William Morrow). In addition, we wish to offer special thanks to the many men, within the men's movement and outside of it, who have reflected on their personal experience as men and helped us to refine our understanding of the "four powers" and how to access them for more healthful and generative ways of expressing the masculine soul.

CONTENTS

Preface: The Return of the King and His Blessingway:
A Human Longing   7

PART 1
HARD WIRING: THE MALE SOUL

1. Gender Identity, Gender Asymmetry, and
   the Sexual Imbalance of Power   19
2. Decoding the Male Psyche   28

PART 2
IMAGES OF THE ARCHETYPAL KING

3. Historic Images of the Sacred King   59
4. The King in His Fullness   112
5. Generative Man: The Challenge of Kingship for
   Contemporary Man   147

PART 3
MALFUNCTIONS: THE SHADOW KING

6. The Shadow King as the Tyrant Usurper   159
7. The Shadow King as the Weakling Abdicator   171

CONTENTS

PART 4
ACCESSING THE KING WITHIN

8. Historical Patterns of Accessing the King   181

9. Welcoming the King into Our Lives   198

10. Dancing the Four Quarters: The Challenge of
    Masculine Wholeness   236

AFTERWORD

The Return of the True King   251

APPENDICES

A: Decoding the Diamond Body: Beyond Jung   259

B: Archetypes and the Limbic System   268

C: Archetypes and the Anima   273

Notes   282

Bibliography   313

Index   327

Thou hast stood as king upon the unyielding land
And caused it to flourish
In thy form of "Ptah, the Risen Land,"
In thy manifestation as the Unifier.
What thy mouth created by speaking,
What thy hands shaped according to thy heart,
Thou hast raised up out of the waters of chaos!

—Based on a translation from an ancient Egyptian hymn
of the second millennium B.C.E.

THE KING WITHIN

From Mind Through Hand (with opposable thumb!) to World:
The Archetypal King Creating (William Blake's *The Ancient of Days*)

PART 1

HARD WIRING: THE MALE SOUL

1

GENDER IDENTITY,
GENDER ASYMMETRY,
AND THE SEXUAL
IMBALANCE OF POWER

INCREASINGLY TODAY, MEN AND WOMEN ARE STRUG-gling to live in a twilight world of gender confusion. Anxiously they wonder what, if anything, constitutes their own unique sexual identity. Women don business suits and become bankers and lawyers. Men clean house and learn to change diapers. These shifts in traditional work roles may be all to the good. But are there any real differences between men and women? If not, what joy is left us in sexual union? Have we become interchangeable parts, androgynous to the core?

Some teach us to feel ashamed of our sex-specific differences. Supporters of radical androgyny go so far as to discourage research into the dissimilarities in brain structure, or in the chemical, hormonal, or instinctual configurations that may influence some culturally exaggerated scripts.[1]

Some theorists offer stereotyped ideals of "feminine" psychological characteristics, now alone deemed fully human.[2] Boys are said to be developmentally inferior to girls. Men are held to be biologically and emotionally inferior to women. Some radical feminists assert women would be better off without men entirely—or that male children should be genetically or socially engineered to eliminate "masculine aggressiveness."

This is not to say that all feminist criticism is invalid. The feminist critique of patriarchal societies makes a great deal of sense. Patriarchy *does* tend to institutionalize a particular kind of masculinity, prone to exploiting and oppressing other human beings, other species, and the environment. But oppressive, "macho" societies deny *men* their mature masculinity as certainly as they degrade women and feminine attributes. Typically a small minority of underdeveloped males at the top of the social pyramid will control power and wealth to the exclusion of all others, male and female. They rank these others in a descending order of usefulness to themselves, and defend against them with all the force of their inflated self-regard. Patriarchy is therefore a manifestation of the infantile grandiosity suffered by its leaders.

Patriarchy is set up and run not for men as a gender or for masculinity in its fullness or in its mature expressions but rather by men who are fundamentally *immature*. It is really the rule of boys, often cruel and abusive boys. For the most part, we believe human societies have always consisted of boys and girls more or less unconsciously acting out their immature and grandiose fantasies. Our planetary home more often than not has resembled the island world in William Golding's *Lord of the Flies*. Thus our societies have, on the whole, opposed the realization and expression of *both* mature feminine and masculine psyches.

Brutalized children—and for most children in most times and places brutality is a commonplace—become brutal adults. But they are not really adults. They can only pretend to be adults while they still operate on a level of childish self-aggrandizement. The developmental crippling that generates patriarchy is not however the sole responsibility of childish males. Immature males *and* females are unconscious partners in the socially sanctioned repression of children. A child's sense of self is distorted by a mother who fails to confront her own emotional issues, and her own unresolved needs for power and adulation. The therapist Alice Miller has written a pioneering series of books that addresses poisonous pedagogy,[3] as she calls this problem. Childish men and women never outgrow being self-interested and self-involved, and they pass their own wounds on to their children. Mature men and women find the ways to be selfless in their regard for others, even as they are manifestly self-caring.

In sum, we feel it is wrong to view patriarchy as the expression of a mature masculinity or of masculinity in its essence. Patriarchal societies are out of balance partly because at their helm are unbalanced men. And while we abhor the often horrific abuses of patriarchal systems, we also remember that males helped generate, from earlier urban neolithic cultures, all the higher civilizations we know from recorded history.[4] The efforts of dynamic, life-engendering men have left an astounding record of discovery and achievement. Clearly the energies of men, in partnership with women and their feminine energies, have fueled (and will continue to fuel) the significant advances of imagination and social organization that characterize our species. Men of the past, in every tribe and nation, have struggled to learn how to use their power to bless the human community. We continue to struggle today.

Lost in Childhood:
Failed Initiation (Egyptian figure of mourning)

Defining masculine and feminine characteristics has led to much discussion. After years of research, depth psychologists and others argue that each sex carries both the psychological and physical traits of the other.[5] No man is purely masculine, just as there is no purely feminine woman. Jungian psychologists call the feminine characteristics of the male psyche the Anima; the female psyche's masculine characteristics they call the Animus.

Both the Animus and the Anima develop in complex fashion as the personality grows to maturity. Neither men nor women can reach psychological maturity without integrating their respective contrasexual other. A man's female elements enhance his manhood, just as a woman's male aspects enhance her womanhood. Typically masculine characteristics are dominant in a man, as are feminine characteristics in a woman. Of course there are exceptions, but this is usually the case. Central to all these discussions is the question of whether masculinity is in its *essence* more coercive, more abusive of power, more compulsively dominance-seeking than femininity. Many have implied or argued that biological gender differences *necessitate* rigid sex-role differentiation and make masculine dominance *inevitable*.

For example, the changing history of male and female roles within the Israeli kibbutzim are presented as evidence of innate masculine and feminine characteristics.[6] The kibbutzim were founded as farming communities in the late nineteenth century under the influence of Marxist ideals. Men and women were viewed not only as equal, but as inherently the same. In the fields, women worked the same long hours as the men. In the kitchens, nurseries, and children's dormitories men worked the same long hours as the women.

As the years passed, however, an unexpected development occurred. Slowly the women left the fields, the traditional areas of men's work. More and more they specialized in the work of the kitchens, nurseries, and dormitories. Gradually, the men specialized in the field work. Against the enormous pressure of kibbutz ideology most men and women sorted themselves into "traditional" gender-specific roles. Was this the result of biology or immature manipulation of masculine power? According to sociobiology, primate ethology, and brain-structure/hormonal research, there *may* be instinctual biological roots for such tendencies in social behavior.[7] In addition, the anthropologist David Gilmore, in his *Manhood in the Making*—the first extensively documented cross-cultural examination of the "cult of manhood"—strongly indicates a widespread societal support for a division of social and work roles among men and women.[8]

Even if it could be proved, however, that some traditionally masculine or feminine *tendencies* may be inherited this would not be a basis for justifying the usual caricatures of these traits. Above all, it does not justify the assumption that men are inherently violent, inordinately aggressive, insensitive, and uninterested in intimate relationships, nor that women have a monopoly on gentle, nurturing, emotional, and intuitive behaviors. Probably the most accurate argument is that men are more "hard wired" for some psychological tendencies and women for others. Unfortunately, historical cultures nearly always have amplified rather than helped us compensate for these tendencies.

Important as all these considerations may be, in this book our purpose is not to focus on gender difference. We intend rather to advance understanding of the deep masculine and the challenge of stewarding masculine power. *For whatever the source of masculine abuse of power, it is our responsibility as contemporary men to understand it and to develop the emotional and spiritual resources to end it.* We want to help men express what psychoanalyst Erik Erikson termed the "generative man" within themselves.[9] We will do this by exploring how masculinity is anchored in the place where body, instinct, mind, and soul arise in men.

Contrary to those thinkers who, with Reinhold Niebuhr, regard power itself as inevitably leading to evil,[10] we believe it is possible to steward power responsibly. The drive toward attaining personal and corporate empowerment is as much a part of our instinctual makeup as eating, sleeping, and procreating. We cannot wish away what psychologist Alfred Adler called the "will to power,"[11] the desire to overcome. "We shall overcome" is not just a civil-rights rallying cry—it is a human instinct to achieve efficacy and competence in adaptation. We cannot and should not raise our children to eschew this primal and ultimately life-enhancing instinct.[12] The issue should never be how to get rid of the urge for power, masculine or feminine. The real issue is how to steward it, and how to channel our other instincts along with it into life-giving and world-building activities.

THE PROBLEM OF THE MODERN
ATTACK ON MYTH AND RITUAL

The creative use of instinctual male energies, like the good use of any energy source, requires maturity. Human maturity has probably always been a rare commodity. But we believe it was, at least in some respects, more available in the past than it is today. It was more available even in patriarchal states, with all of their drawbacks, than it is in our modern societies. In the past there were powerful rites of initiation presided over by ritual elders to help boys and girls remake themselves into men and women capable of assuming their social responsibilities.[13] The scope of these premodern initiation rituals was often limited by inflexible cultural norms. But they did provide boys and girls with workable blueprints for achieving gender-specific maturity and were based on mythic visions of the tribe's view of the best in human nature—their normative vision of the possible human.

An apprentice electrician must be initiated by an experienced master into the mysteries of electricity's sources, methods of generation, and technologies of distribution. Whatever the apprentice does not take care to understand is a danger to him, because electricity carries force enough to kill him. In similar fashion all human beings need to be initiated into the wise and life-enhancing uses of human psychological resources. Where misunderstood, the energies of our psyches can wreak havoc upon our lives. Despite the elaborate training our modern society provides an individual mastering a trade, we do not think to offer anything similar to the man who wishes to master his own psyche. But our lack of teachers doesn't change our need to learn how to access the powerful energies of our deep souls.

Essentially, the process of initiation removes our Ego from the center of the universe. When a society abandons initiation rituals, individual Egos lose an appropriate means of learning this valuable lesson. Life circumstances will urge the same lesson upon the Ego eventually, but perhaps in a very painful, inopportune manner. But by far the most serious consequence of ceasing initiation practices is the loss of a periodic social forum for considering the nature of maturity. A society has to know what maturity is before it can pass the knowledge on. It's as if we no longer have a map to get us to maturity. If you don't know where something is, and you don't have a map, how do you get there? A few will stumble across the destination. But most of us end up getting hopelessly lost. When people bemoan our culture's loss of values, in part they are missing the old transformative rituals—for rituals provide a structure within which social values can be recalled and reconsidered.

In many tribal societies initiation ceremonies are still given the prominence they deserve. Through ritual training and the special imparting of carefully stewarded wisdom, the Ego is displaced into an orbital position around a Transpersonal Other. The Ego may experience this Transpersonal Other as any kind of group or task to which the individual pledges his or her

loyalties, best efforts, even his or her life. In premodern societies, such group tasks and loyalties are always themselves
ultimately subordinate to and given meaning by a greater
Transpersonal Other, which religions of the world call "God."

As a complete cultural system, modernity has largely
turned its back on God, on effective processes of initiation, on
ritual elders, and even on family, tribe, and nation. Consequently, an individual Ego can no longer reach the sober but
joyous realization of its *non*central position in the psyche and in
the wider universe. Nature fills the vacuum modernity has created with our modern Egos, which expand terrifically to fill the
empty space. Where a powerful Transpersonal Other is missing,
God is replaced by unconscious pretensions to godhood.

An individual psyche, bloated by dangerously distorted
assessments of self and others around it—family, friends, lovers, company, nation, and perhaps the entire globe—must pay
the price for its infantilism. Corrupt politicians, money-hungry
yuppies, drug dealers, wife (and husband) abusers and new
racists are but a few examples of infantilism run amok. Petty
dictators, self-styled fundamentalist "messiahs" and their ter-
rorist henchmen, Khmer Rouge genocidal murderers, Chinese
Communist-party bullies, international oil company executives,
among many others, cause the social and environmental devastation that always accompanies the Ego inflation of the human
psyche unchecked by a sense of limits grounded in a Transpersonal Other. These would-be men and women have failed to
grasp a sufficiently wide and deep vision of the archetypal realities upon which our psyche is founded. It is time we look
again to these deep structures and draw from them the psychic
support our modern era so desperately needs.

DECODING
THE MALE PSYCHE

CARL GUSTAV JUNG FOUNDED THE SCHOOL OF ANA-
lytical or "depth" psychology that provides the overall
framework of our work.[1] We rely heavily also on insights from
theorists of other schools such as Sigmund Freud, Erik Erikson,
D. W. Winnicott, Heinz Kohut, and Alice Miller. But we believe Jung's approach is the only one to provide a truly transcultural understanding of our human psyche. His is also the
only approach to adequately bridge the gap between modern
science and the mythological and spiritual traditions of our
species.

Jungian depth psychology values the mysteries of the human soul. Dreams, visions, symbols, images, and cultural achievements arise from those mysterious depths that the world's religions understand as the "spiritual dimension." Depth psychology embraces all human experience as authentic to the psyche. Consequently, phenomena such as the "soul," "demonic possession," "revelation," "prayer," or "god" are completely compatible with scientific truth. Because all experiences are psychological, all are real, no matter how strange.[2] Above all, *any* human experience is both *based on* and *perceived by* the deep psychological structures within us.[3]

Before we explore the deep structures of the male psyche, it will be helpful to define a few Jungian terms.

MYTH: For depth psychologists myth does not imply a naïve, untrue, prescientific tale about the origins of the world or humankind. Myths are true stories that describe the ways of the psyche and the means by which our psychological energies interact.[4] Myths project our inner dynamics onto the outer world and allow us to experience it through the filter of how we think and feel.[5]

Since in a real sense we *are* the universe and the universe is us, myths often accurately describe the workings of the larger universe by using anthropomorphic images. That is to say, we are products of the universe in the same way that galaxies, oceans, and trees are. It would be a very strange thing indeed if our psyche did not mirror the structures found outside in the cosmos. An immediate and intimate correspondence between *inner* and *outer* is fundamental to our nature as beings. If no such link existed, we would be unable to acquire any realistic or workable knowledge of the world. We would be unable to survive. Ultimately, it is possible that *inner* and *outer* are purely subjective, pragmatic distinctions made by our consciousness in order to navigate within a mystery it cannot fully fathom.

Creation myths illustrate this beautifully. In the Bible, the

Hebrew God Yahweh creates the material world by speaking. He says, "Let there be such and such!," and there is such and such. Behind this concept of creation stands the idea that naming something brings it into existence. Of course, modern science maintains the world did not come into being through a divine uttering of words or the naming of material objects. The biblical account does not convey a scientific truth about the world's origin. The truth it speaks is psychological.

Human consciousness at its height is developed largely by the mastering of words. Arising from language, at the same time it gives rise *to* language, consciousness creates our experience as it defines creation. The words we use for things allow us to distinguish *this* from *that*. They also profoundly color how we think and feel about those things. What we cannot name is therefore not fully real or fully experienced for us. As far as our psyche is concerned, an unnamed thing is "uncreated."[6] Thus the biblical image of Yahweh creating the world by naming it is true to human psychological processes. At the same time, if we assume there is an intelligence behind the created world, it might be true that that intelligence manifested the universe through some process analogous to the human use of language. If this were so, the biblical story would be working both as a psychological parable and as a visionary expression of a process that really is occurring.

EGO: When Jungian psychoanalysts talk about the Ego, they usually mean the "I" we normally think of as ourselves.[7] The Ego is who we believe ourselves to be, the part of our psyche we identify with our name. When we say, "*I* feel this way about something," or "*I* think I'll do that," the Ego is probably speaking. Jungian theorists sometimes define the Ego as a *complex*. By this they mean a structural element of the total psyche that exhibits certain specific features. The Ego operates in what we imagine to be our capacity to think rationally, in our feelings, in

The Sacred King Making Words
(King Barrakab of Sam'al with his scribe)

our ability to will actions, remember the past, and create the future, and in our encounter with consciousness.

In reality, however, the question of the Ego is more complicated. Often "I" am not the one who is thinking, feeling, acting, willing, or deciding. Rather some *autonomous complex* other than the Ego may temporarily "possess" it and make it operate out of the complex's perspective. Since the Ego is largely unaware of these other complexes, it is tricked into the illusory feeling of holding a solitary place in the psyche, and into an accompanying illusion of its "free will." According to

Jung, the other complexes operate largely from the personal unconscious, but may also be anchored in a transpersonal unconscious which exerts a deeper influence on the psyche.

CONSCIOUSNESS: Consciousness is not confined to the Ego. The *sub*conscious or *un*conscious is itself conscious. It is only unconscious—invisible and indistinct—from the *Ego's* perspective.[8] Personal complexes other than the Ego, and the deeper transpersonal psychological structures of the unconscious, can be conscious of each other and of the Ego, and they operate out of their own agendas. The case of multiple-personality disorder demonstrates this clearly. Here highly activated complexes usurp the place of the Ego in the daily affairs of the afflicted person, causing him or her to behave in ways the Ego neither wishes nor sometimes even remembers afterward.

What is true for people who suffer multiple-personality disorder is true, though to a lesser extent, for all of us. We all at times act in ways contrary to how our Ego wills us to behave, perhaps through deep mood swings and emotionally violent outbursts of fear and rage. When we return to a state of Ego consciousness, we say such things as "I went out of my head" or "I don't know what came over me." What came over us, like a wave of energy that shifted our whole mode of perceiving, feeling, and acting, was an autonomous complex, another consciousness from within the total psychic system that is our Self.

Autonomous complexes are usually (though not always) organized around traumatic childhood experiences.[9] During early traumas, our emerging Egos split off and repressed aspects of the psyche that parents, siblings, or society found unacceptable. These split-off aspects could be thoughts, feelings, images, or associations. Often they are valuable and worth recall. They may carry hidden talents, intuitions, abilities, or accurate feelings that would make our personalities wiser and more complete if we could reintegrate them. Until reintegration can occur, our psyches are like the pieces of a broken mirror, which hold in fragments what was once a complete reflection. Through all our complexes, including the Ego, and the vast territory of the unconscious, consciousness pervades our psyche.

ARCHETYPES: Archetypes operate at a level of the psyche deeper than that of the personal unconscious with its autonomous complexes. They are the hard-wired components of our genetically transmitted psychic machine.[10] They are the bedrock structures that define the human psyche's own nature, and make it the same, regardless of the culture in which an individual lives. In this sense archetypes represent transpersonal human psychological characteristics. They are dynamic, energic elements in all of us. They well up and fall deep within our unconscious like tidal pulls. Our daily life is influenced by these energies in ways we can never fully understand.

Jung declared that the archetypes are equivalent to the instincts of other animals. He located them in what he called the *collective unconscious*.[11] The existence of an unconscious, or what many called the subconscious, had been noted for some time. But Freud was the first to make it the focus of major psychological investigation. Before him, even where psychologists acknowledged the subconscious mind's existence, they usually dismissed it as an inert repository of forgotten or repressed experiences.

Freud's interest in the mind's possibilities had been aroused during his medical studies with the great Parisian hypnotist, Jean Martin Charcot. Charcot dismissed the results of his own experimental demonstrations as stemming from patient hysteria. Whatever their source, the hypnotic manifestations witnessed by the young Freud convinced him he'd found a rich field for further study.

Common to all of us, Freud's life work implied, was a subconscious deeper than a particular personal one. He called this instinctually based subconscious the *Id* (the Latin word for "it").[12] This wild, primitive Id was responsible for all kinds of enormously powerful and irrational impulses, especially aggressive sexuality.

Classic Freudians have tended to regard the subconscious as more or less unstructured. But a number of neo-Freudians maintain that the deep psyche, far from being chaotic, is characterized by structure. Erik Erikson talks about "instinctive structures" and "preformed action patterns," which, under appropriate circumstances, call up "drive energy for instantaneous, vigorous, and skillful release."[13] He proposes the existence of "a general psychic energy (instinctual force) which can be put to use by a variety of preformed and relatively autonomous instinctive patterns."[14] He also says, "the action patterns—the modes and modalities—are all present in the ground plan from the beginning, yet they have their special time of ascending."[15] His thoughts come remarkably close to the Jungian conception of time-and-circumstance-released archetypal "action patterns" from the collective unconscious.

Jung pushed the exploration of the collective unconscious structures a step further. Stored within them, he claimed, are both the human psyche's archetypal building blocks and the accumulated collected memory of the entire human race. He reached this conclusion because he discovered that symbols, images, myths, and Gods from different cultures and epochs bore striking resemblances to one another and also to the images that appeared in his patients' dreams. According to his conception, the collective unconscious is the source and the limitless reservoir of all the images recorded in human art, mythology, and religion. From it leap both the poet's song and the scientist's insight. From it flow the signal dreams which have implication often for an entire society as much as for their dreamer.

The psyche's archetypal structures serve as conduits for great charges of primal psychological energy. Because of their own dynamic configuration, they mold this energy, imparting to it their particular patterns. Psychologists call this life-force in psychic form the *Libido*.[16] Freud believed it is fundamentally sexual. Any expression of the Libido redirected into pursuits other than sexual ones he called "sublimations." Jung, on the other hand, believed that the Libido is a generalized life force that expresses itself through imaginal and spiritual impulses, as well as through sexuality.

For any individual the archetypes may be creative and life-enhancing or destructive and death-dealing. The result depends in part on how the Ego is able to relate to them based on its own developmental history. Properly accessing and using the Libido available to the psyche amount to a sort of psychological technology. If we learn the technology and use it properly, we can use the energy to make generative men and women of ourselves. But if we fail to learn how to use these vast energy resources, or misuse them, we will be courting our own destruction, and we may take others with us. If we try to ignore the archetypes, they exert their mighty influence upon us nonetheless. They bend us to their nonhuman, sometimes *in*human wills. We must therefore face the evidence depth psychology and other studies have provided us. We are not as free of instinct or unconscious content as we have been encouraged to believe. Genuine freedom for the Ego results from acknowledging and properly accessing the chemical fires that burn hot in our unconscious minds.

Some Jungian analysts romanticize the archetypes.[17] They encourage their patients to find and claim the particular archetype or myth that has organized their lives. Life then becomes a process of affirming and living out this myth. In our opinion our goal should not be to identify with an archetypal pattern, or to allow a mythic expression of it to make our lives what it will. We believe that when we romantically *identify* with any archetype we cease to be viable human beings moving toward wholeness. If we are drawn to an archetype by its seductive power, its promise that we can shirk our individual responsibilities and the pain involved in being a person with a personal Ego, we will be crushed by the sheer weight of unconscious compulsive impulses.

On the other hand, our goal is not to become *ordinary* in our quest for psychic health. We must not lose the vital connection with the libidinal energy the archetypes supply us so that we can live our lives fully, energetically, and creatively. Our goal is to learn how to *differentiate* ourselves from the archetypes without completely *disassociating* ourselves from them. If we learn to access them successfully, they become resources of energy both for our personal lives and for healing our planet—we become more radiant in every area of our lives.

More precisely stated, our objective is to develop mature Ego structures strong enough to channel useful libidinal energy into our daily lives. We can begin by making ourselves conscious of how archetypal energies already possess us. Only then can we begin to access them creatively, through a process that provides us with a greater sense of free will in the choices of our lives. The effort to achieve liberation for ourselves will in turn motivate us to help others do the same. Our renewed energies benefit ourselves and others on all the levels of our psychic organization: the personal, the familial, the communal, national, and global.

SHADOW: Jung himself occasionally identified the Shadow with the totality of the unconscious. But most depth psychologists view the Shadow as an individual, multifaceted contra-Ego, of the same sex as the Ego.[18] If the Ego is a photograph, the Shadow is its negative. Standing in direct opposition to the Ego, the Shadow is an autonomous complex, which holds opinions, expresses feelings, and generally wills an agenda radically different from the Ego's.

Like most autonomous complexes, the Shadow results from childhood trauma. Those qualities of a person's total psyche that are diametrically opposed to the emerging Ego, and which the Ego rejects because of the pressures of the childhood environment, coalesce in the unconscious. There they form a distinct, conscious, willing entity. Unless reintegrated later in life, they forever seek to sabotage the Ego's plans and behaviors.

We have all had the experience of willing one scenario and living quite another. For example, we intend to remain friendly while visiting our in-laws, but then find ourselves drawn irresistibly into arguments and confrontation. Our Egos want to maintain an image of family harmony. Our Shadows, unable to tolerate such hypocrisy, and feeling real animosity toward our in-laws, compel us to behave in a more honest, if more destructive, way.

The animosity we feel is ultimately toward ourselves, but it often takes a lot of work before we can realize this. The Shadow endorses this work because it longs for reintegration. It is the Shadow's method to lead us into holding our impossibly defensive, illogical positions—in order to confront us with whatever psychic complexes we would rather forget. Our "real world" hatreds are most usually against these inner complexes, and our Shadow works by *repetition compulsion* to call our attention to them.

Rather than face any rejected qualities, either positive or negative, within ourselves, we frequently deal with our Shadow by projecting those qualities onto others.[19] As an Ego, we don't project them. But our Shadow does so in order to focus our interest on its feelings, wishes, and agendas. Our Shadow induces us to see other people we disapprove of or dislike in colors that are perhaps only marginally like their "true" colors but which *are* colors that the Shadow itself possesses.

Jung believed withdrawing a projection of the Shadow and owning it as a part of ourselves requires enormous moral courage. He also believed that what we will not face within our psyche we will be forced to confront in the outer world. So, if we can claim our Shadow's qualities, and learn from them, we defuse much of the interpersonal conflict we would otherwise encounter. People who have served as the screens for our Shadow's projections become less odious, and more human. At the same time, we experience ourselves as richer, more complex, and more powerful individuals.

THE TRIANGULAR STRUCTURE
OF THE ARCHETYPES

In this book our definition of the Shadow includes this traditional Jungian understanding, but introduces another archetypal, transpersonal aspect to it as well. We believe masculine and feminine archetypes possess their own Shadows. The King, the Warrior, the Magician, and the Lover are the masculine archetypal structures we have undertaken to study in this series. In one sense these archetypes are operating at more primitive levels than the Ego accessing them, and each has its own Shadow.

In our extended definition, a Shadow always manifests where there is an immature, fragmentary psyche, because splitting is always a symptom of unintegrated development.[20] In the traditional Jungian view of maturity, wholeness is achieved to the degree that the split between the Ego and the Shadow is overcome. In other words, psychological maturity is a measure of how thoroughly the Ego is able to integrate the Shadow into its consciousness.

We maintain that the Ego/Shadow split represents a Shadow system in itself. The split actually involves the Ego in the *bipolar* Shadow of one or more archetypes. In this situation our Ego usually identifies with one pole of the archetypal

Shadow and disassociates from the other. In our view, then, the Shadow can still be regarded in the traditional way as the psychic area from which the Ego is divided but, more fully, as a bipolar *system* characterized by splitting, repression, and projection *within* the energy field of an archetype.

For a long time psychologists associated "bipolar disorder" almost exclusively with the manic-depressive personality.[21] Then, in his *Modern Psychopathology*, Theodore Millon extended the idea of bipolarity to include passive and active dimensions in all the major disorders of personality.[22] In a similar fashion, some Jungians have described a bipolar relationship between certain archetypes (though they are not in themselves personality disorders). That gave rise to such archetypal pairs as the senex-puer (old man–eternal boy), the domina-puella (old woman–eternal girl) and others.[23]

In the case of the Warrior archetype, for example, neither the Sadist nor the Masochist (the two poles of the Warrior's Shadow) represents personal growth or fulfillment. The full embodiment of the Warrior is to be found in a third transcending option that integrates the two poles into a creative psychological structure. Since they define psychic wholeness, archetypes always reconcile opposing forces in this way. Both of the opposing poles in the archetypal Shadow systems contain qualities essential for psychological health. But if left in their state of chronic tension, they will condemn the Ego to a fragmented and immature existence. Guided by the archetypes in their transcending fullness, a mature personality integrates these important qualities by reconciling the divisions in the archetypal Shadow.

Our refined understanding of how the archetypes work suggests interesting analogies with other schools of thought. The psychologist Alfred Adler, a contemporary of Freud and Jung, believed personality disorders appear both in active and passive

**THE TRIANGULAR STRUCTURE OF
THE ARCHETYPES OF THE MATURE MASCULINE**

THE KING IN HIS FULLNESS

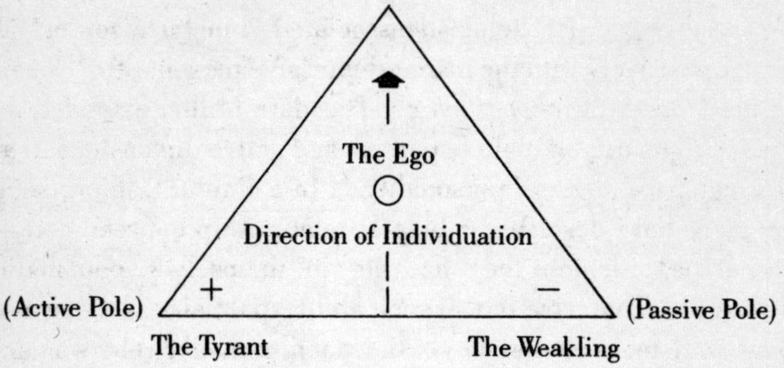

The Ego

○

Direction of Individuation

(Active Pole)   (Passive Pole)

The Tyrant   The Weakling

THE WARRIOR IN HIS FULLNESS

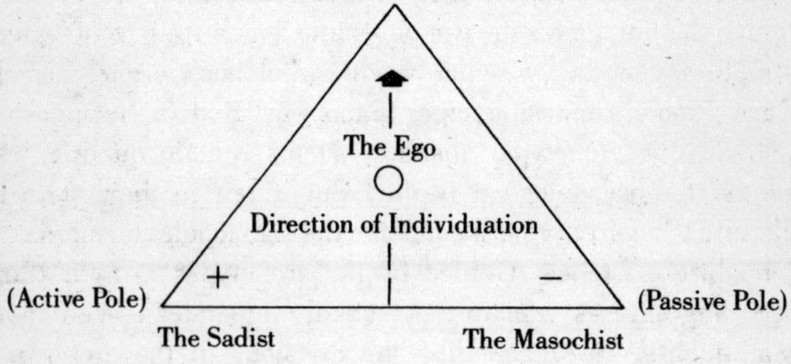

The Ego

○

Direction of Individuation

(Active Pole)   (Passive Pole)

The Sadist   The Masochist

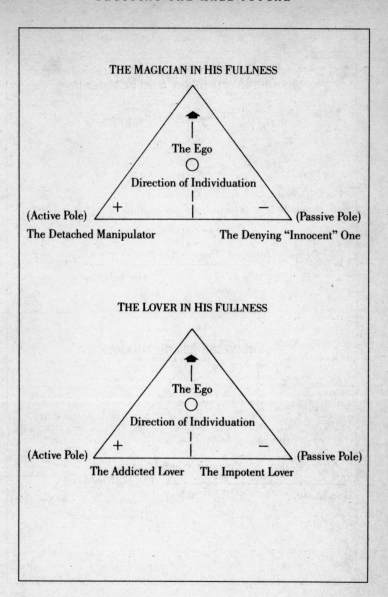

THE MAGICIAN IN HIS FULLNESS

The Ego

Direction of Individuation

(Active Pole)

(Passive Pole)

The Detached Manipulator

The Denying "Innocent" One

THE LOVER IN HIS FULLNESS

The Ego

Direction of Individuation

(Active Pole)

(Passive Pole)

The Addicted Lover   The Impotent Lover

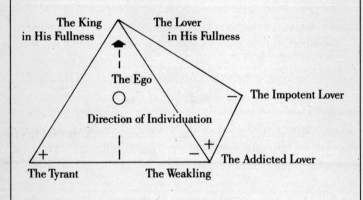

modes in a way similar to our view of how archetypal Shadow systems work. The Christian theologian Paul Tillich grounded his thought with a belief in what he called the "ambiguities" of space and time in the created world. He believed that these ambiguities find their resolution in a third, higher reality "above" history.[24] The impulse to achieve this comes from the "Spirit." The German philosopher Hegel saw the forward movement of the universe as occurring through a "thesis, antithesis, synthesis" process in which each synthesis became a new thesis, and so on in a continual upward program of evolutionary complexity and integration.[25] Alfred North Whitehead, the great twentieth-century American philosopher, sees the whole "adventure of ideas," ideas that *create* the world, as a process by which God lures the created world forward in tiny increments, which he calls "occasions."[26] These occasions are like Hegel's theses, and God is the ever-changing antithesis. Whitehead calls this unceasing process "creative advance."

Similarly, Jung drew from his alchemical studies the idea of the *coniunctio oppositorum* ("union of opposites")[27] impelled by a "transcendent function"—the conceptual equivalent to Tillich's "Spirit" and Whitehead's "lure." Jung believed it is essential for the Ego to balance opposing images, feelings, and points of view without allowing either of the opposed sides to disappear into the unconscious. Eventually, when this struggle is consciously experienced with all the suffering it demands, our psyche can follow a transcendent third possibility into greater wholeness.

Jung's followers have largely neglected the Ego's vital role in determining how the archetypes will shape our everyday lives. With our model of the triangular structure of the archetypes, an individual can take care to see that the archetypes will manifest in their fullest form rather than in their Shadow structures. An Ego that does not properly *access* an archetype will be *possessed* by that archetype's Shadow, and left oscillating between the Shadow's two poles. At one the Ego will suffer *positive inflation* (explosion) and at the other *negative inflation* (implosion). Separated, the Shadow's two poles express a pathological darkness, which is only "enlightened" by polar integration into the transcendent third of the archetype. Their pathology is transformed by the Ego into a creative advance.

The action of the Ego is the key to this transformative experience. The Ego and the elements of the archetype exercise a kind of gravitational pull on each other. To allow transformation, the Ego must position itself "above" time and space, in the domain of the Spirit, or the collective unconscious. The Ego will serve ultimately as an occasion for the archetype's expression in time and space. Unless the Ego can work above the spatiotemporal dimension, the archetype will appear largely in its fragmented polar aspects, and the Ego will attract these to itself. In the Spirit's domain, the Ego can instead keep its proper fix on the lodestar the archetype's transcendent third represents.

The archetype's bipolar arrangement in time and space is portrayed in the mythic image of the Symplegades, the Clashing Rocks the Ego must pass between in pursuit of the archetype's transcendent third.[28] The Ego needs to be *lured* by this full expression of the archetype to experience creative advance on its own and in the world. And the archetype needs the Ego in order to experience itself in space and time, and to recover its lost Shadow fragments. The act of recovery empowers the archetype's ongoing creative action in the world.

According to our theory, there are four foundational archetypes of the mature masculine (as well as of the immature masculine). Each of these triangles—King, Warrior, Magician, and Lover—since they are interdependent aspects of the single masculine Self, fit together into a pyramidal form. The pyramid as it has appeared throughout the ages can be interpreted as a symbol for the masculine Self. Pyramids from Egypt to Mesoamerica, from Mesopotamia to Hawaii, are representations of the universe in miniature and often display a layered or stepped form. The layers of the pyramids nearly always stand for the layers of the universe, the different cosmic levels of reality. By ascending the pyramid, an individual climbed from the profane dimension to the sacred, from the less divine to the fullest manifestation of divinity.

This idea parallels ours about the "upward" direction of the Ego's individuation from a less integrated (profane) state to a fully integrated (sacred or "divine") state. A man's Ego must ascend the four faces of the stepped pyramid of the masculine Self, thereby overcoming the bipolar Shadow split at the base of each of the faces. The Ego must keep its eye on the capstone of the pyramid, which represents the fullest expression in an individual life of the four archetypes in perfect unity. This ascent of Ego-consciousness, according to Jung, is always a matter of reconciling opposites and of integrating split psychic materials. As a man's Ego ascends through each of the triangular structures of the archetypes, he becomes more integrated and whole. And he is better and better able to access the archetypes in their fullness at the top of the pyramid. On the King side, he integrates the Tyrant and the Weakling. On the Warrior face, he integrates the Sadist and the Masochist. On the Magician surface, he integrates the Detached Manipulator and the Denying "Innocent" One. And on the Lover side, he integrates the Addicted Lover with the Impotent Lover. Each of the poles of the split Shadows of the four major archetypes possesses insights and strengths that, when the Ego integrates them, contributes to a consolidated sense of Self. Each of the bipolar opposites, when united, reveals the "transcendent third" of the archetype in its fullness. By overcoming the splitness in the bipolar archetypal Shadows, a man comes to feel inwardly empowered. And, in a sense, while he is *building* internal masculine structure he is also *discovering* the pyramid of the masculine Self, which has always been within him, at his core.

The "Mountain of God" at the Center of the Urban Complex
(The Temple Tower Esagila at Babylon: a reconstruction)

From Xibalba to the Skies
The Levels of Reality in the Maya Pyramid (Tikal)

Teotihucán:

Raising the King-Energy and Generating a World

Stairway to the Sky:

Khmer Temple-Mountain of Koh Ker (tenth century C.E.)

Pyramid Power:
Great Morai Pappara, Otaheíte (Tahiti)

The Masculine Self on a Monumental Scale:
The Pyramid of Khufu (Giza)

THE ARCHETYPES AND
BRAIN STRUCTURE

Startling resonances are being discovered between the fields of brain research and depth psychology. In his book *Archetypes: A Natural History of the Self*, the psychologist Anthony Stevens has extended the exploration of areas of the brain that may be the loci of archetypal forms.[29] He tries to explain Jung's theory of personality types in terms of brain structures. Jung's intuitive types, he speculates, might be using predominantly their Right Brains, and those who favor their Left Brains would correspond to Jung's thinking types.

Briefly, the Right Brain (the right hemisphere of the cerebral cortex) "thinks" in images and symbols, grasps situations and patterns as wholes, and is the primary center for the generation of dreams, visions, and fantasies. The Left Brain (the corresponding left hemisphere) thinks sequentially, analyzes situations and patterns logically, and uses language in its cognitive processes. Many locate the Ego entirely in the Left Brain. In contrast, Stevens proposes that while the Ego may function most of the time in the Left Brain, it also draws on the Right Brain. Consciousness, he says, is a pervasive function of the whole brain, though Right and Left Brain modes of consciousness are quite distinct. The personal unconscious and its various complexes seem to manifest in the Right Brain. By dreaming, the Right Brain communicates with the still primarily Left Brain–identified Ego.

Rather than locating the archetypes in the Right Brain, Stevens proposes that they arise in deeper, older layers of the brain, layers that, according to brain researcher Paul MacLean, have remained largely unchanged for millions of years of animal evolution.[30] The dihemispheric cerebral cortex we think of as the human brain is only the most recently evolved element of

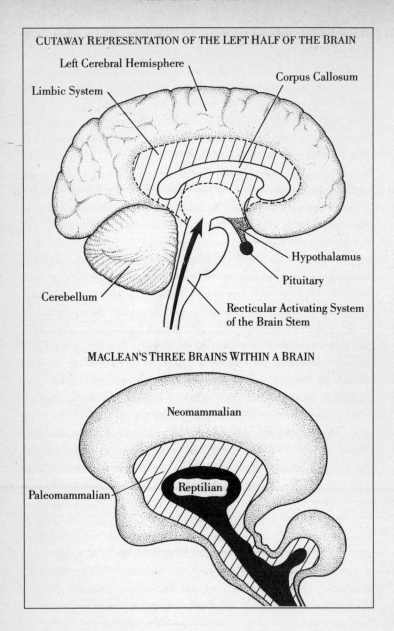

CUTAWAY REPRESENTATION OF THE LEFT HALF OF THE BRAIN

Left Cerebral Hemisphere

Corpus Callosum

Limbic System

Hypothalamus

Pituitary

Cerebellum

Recticular Activating System
of the Brain Stem

MACLEAN'S THREE BRAINS WITHIN A BRAIN

Neomammalian

Reptilian

Paleomammalian

three distinct neurological regions. Before it, in ascending order of antiquity, come the neocortex, or neomammalian brain, apparently responsible for cognition and sophisticated perception; the midbrain, or paleomammalian brain (limbic system), which seems to generate the basic emotions of fear and anger, affiliation, and maternity as well as species-characteristic individual and social behaviors; and the upward growth of the spinal cord, the reptilian brain, or R-complex, responsible for basic life activities, also probably the seat of our most basic instincts and our routine-driven behavior patterns. These three brains within a brain function relatively autonomously. Our process of psychological integration is, in part, an attempt to unify and synchronize these three regions of the brain.

If archetypes arise, as Jung believed, at a fundamentally instinctual level, then it could be that they originate in our most primitive region, the reptilian brain. Elaborated as they pass upward through the paleomammalian and neomammalian brains, the imagistic, intuitive structures of the archetypes would rise primarily into our Right Brains. But since our Ego's experience of the archetypes will also be mediated via the Left Brain, they will also be influenced by the linguistic and logical modes of thinking centered there. Archetypes hold a sense of otherness[31] perhaps because they originate in levels of the brain so much deeper than the source of Ego-consciousness, and then must be translated into terms that make sense to the Left Brain. Archetypes in their fullness involve *both* Left and Right Brain functions. This is clearly the case with the four foundational archetypes of the mature masculine, which we are outlining in this series. Certainly the rational, strategic, and emotionally detached modes of the Magician and the Warrior are characteristic of Left Brain processes, although they seem to draw secondarily on Right Brain functions, and the visually oriented, aesthetic, intuitive modes of the Lover are characteristic of Right Brain functions, although the Lover seems to draw on

Left-Brain processes. We attempt a more thorough discussion of the origin of the four archetypes of mature masculinity and the brain's limbic system (paleomammalian brain) in Appendix B. This field of inquiry is wide open to exciting future research.

COVERGENCE OF THE
MATURE MASCULINE ARCHETYPES

Depth psychologists often merge the mature masculine archetypes. Because only the most perfectly realized Ego apprehends an archetype's full expression, for most of us they retain a degree of mystery. The very images and symbols archetypes use to communicate to us refer beyond themselves to other images and symbols in an almost infinitely complex way. For example, the phallus, the cross, the tree, the axis mundi, the spine, the sacred mountain, and the pyramid can each be read symbolically as aspects of one another.[32] There are dangers, however, involved with overinterpretations. An individual can easily lose himself, as Yeats was warned in the course of his occult researches, along the Path of the Chameleon, a labyrinthine trail of correspondences. Besides this, the four basic archetypes that influence a mature man, the King, the Warrior, the Magician, and the Lover, are the fragments of a primevally whole Self, and complement each other to such a degree that no one of them receives its fullest expression without incorporating the others.

These archetypes have historically merged and diverged again in a bewildering variety of configurations. Rain magicians, for example, give rise to rain kings, who appoint priests to elect warrior kings, who commission other warriors to serve magicians who themselves become kings. A mortal king, to the extent that he fully expresses the archetypal King, is a warrior who enforces order within his kingdom and who may take military action to extend his kingdom. He is also a sacred king, the high-priest magician who mediates between the spiritual dimension and his people.[33] He is also a lover, of his people, and in a special sense of his sacred queen, since he cannot rule legitimately or effectively unless their union is fruitful.[34] Despite these uncertain boundaries, it is useful to distinguish masculine archetypes, in order to enhance the Ego's capacity to access these psychic structures in all their richness and complexity.

THE ALPHA MALE:
A PRIMATE PREFIGURATION OF THE
SACRED KING

Chimpanzees are our closest living animal relatives.[35] Their genetic profile is over 98 percent identical to ours.[36] Primate ethology research suggests close correspondences between their social structures and interpersonal behaviors and ours. It seems likely that similar psychological processes are at work.[37]

While of course we cannot *know* fully what other animals feel and think, in many ways we cannot be sure we *know* what another *human* feels or thinks. In either case we make judgments based on observable behaviors. Our great advantage in observing humans obviously is spoken language, but we still have the subjective task of interpreting linguistic signs. Chimpanzees, while they cannot speak, *can* communicate with us in sign language and through other quasi-verbal methods designed by researchers.[38] In addition, their complex range of body signals bears a striking resemblance to our own body language. It seems reasonably safe to assume that when chimpanzees *appear* to be fearful, wrathful, submissive, loving, or awed, they are in fact experiencing these emotions. Probably their emotional experience is less self-conscious and complicated than ours, but still it offers clues into primate psychology, including our own.

King, Warrior, Magician, Lover:
The Alpha Male "Displaying" (Figan as Alpha Male at Gombe)

The hierarchical power blocs and coalitions of chimpanzee society center around a dominant adult male ethologists call the *Alpha Male*.[39] Successful Alpha Males are usually mature and physically powerful. They display foresight, courage, and what can only be called "character." Alpha Males exhibit many behaviors common to the sacred king, the specific archetypally inspired figure we'll be exploring in the pages to come.

Alpha Males surround themselves with male "knights" to help support their claim to power in their "realms." These

The Alpha Male Defending His People (at Gombe)

males exhibit characteristics of what David Gilmore calls the "cult of manhood" in human males. Like their human counterparts, chimpanzee males are protectors and providers for the females and the young of their societies.[40] The Alpha Male is our first look, long before the curtain of human history rises, at the *Lord of the Four Quarters*, a title ancient Mesopotamian kings used to describe their central position in what was for them a quadrated cosmos.

We believe the Alpha Males among chimpanzees, gorillas, and other primates are working out of archetypal structures similar to those of their human counterparts, albeit on a much more primitive level. They impose order on the frequent chaotic outbreaks in their "realms."[41] They settle disputes, and at their best seem to inspire admiration and respect in their "subjects." In return they defend their subjects with great ferocity and at times pay for their efforts with their lives.[42] Decisions—over when to move the tribe to different feeding grounds, for example—seem largely to be theirs.[43] Alpha Males enjoy the trappings of authority and wealth, often in terms of desirable females, for example, but often behave generously, even altruistically. We can see in the Alpha Male the primordial energic structures of the masculine Self.

Human males experience this Self in a significantly more elaborate form. In one sense the gap between the Alpha Male and the sacred kings of human history is an enormous one, millions of years long. In another sense, however, the gap is incremental. If Stevens and others are right in their analysis of human brain structure, there is an Alpha Male within us.

We offer this book and the series as a whole to the man who is looking for an operator's manual to the psyche, and to the woman who wants a guide to the hard-wiring of men, and to her own inner masculine as well. Just as no jet pilot would try to fly a 747 without knowing its capabilities and instruments inside and out, the only way to "fly" successfully an immensely complicated male psyche is to know it inside and out, with a clear understanding of how to access its archetypal energy systems. The mindful use of this energy will bring a man safely into his mature manhood.

PART 2

IMAGES OF THE ARCHETYPAL KING

HISTORIC IMAGES
OF THE SACRED KING

D EPTH PSYCHOLOGY INFERS THE EXISTENCE OF AR-
chetypes in the collective unconscious in part by the startling correspondences between the guiding images of very
different cultures. These images surface in myths, in philosophical and theological speculations, in artistic productions, in
scientific achievements, and in institutional and societal designs. Though some disciplines emphasize the *differences* between cultures, as depth psychologists we, like the
sociobiologists and other researchers,[1] are most concerned with
similarities.

We believe there is an archetypal structure within the

collective masculine psyche behind both cultural and psychological expressions of kingship. We base our conclusions on the comparative study of world history, and evidence from the theory and clinical practice of depth psychology, as well as upon the most recent findings in the fields of brain-structure research and ethology.

The archetype of the King in its fullness involves a structure made up of a number of distinct lines of force. These are coiled in a kind of dynamic cable. Three of these lines of force reveal the presence of the other archetypes we are delineating in this series *within* the archetype of the King—Warrior, Magician, and Lover. The archetype of the King combines these energies, adds a fourfold dimension of its own (see Chapter 4), and integrates all of these forces in the nearest approximation of a transpersonal masculine Self we can imagine. A man can make his first personal connection with these archetypal forces at any point along one of the several available lines. The task is from there to tap into the other forces in the cable, and finally to integrate all these newly accessed energies into his psyche.

The archetype itself is an eternal, constant construct within the masculine psyche.[2] But cultures vary in the kinds of King energy (which lines of force) they draw upon. Some believe their most useful connection is to the King with his fructifying powers. Others summon the King's aggressive, military powers.

The different King forces a given society taps into demonstrate that society's particular Ego-archetype configuration. The ancient Egyptians, for example, believed every pharaoh to be divine and inviolable. They identified the mortal king with the King archetype. When a mortal king is identified with the King archetype to this degree, he becomes almost always inflated and grandiose, and will likely deprive his people of full selfhood. To the extent that the men in his kingdom believe him to be the *unique* embodiment of archetypal masculine energies, they are personally deprived of experiencing this embodiment for them-selves. A man's blending of human and "divine" energies is essentially the experience of what we are calling an Ego-archetype axis. A man deprived of the inner experience of himself as the Lord of the Four Quarters[3] in his own right and in his own "realm" is a man impoverished and limited.

If a mortal king is not completely identified with the King archetype, he and his subjects have a much better chance at archetypal integration. The ancient Hebrews believed their kings to be mortal, often even foolish.[4] Therefore their kings were *servants*, as much as they themselves were, of a Transper-sonal Other in the form of the *archetypal* King. While *all* kings, whether *identified* with the archetypal King or viewed as *distinct* from the archetype, were *servants*, the Semitic kings in general and the Hebrew kings in particular were in an advantageous position to exercise "servant leadership" (see Chapter 10). If a *mortal* king, as in this case, is seen in his full humanity and fully distinguished from the *archetype* of the King, then he and the men in his realm have a much better chance of experiencing themselves in a mature way. Such an experience of Ego-subordination to *the* King is a healthy way for men to live their lives. In this Ego-archetypal axis[5] the Ego is able to guide the archetype's enormous energies into creative expression in the world and to receive the life-giving Libido of the archetype without being overwhelmed and possessed by it.

Of course, not every ancient Hebrew took advantage of the opportunity to infuse his Ego with the archetype's life-giving Libido. And there were times when his theoretically fallible kings, such as David and Solomon, were accorded almost super-human status.[6] Similarly, the ancient Egyptian found at times the means to depose his theoretically divine pharaoh.[7] Rather than declaring all pharaohs mortal, and thus distinct from the King, the particular offending pharaoh was declared a usurper and a fraud, not a genuine incarnation of the archetype.[8]

Hebrew and Egyptian traditions of kingship provide two useful poles to limit our study. Other cultural traditions of the Ego-King relationship lie, as we will discover, between them. We will focus on these cultural Ego-archetype axis traditions, and not on the history of dynastic and societal struggles to manipulate the office of the king.

The study of sacred kingship in historical times has a substantial background. The ancient Greek and Roman historians as well as later medieval, Renaissance, and post-Renaissance theorists have contributed valuable on-site evaluations of reigning monarchs as well as elaborate philosophical justifications for and critiques of kingship.

Sir James Frazer began the modern comparative mythological and anthropological study of sacred kingship in his now classic work, *The Golden Bough*.[9] Jung also explored the field, fascinated by the question of how such a tenacious and pervasive mythic formulation might manifest in the deep structures of an individual psyche.[10]

In *Roots of Renewal in Myth and Madness*,[11] the Jungian psychiatrist John Weir Perry demonstrated the dramatic restorative effect the archetype had on the psychological health of severely wounded people. He then turned his attention to a transcultural investigation of the archetype of the King. His book *Lord of the Four Quarters* includes mythological texts about the King-Gods alongside legends and historical materials about the sacred kings believed to have incarnated the Gods of the myths.

Mircea Eliade,[12] perhaps the greatest scholar of comparative religion and mythology, has contributed enormously to our understanding of rituals and myths among premodern peoples, including the rituals and myths associated with sacred kingship. For premodern peoples, Eliade noticed that the sacred dimension of reality was by far their most important mode of experience.[13] This sacred dimension was the locus of what Eliade called the "superabundance of divine energy," and existed in the timeless time creation myths speak of, a time "above" our earthly time.[14] Spatially the sacred mode was located above and below our earthly plane, in the heavens and in the underworld.

The everyday experience of time and space Eliade called "profane." Profane *time* began at the world's creation. Profane *space* encompassed all those physical locations in the material world never shaped by divine powers, and also those discarded from sacred space by the Gods. When sacred time and space erupted into the profane mode, they made the earthly dimension "real." Creation was the product of divine energy materializing in the sterile and chaotic profane dimension.

Creation for premodern peoples began at the center, and radiated out in every direction.[15] Eliade found that most of these peoples located the creation site at the center of their territories, where stood a sacred tree, a sacred mountain, the throne or dais of the sacred king, his audience hall, his holiest temple, and by extension his entire capital city. These cities, and the palace-temple complexes they enclosed, often were constructed as miniatures of the cosmos.[16] Since they were located at the point where sacred energy had broken into the profane dimension, these locations were believed to carry enormous charges of divine, or in *our* terms, archetypal energy. Rituals at the temples and palaces were designed to activate or deactivate this energy.[17]

The absolute center was conceived of as a radically energized vertical axis, which Eliade called the *axis mundi*,[18] securing the sacred dimension to the profane. Along this central axis the divine energies could travel up or down and gain access to the earth plane. Priests and shamans, either by innate psychic gifts or ritual consecrations, could also travel to the heavenly and infernal regions at will.

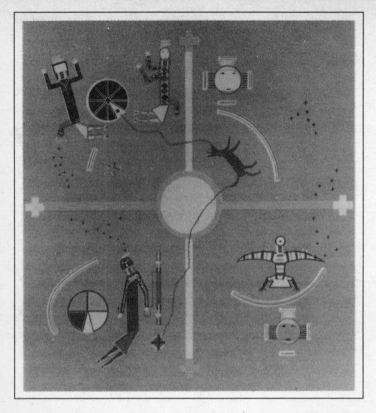

The Universe as Mirror of the Psyche: The Four Quarters with the *Axis Mundi* at the Center (Navajo sand painting of the myth of Coyote)

The sacred king was usually the foremost interdimensional voyager. He could constellate the *axis mundi* wherever he happened to be. By performing religious rituals and ceremonies, or simply by entering into a shamanic trance, he would create the center of the world. He was a sort of portable axis. But especially at times of high ritual he could, like the characters in the *Star Trek* series, "beam" himself up or down along the axis of radiant energy that bound the levels of reality.

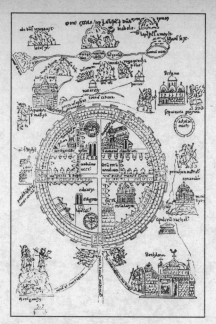

Divine Order on the Earth Plane:

The Quadrated City as Microcosm of the Universe

(twelfth-century plan of Jerusalem)

The Sun-Power and the Mystery of Time:

Masculine Consciousness Enthroned Among the Aztecs

(scale-model Aztec temple surmounted by a calendar stone)

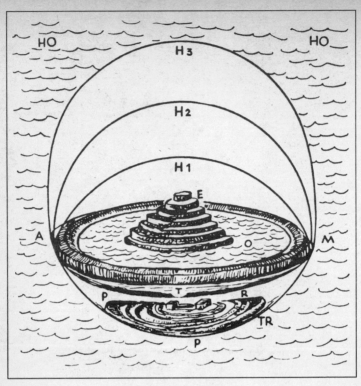

The Babylonian Universe:
Earth as the Sacred Mound of Masculine Consciousness
Rising from the Waters of the "Feminine" Unconscious

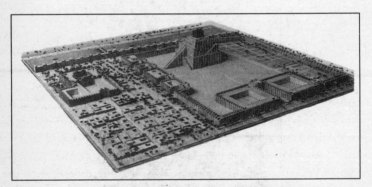

Where the Archetypal King Intersects the Earth Plane:
Temple as "Transporter" Room

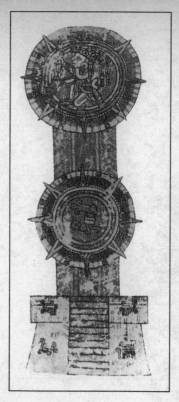

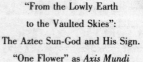

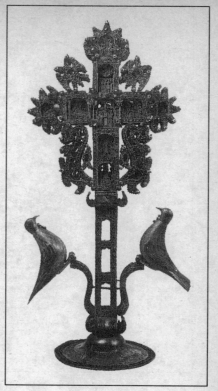

"From the Lowly Earth
to the Vaulted Skies":
The Aztec Sun-God and His Sign.
"One Flower" as *Axis Mundi*

The Foliated Cross as Tree of Life/
Axis Mundi with Birds,
the Symbols of Spirit
(Greek, dated 1654)

Whether he was thought of as divine or mortal, the king's task was to further and steward the creation the Gods had entrusted to him.[19] According to Eliade, any time the *axis mundi* was conjured and traversed by the spirit of the king (or his high priest or shaman), the ultimate purpose was always world building.[20] World building accomplished a new transfusion of sacred energy into the profane world, with a resulting regeneration of creation. Without regular transfusions such as these, premodern

Axis Mundi as Tree of Life:
Transfixing the Planes of Reality
(eighteenth-century engraving of the Teutonic World Tree,
Yggdrasil, from Finnur Magnússon's *Elder Edda*)

peoples believed the earth plane would degenerate into sterility
and chaos. Among the rituals used to secure this sacred energy
were seasonal and new-year festivals, and the sacrifices, coro-
nations, marriages, and jubilees of the kings. The king's ritual
journeys assured as firmly as his governmental and military activities the continued stability and fertility of his kingdom.[21]

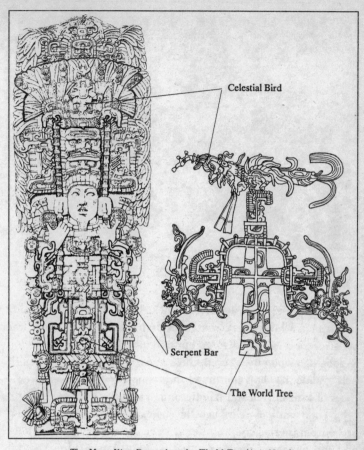

Celestial Bird

Serpent Bar

The World Tree

The Maya King Dressed as the World Tree/*Axis Mundi*
(18-Rabbit at Copań, 711 C.E.)

TRADITIONS OF SACRED KINGSHIP

Africa is a name still fraught with magic. Despite the changes of the modern era, Africa still has the power to conjure images of limitless grassy plains, impassable rain forests, and fantastic beasts; images too of fierce warrior tribes and their charismatic

The Asante King: Glorious Insulation

kings, resplendent in ostrich plumes, leopard pelts, and gold, proud men whose every word was divine law. While such images are increasingly divorced from reality, there was a time not so long ago when the sacred kings of Africa still ruled in wealth and grandeur. They continued the immemorably ancient traditions of kingship of the Nilotic and sub-Saharan peoples.[22]

Thousands of years ago the majestic office of the pharaoh arose from these same traditions. Even today among the Nilotic and sub-Saharan peoples we find powerful kings ruling, as did the pharaoh, in seclusion from their subjects. The king is often hedged around by elaborate and inviolable taboos.[23] He may not allow his face to be seen even when he is holding public audience. He must observe a host of daily ceremonies and rituals designed to make of him a veritable God on earth. He is aided by a council of elders, including warriors and statesmen, but closest to his side is the high priest or witch doctor.

He is often referred to as a "rain king"[24] since his primary function is to assure a sufficient rainfall for the crops, herds, and game animals his subjects depend upon. The rain kings achieve their control over the weather, it is believed, through their mystical oneness with all of nature and with their regular communion with the Gods. The "rain magician" still to be found serving some African tribes may historically have been the prototype for the African sacred king. The king is regarded as a temporary vessel carrying the power of the divine kingship, what *we* recognize as the King archetype.

When the power begins to fail a king, it is thought that the man's mortal frailty has begun to block the King energy. The king may hold office only as long as this fructifying power remains with him. Even modern times have seen a failing African king ritually murdered, so that a more vigorous man may be designated as his successor.[25]

The early kings of Africa drew on all four of the mature masculine archetypal energies. Besides the evident manifestation of the King, the Magician was present when the king invoked the powers of nature for the benefit of his people. The Warrior enabled the king to enforce law and order within the realm, and to defend and extend its boundaries. The king's sacred marriage to a primary queen, and his taking of a harem, were performed as acts of sympathetic magic designed to draw down the procreative energies of the cosmic Lover.[26]

Egypt's ancient civilization developed after desertification forced a number of North African tribes to migrate into the Nile River valley.[27] By 4000 B.C. these various tribes had united into two kingdoms, Lower Egypt in the Nile's northern delta, and Upper Egypt in the river valley to the south.[28] Their "upper" and "lower" designations are the reverse of what we might expect because they were taken from the direction of the all-important river's flow, and not from geographic orientation.

Each kingdom was a highly complex, hierarchically orga-

The Sacred King of Egypt: Empowered by the Feminine
(the Pharaoh Mycerinus with Hathor and the Goddess of the Jackal
Nome, Old Kingdom)

nized society of priests, scientists, engineers, scribes, lawyers, physicians, landholders, merchants, and peasants, presided over by a sacred king.[29] These predynastic kings were credited by the early Egyptians with the creation of civilization. Certainly archaeological evidence demonstrates that sacred kingship flowered just as the Egyptian social system emerged. And the ancient myths link Osiris, the legendary first sacred king, with the birth of civilization.[30]

After teaching the Egyptians all the arts of culture, the god-king Osiris was slain by his evil brother Set, who during his subsequent rule reversed much of the good work Osiris had done. When Osiris was resurrected from the dead by his wife, the Goddess Isis, he became the Lord of the Dead. Later, Osiris's son Horus defeated Set and restored Egypt to its road to glory.

The transition period between Egyptian predynastic and dynastic civilizations witnessed a sudden outpouring of creative intellectual activity.[31] This is the period when the monumental stone temples and monuments were raised, when written languages appeared, and when the fields of medicine, astronomy, and mathematics were codified and extended. Three thousand years later, the ancient Greeks built much of their scientific and philosophical systems on an Egyptian foundation.[32] Through the Greeks our entire Western culture owes a debt to Egyptian engineering, mathematics, medicine, and theology. Egyptian conceptions of the immortality of the soul, the incarnational character of human being, a last judgment, heaven and hell, the essential unity of God, Madonna and Divine Child, the Trinity and the Logos, inspired Christian versions of these same ideas. Although other ancient cultures often held such ideas (they are archetypal), our own understanding of them is built upon the Egyptian.[33]

Upper and Lower Egypt were united about 3200 B.C. by a pharaoh of Upper Egypt, Menes, or Narmar, into the first nation-state in history.[34] The traditions of sacred kingship founded by Menes lasted for the next three thousand years.

According to Egyptian belief, the pharaoh was the living incarnation of the high God, Ra (the sun).[35] Ra, the original King-God, had given birth to himself at the dawn of creation. From him all the other Gods and Goddesses and the created world with its myriad life-forms had flowed. Ra was the source of life and the sustainer of all things. He had founded the original order (Ma'at) by which the created world was made and according to which it continued to flourish, both in the realm of nature and in the social sphere. The pharaoh was at once Ra the father and Horus the son. This same Horus was also the son of Osiris, as Ra and Osiris were held to be two aspects of the same divine mystery.[36]

Ra lived in the timeless world of the high heavens. Through his son, he maintained life-engendering contact with the things he had made. The pharaoh alone was the conduit for *ka*, the life-force Ra poured into the world to animate all things.[37] The pharaoh's every action was an expression of *Ma'at*, Ra's divine order. Ra's first creation out of chaos was the Primordial Hill.[38] Upon this hill sat the pharaoh's throne, by the symbolic device of the raised dais.[39] From the pharaoh's throne the ordered universe radiated in every direction.

The Egyptians believed their very souls came from the pharaoh's ka. He was literally, as the point of contact between the human and the divine, the "giver of life" and the "father" of his people. He had also, as the "raging bull" and the "wrathful lion," the power to take souls away.[40] He fought Ra's battles against darkness and death. Where there was injustice and disorder the pharaoh brought retribution and the restoration of Ma'at.[41]

As high priest of Egypt, through his harmonious participation with the fabric of Ma'at, he drew upon the power of the Magician. He called upon the Warrior's energy to defend the citizens of the created world (the Egyptians) against the hordes still ruled by Set (everybody else).[42] Ra also demanded that he extend the boundaries of creation. Thutmose III, the greatest warrior of the pharaohs, pushed Egypt's borders as far as the Tigris and Euphrates rivers in Mesopotamia.[43]

The Lover manifested in the pharaoh's love for his nation. He protected his people from malevolent humans and spirits alike; for the people he was their "strong wall" and their "shady tree." He loved the Goddesses through the person of his sacred queen, and with many other wives and concubines besides. It was essential he produce an heir.[44]

Besides such a necessary and concrete demonstration of virility and life-force, the pharaohs had to celebrate a self-rejuvenation festival called the ḥeb sed.[45] Through trials of physical endurance the pharaoh proved he still could serve as a channel of divine energy. Scholars believe this ḥeb sed festival was a substitute for an earlier tradition of periodically sacrificing the king.

Upon his death the pharaoh ascended to heaven. There he was reunited with Ra, his father. Horus would then incarnate in the heir, so continuing the divine presence on earth. Since Ra was also an aspect of Osiris, the pharaoh reunited with him as well, and so became the Lord of the Dead. Thus he had the power to enable pious Egyptians to live forever beyond the grave.[46] The pharaoh was seen therefore as the benevolent source of life on earth, and beyond the grave as the stern enforcer of divine order. His people looked to him to supply their every need, and he was the individual uniquely empowered to provide for them.

Originating in the Caucasus region of Western Asia, the Indo-Aryan diffusion[47] spread, by a series of invasions, a group of tribes throughout India, Iran, the Near East, and Europe. These invasions began in the second millennium B.C. Descendants of

the conquerors include the Greeks, the Romans, and the Teutonic peoples. All of the Indo-Aryan groups drew heavily on
Warrior energy. All organized their societies under warrior
kings, in rigid hierarchies of professions and classes. The Magician also figured effectively in their elaborate theological systems and their various sciences and technologies

India, fabled land of desert and jungle, of tigers and elephants,
of golden palaces and garden-festooned temples, has cradled in
her valleys some of the world's foremost religions—Hinduism,
Buddhism, Sikhism, and Jainism. From this home of sophisticated metaphysical and theological traditions, Indian spirituality spread throughout the Mediterranean area during the fourth
century B.C., the time of Alexander the Great. Indian thought
was a major influence on the pre-Socratic philosophers of
Greece, and through Plotinus, on the theology of the Christian
Church.[48] India's Gods are legion. Indra, Varuna, Krishna,
Rama, Vishnu, Shiva, Brahma—King-Gods all of them, providing, protecting, and procreating in myth and legend. It is
they who engendered divine order, *Dharma*, in the events of the
material universe.

In premodern times the Indian rajas were believed to be
composed of particles of the Gods.[49] A raja was the living
embodiment of Dharma.[50] The souls of all living things were
drawn upward into the spiritual dimension through this sacred
king, the people's holy vessel.[51] Though theoretically the raja
could betray his divinity, transgress against Dharma, and be
deposed, some Indian commentators insisted that the king's
divinity was so entire that he could flout human conventions
with impunity. For these apologists even the raja's cruelest and
most abusive actions were expressions of a godly nature. He was
titled, as were the Gods, the Lord of the Four Quarters.[52]

Through his every word and deed the raja was inextricably
bound to the fructifying and desolating powers of nature. He

was the unique source of life and blessing, of rain and abundance for his people. He was also their source of eternal life, and their wrathful judge. Because his person was a holy vessel of divine energy, he had to be sealed off from the profane dimension of the earthly plane. His daily life was bound by ritual, serving to isolate, conserve, and contain his sacred powers. He could not touch the ground with his bare feet lest his divine energy immediately drain from him. To his subjects, he was both high priest and military leader, whose Dharma filled him with radiance, and whose battlefield prowess knew no equal.

Persia's king sat on a golden throne ornamented with richly worked tassels, fringes, and purple silk cushions. Around his head burned the holy flames of the supernatural *xvarnah*.[53] And above him the winged sun disk of Ahura-Mazda,[54] the Creator, God of light and fire, flashed a warning to any agent of darkness who might be seeking to destroy the creation. His Persian empire, centered in what is now Iran, at its height stretched from Mongolia to Egypt, and from Arabia to the shores of Greece.

The Persian king wore a veil in order to protect his subjects from the fiery effulgence that emanated from him. He was the holy container of *khshathra*, the "charism of rule,"[55] and he dedicated his life to the overthrow of demons and all their impious works. The Persian monarchs were heirs of the Mesopotamian and Egyptian civilizations, and converts to the Zoroastrian faith. Their ferocity was a symptom of their determination to re-create the world through an injection of Ahura-Mazda's light and truth into the tarnished dimension of space and time. Their earthly battles were echoes of the profound struggle fought on all levels of sacred space and time between the forces of light and darkness. At the end of history these kings were destined to fight side by side with the heavenly Savior and share in the triumph of good over evil.[56]

The Sacred King as Anglo-Saxon War-Leader
(Arthur's knights in armor, from an illustration by Gustave Doré
for Tennyson's *The Idylls of the King*)

*   *   *

Teutonic tribes were among the Indo-Aryan warrior nations to share in the conquest of Europe from the sixth century B.C. through the sixth century A.D.[57] In the process, they subdued or displaced the Celts and the other peoples of central, southern, and western Europe. These "barbarians," as the Dorian Greeks termed the bearded Teutonic hordes, invaded the Mycenaean city-states and eventually joined with the natives in establishing the culture of classical Greece. They conquered Italy and founded Rome. Later still, they engineered the collapse of the Roman Empire in the West, settling afterward in the cultural spheres that became the modern nations of much of Europe.

The Vikings were one of the notorious Teutonic tribes, whose campaigns reached as far as Moscow, and who founded the Russian nation. Among these tribes, too, were the Anglo-Saxons, who took Britain back from the Romans, driving the romanized Celts into Cornwall and Wales in the process. Much later various amalgams of these peoples—the Normans, the French, the Dutch, and the Germans—through their colonial policies profoundly altered the geopolitical situation of the planet.

The early Anglo-Saxons believed in a sacred kingship very similar to that of their cousins in Iran and India.[58] The Anglo-Saxon king was held to be descended from Wotan, or Odin, the high God of the Teutonic pantheon. Wotan could be wise and kindly, but had also a fierce and militaristic aspect, strongly paralleling the other King-Gods found throughout Indo-Aryan and Semitic cultures.

Descended from Wotan, an Anglo-Saxon king was believed to be filled with Wotan's creative powers and destructive might. The sacred king was the warrior chief of his people. Because of his divine ancestry he was also the high priest. Through ecstatic communion with his divine ancestors, he assured the well-being of his realm. He was in mystical communion with the forces of nature. He called his divine energy "luck," a cognate of the Iranian *khshathra*. As his luck went, so went his kingdom.

In the earliest times when his luck failed he was sacrificed and a new, luck-bearing man from the sacred kin was elected. After his death, the king became a God. In the sacred dimension beyond the grave, he continued to care for his people. A little reverie allows us to picture what this posthumous contact may have been like:

Imagine a morning sun rising through the angled trees of a northern forest, rousing the spirits of the beasts, lighting the broken grasses along a path to a man-made hill. Asleep in his barrow is the king, entombed with his iron weapons, his chariot and horses, an amber pendant and a boar-tusk necklace. Though the body of the king rests, his soul is alive in the forest. It speaks in the wind, it shouts in the thunder. It cups the waving grain in invisible hands, urging it to grow. At the barrow, when his son comes with the priests and the whole folk to do him honor, the soul of the king whispers in his son's ear, uttering oracles concerning future triumphs and impending disasters. A God now, the sacred king guides his people with all of his accumulated wisdom and the strength of his supernatural will.[59]

When we move from the Near East and Europe to Central Asia, we move into Magician territory. The kings of Asia turned the Warrior's virtues of emotional detachment and rigorous self-discipline inward in order to achieve a continual state of communion with the spirit world. The remainder of the Warrior energy these kings split off and vested in various ministers at the royal court. The sacred king in these countries has been otherwise entirely encompassed by the Magician, and the Lover in his spiritual aspect. He lives his life at a distance from the world and in intimate union with the Buddha's "essence of mind."

Embodying the Archetypal King at the Center of the Universe
(twelfth-century Tibetan painting)

*   *   *

Tibet saw the emergence of sacred kingship in the seventh century A.D.[60] The king soon found his claims to divinity supported by the Buddhist religion, which was making headway against the native Bon faith at this time. The Tibetan king was the *dharmaraja*, the embodiment of the sacred order on the earth plane. And yet he had little to do with the actual governance of his people. The administrative and military duties were delegated to powerful functionaries, and priests saw to the people's religious needs.[61] The Tibetan king was expected to live his life as a holy ascetic, unaffected by the affairs of profane reality, and beyond all feminine charms. Only so long as he could sustain this monastic ideal would the rains fall and the people prosper. If the king's *mnga' t'ang* became corrupted, drought would follow and the kingdom would perish.

Fresh mortal vessels for the incarnation of Dharma were always provided by a ceremonial system that sacrificed the reigning king when his heir turned thirteen. The coronation ritual following returned the world to the untainted state it had been in when fresh from the hands of the Gods. Upon his death the former ruler became a divine ancestral spirit; he continued to live on in the person of his son. All deified Tibetan kings became one with the mythological ancestor king. It was said the ancestral king, lost in the mists of prehistory, had descended from the land of light in order to inaugurate the rule of Dharma in the created world.

The intricately worked mandalas of Tibetan Buddhism are hypnotic images of the sacred center their kings were expected to hold. Around this still point swirl Gods and Goddesses, angels and demons, saints and sinners, and the whole of the created world. At the center all is harmony and bliss, resolved into the tranquil light of Buddha Consciousness.[62]

*   *   *

China's divine emperor was called the "unique man."[63] His physical and spiritual person was again the universe's center. In the Chinese character for emperor, 王, he is represented as the vertical *axis mundi* holding together the earthly and heavenly planes. The "son of heaven," he ruled by the "mandate of heaven."

As the supreme embodiment of the sacred center the emperor ruled a created world that expanded intricately on every side in Chinese-box fashion. His palaces and temples were built to duplicate in miniature the structure of the universe. The sacred city around the palace-temple complex was a further replication of the cosmos. The rest of the kingdom drew its sustenance from this center, and extended the divine presence to the limits of profane space and time. Beyond its borders were chaos and death.

The Chinese regarded themselves as the "true" people, imbued with an overflow of the *teh*, or life-force, which their emperor shared freely with them. As high priest, the emperor performed sacred seasonal rituals in the Hall of Light where the teh was concentrated. From this central hall teh was distributed, just as Ma'at and Dharma were distributed, among all living things in the kingdom.

On T'ai Shan, the holy mountain, the emperor was ceremonially sacrificed (through an unfortunate proxy), and then resurrected. By this sympathetic magic the whole universe returned to its original chaos and then was regenerated. The emperor's power was renewed so that he could pursue Heaven's command to defeat the forces of chaos and extend the boundaries of the created world. Within the borders of the Chinese world the emperor brought abundance, fertility, joy, and peace to all of his subjects. He manifested both mercy and wrath, reflecting in his sacred moods the benevolent and wrathful seasons in the cosmic order.

Huang-Ti, the "Yellow Emperor," was the mythological

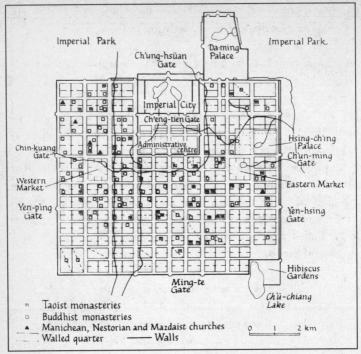

The Chinese City as Microcosm of the Universe

(Ch'ang-an during the Sui and T'ang dynasties)

paradigm for succeeding historical emperors.[64] According to legend, he was conceived by a concubine who happened to glance up into the sky as a bolt of lightning flashed toward the constellation of the Great Bear. Huang-Ti dedicated himself to scholarship and reflection, drawing upon the Magician energy that came to characterize Chinese kingship for three thousand years.

His magic power came from learning the secret harmony of all things. By obeying the mystical numbers that governed the dynamics of heaven and earth, he established cosmic order in

The Tao Employed: The Hsi and Ho Brothers Commissioned
by the Emperor Yao to Organize the Calendar and
Pay Respect to the Celestial Bodies

China, and in so doing made civilization possible. He was "firm and just and embraced the whole world."[65] Nature conformed to his wishes and through him abundance was offered to the Chinese people.

After he had reigned nineteen years and his kingdom was at peace and prospering, Huang-Ti heard that the great sage Kwang Khang-tze was living on the summit of a sacred mountain near the capital city. Huang-Ti went on a pilgrimage to learn from Kwang Khang-tze. He explained he hoped to learn "to direct the yin and yang, so as to secure the comfort of all living beings."[66] Kwang Khang-tze instructed the emperor in the mysteries of the yin and yang (the masculine and feminine energies of the universe) and other mysteries of the *Tao*, the "way" of things that underlay teh.

Kwang Khang-tze taught the emperor that he could accomplish all things solely through attention to his own inner psychological and spiritual condition.[67] The Taoist ideal proclaimed that all things would work together in harmony as long as the emperor's own inner life was harmoniously ordered. This Taoist concept makes a certain degree of sense in terms of the conclusions of depth psychologists. On the basis of extensive evidence it seems that our outer worlds do reflect back to us the dynamics of our inner lives in the persons and events we encounter.[68]

Korea's Pak Hyŏkkŏse, the "man who rules by light," agreed to take the form of a human being and descend to earth in order to establish civilization among the peoples of Korea.[69] He dropped to earth at the foot of the sacred mountain and founded the Silla kingdom. As he touched the ground, the birds and animals began to dance, the sun and moon shone more brightly than they ever had before, and the earth shook for joy. The whole mountain shone in the radiance that enveloped him. He set up the sacred kingship of Korea and taught the people his divine knowledge of agriculture, mathematics, government, written language, science, the trades, and the arts.

Japan's samurai tradition was brought frighteningly home to the American sailors who watched wave after wave of kamikaze pilots slamming their explosive-laden planes into the decks of U.S. warships. These young Japanese seemed completely out of their minds to the Americans. But to their countrymen, they were heroes. Inspired by the self-sacrificial ideals of the samurai of medieval Japan,[70] they followed the emperor's behest to spread the light of the "rising sun" beyond the borders of Japan.[71] Their white flag's central image of the blood-red dawn sun, rays flashing outward to vanquish the darkness of the rest of the world, symbolized their holy cause.

Japan's kingship ideology reached full expression between the fourth and eighth centuries A.D. The first divine emperor, Ojin, established his rule at Naniwa, near Osaka. He and his descendants were referred to as "children of the high-shining sun." To the Japanese the sun was the God of enlightenment, life, and cosmic order.

By the eighth century Japanese emperors were believed to be incarnations of the Sun God.[72] The emperor was given the title *akitsu-mi-kami*, "the sun who has manifested himself in the phenomenal world as a human being." As god-kings the emperors became the supreme mediators between the human and the divine. One of the emperor's most important duties was to annually distribute the sacred rice seed, which initiated the planting season. This ceremonial action was both a symbolic and a tangible expression of his life-bearing powers.

Closely associated with the emperor were ministers who specialized in either military or religious matters. Over these formative centuries a vast bureaucracy was developed on the Chinese model. As in China, the emperor became a "sage king" who fostered the growth of a large intellectual elite. His palace was the sun's center in the world, and from it he beat back the forces of darkness. His enthronement signaled the re-creation of the universe.

Maya civilization (at its height from approximately the first century B.C. to the tenth century A.D.) arose in the context of the enormous creative energies unleashed by the emergence of the sacred kingship.[73] The Maya built vast stone cities in the steaming jungles with huge palaces and soaring pyramids topped with ornately decorated roof combs. A profoundly mystical attitude toward time was characteristic of the Maya, who could calculate unimaginably distant dates in a prehuman past. Efficient, stratified societies, flourishing arts and sciences, and innovative agricultural technologies were also theirs. Their temples, the collective conception of priests, architects, astronomers, and engineers, were designed to be microcosms of a multidimensional universe. The temples served, for the Maya, as power centers whose function was to raise the sacred life-force and then ritually distribute it for use throughout the kingdom.

The sacred Maya king was the ceremonial conduit for this power. Again through a reverie we can combine pieces of archaeological testimony into a vivid scene:

On the pyramid platform, high above the surrounding jungle, before the door to Xibalba, the underworld, the king pierces his tongue with a stingray spine. He then draws a rope though the perforation. He catches his blood in a bowl of paper scrolls, so that when the scrolls are burned he can behold the Vision Serpent in the rising smoke.

From the Vision Serpent's mouth the heads of his divine ancestors appear. Trembling with the force of energy of the World Tree he has constellated, the king hears the voices of the Gods. They speak perhaps auspicious words about the war he will soon have to fight to secure noble captives for temple sacrifices.

A Maya Power Plant: Copán

The king's quetzal-feathered headdress and jaguar robe signal his divinity to all. Through his magical acts and his military prowess he regenerates a dangerous world. He is high priest of the sun, commander in chief of the warriors, administrator, judge, and architect—his kingdom's welfare depends entirely upon him. As divine *ahau* his word is the word of the ancestor kings and the Gods. A giant invisible jaguar spirit rears behind his throne, a deadly threat to any who might doubt that this ahau is protected by the unseen world. Through the king the realm of the Gods and demons can work its will, for good and evil, upon all the life-forms of the earthly dimension.

Central Mexico, far to the north, supported the great civilizations first of the Toltecs and later the Aztecs. These peoples emerged from the same cultural horizon as the Maya had.[74] Though recent research indicates that the Maya were more warlike than had been previously thought,[75] by contrast with their

Bird-Jaguar's Flapstaff Ritual
(Yaxchilań, eighth century C.E.)

northern cousins they were a peaceful people. The sacred kings of Central Mexico were aggressively militant. The Aztecs had an especially insatiable appetite for empire building, all-out warfare, and human sacrifice. [76]

Kingship among the Aztecs developed slowly out of a tribal democracy in which the earliest kings were the first among equals, addressed simply as "reverend speaker."[77] The reverend speaker, though human, was seen as the chief intermediary between the Aztec people and their high Gods, Huitzilapochtli and Tonatiu. Just prior to Cortez's arrival in Mexico, Aztec kingship was transforming into the kind of sacred kingship we have already surveyed.[78] Motecuzoma II (Montezuma to the Spaniards) demanded that he be treated like a living God. This seemed outlandish to many of his subjects, but they were in no position to refuse him.[79]

Behind Central Mexican kingship lay legends of the ancestral god-king Quetzalcoatl, the "feathered serpent."[80] The Toltec priest-kings who succeeded him and incarnated his spirit took on his name as well. He had established and ruled the primordial city, Tollan. Tollan had been laid out from a central pyramid plaza under Quetzalcoatl's guidance, in the directions of the four quarters of the universe. Quetzalcoatl taught the Mexicans all the arts and sciences, and the customs and laws of civilized life.

Prior to this, Quetzalcoatl had created the Fourth Age in the history of the world. As his crowning achievement he made human beings. He had done this by an act of self-sacrifice. He died in order to journey to the underworld, where he stole the sacred bones he needed to make the first people. He sprinkled the bones with his own blood, drawn from his phallus, until they came alive. He then resumed his life in the land of the Toltecs, enjoying being king to his new creations.

He taught his subjects how to harmonize their society with the cosmic order, revealed in the mysteries of the calendar. A

"Truly It Began with Him!"

Quetzalcoatl, the Feathered Serpent

(from a relief at Xochicalco)

great warrior, he extended Tollan's sphere of influence in every direction. He gave to every human being at birth an immortal soul. He journeyed at the end of his reign to the Gulf Coast, setting sail for the rising sun after vowing someday to return. But even after his earthly departure, Quetzalcoatl continued to nourish his creation. As the Mexican poets said: "Truly it began with Him/Truly from Him it flowed/All art and knowledge."[81]

Peru was home to the aggressive Inca people. "Inca" actually was the title for their emperor, and their first, Pachacutec, began an amazing period of expansion.[82] Beginning in A.D. 1438 the Incan armies carried their conquests all the way to the Colombian-Ecuadoran border, and to central Chile.

Not only a great warrior, Pachacutec personally redesigned and renovated Cuzco, the capital city. He initiated ambitious building projects and reorganized Incan society into a hierarchy of trades and professions. Under the leadership of succeeding Incas the people advanced the sciences of metallurgy, medi-

Machu Picchu:
The Splendor of Civilization in the Andes

cine, architecture, and engineering. They built a network of roads and bridges connecting all the cities of the empire. They founded an efficient postal service, delivering messages through a language of knotted cords.

The Inca was believed to be the child of the sun. His word was the will of the Gods. Like most other sacred kings, he possessed a large harem. His many sexual liaisons were magic acts encouraging the universe to rain abundance and bliss down upon the peoples of his empire.

THE SACRED KING
AS MORTAL MAN AND
SERVANT OF THE ARCHETYPE

Up to this point we have been looking at kings who, at least in theory, were *incarnations* of the King archetype. In the societies we've examined, little distinction has been made between the mortal king's Ego and the archetype. The two were more or less merged. Beliefs about the king's divinity were remarkably uniform, whether the kingship emphasized Magician or Warrior energy, and whether the Lover was celebrated in his erotic or in his spiritual and ascetic aspect. In every case the mortal king, reigning at what was believed to be the center of the cosmos, manifested the creative ordering of the earthly level of reality. His world building effected the rise of great civilizations. His procreative powers were held to assure the flourishing of life in his kingdom.

Now we turn to the other pole of the phenomenon of kingship. This pole is typified by a radical *disidentification* of the mortal king's Ego from the archetype of the King.

Mesopotamian relief sculptures from the palaces of ancient Assyria portray their great kings—Ashurbanipal, Shalmaneser, Tilgath-pileser, and others. Attired in scaled body armor and intricately worked crowns, they swing their swords or draw their bows from horseback or from chariot, thighs and biceps bulging with effort. Their expressions are an odd combination of fierce intensity in the eyes and ethereal, tranquil smiles.

These all-conquering muscular giants with long curled beards and flowing oiled tresses are representations of the dynamic calm that is a hallmark of the King energy. Their eyes pierce friend and foe alike, their hands are swift, their movements sure, and their enigmatic smiles are hints of a supreme

The Lord of Joy:
The Assyrian King Ashurnasirpal Quaffing Wine

self-confidence. A winged sun disk above their heads figures the high God, Assur, guiding them in the cosmic combat of light against darkness.

Scholarly controversy surrounds the attempt to understand sacred kingship in Mesopotamia.[83] Some scholars argue for similarities to Egyptian beliefs and practices, emphasizing a number of ancient texts that suggest that the Mesopotamian kings were regarded as incarnations of King-Gods.[84] Others point to what they believe are considerable differences between the two traditions.[85] In Mesopotamia, they argue, the mortal king was considered the *servant* of the King-God, not his incarnation.

Mesopotamian geography determined a very different culture from the one developed by the Egyptians.[86] Egypt's geographic isolation gave her relative security from invasion. Dependable annual floods brought fertile soil from the interior of Africa and ensured flourishing crops. This led to the spiritual optimism that characterized Egypt's outlook and religion.

Between the Tigris and Euphrates rivers, Mesopotamia was situated on a great plain which was extremely vulnerable to marauders from the mountains to the northeast and the deserts of the south. The elements were as violent and insecure as the neighbors.[87] Mesopotamian religion reflected a pervasive sense of insecurity in its preoccupation with demons, magic charms, and exorcism. The Gods were angry and cruel, often for no good reason.[88] The cosmos was constantly on the verge of being overwhelmed by chaos and death. The Combat Myth, present in most spiritual traditions around the world at some level, was a *central* part of Mesopotamian mythology.[89] World making was of paramount importance, to be pursued continually and with the utmost vigor. The people looked to their priests and magicians, their armies and, above all, their kings in a never-ending struggle to affirm life against the forces of destruction.

The basic system of government in Mesopotamia seems to have been village democracy. The earliest kings were elected from town councils and served only in times of crisis.[90] This city-state culture predated the rise of civilization in Egypt by some five hundred years.[91] By about 3500 B.C. the Sumerians of southern Mesopotamia had developed a highly sophisticated civilization with monumental architecture, written language, refined arts and sciences, social stratification, and a complex philosophical understanding of the world.

A permanent city-state kingship was established eventually, out of military necessity.[92] In the twenty-fourth century B.C. the kingdom of Akkad just to the north of Sumeria succeeded in conquering much of the Tigris-Euphrates Valley, and the first Mesopotamian nation-state came into being.[93] With it came sacred kingship. Sargon of Akkad, the conqueror, called himself "He Who Rules the Four Quarters," a title previously reserved for the highest God. Sargon's son made a direct bid for divinity by styling himself "King of the Four Quarters."[94]

By the time of Hammurabi,[95] Babylon's most famous king, the claim to divinity seems to have been dropped.[96] On the stelae proclaiming his code of law Hammurabi pictured himself as the faithful servant of Shamash, God of the sun.[97] Hammurabi stands before Shamash's throne in an attitude of contemplation. Shamash, gesturing with his right hand, imparts the sacred laws to the king. Henceforth, the Mesopotamian kings were seen more as anointed *servants* of the King-Gods than as *incarnations* of the King archetype.[98]

The sacred king was still, however, the chief mediator between divine and human modes of reality. While he may have been mortal, he was still the God's chosen adoptive son.[99] The urban center the king presided over was laid out as a miniature universe and oriented toward the four quarters.[100] The palace was often attached to the temple. The king was the chief priest. On certain holy days only he could ascend to the top of the ziggurat to commune, in the summit temple, alone with the Gods.[101]

At such times the king came before the divine presence on the holy mountain as the representative of all humankind. At other times, such as the new-year festival when the Epic of Creation was recited, he represented the Babylonian God Marduk in his struggle with the great dragon of chaos, Tiamat, and his subsequent creation of the world.[102] This partial identification of king and God implies at least *some* merging of Ego and archetype.[103]

Mesopotamian kings were the codifiers of divinely inspired laws, ancestral to the Hebrew Torah.[104] Babylonian and Assyrian kings were the patrons of huge libraries and of the arts. But while the Magician energy was a powerful influence on Mesopotamian kingship, the Warrior force was even more powerful, especially in Assyria. While the Assyrian kings are occasionally sculpted performing religious ceremonies, they are most usually shown in military guise.[105] We see them leading lion hunts, or mowing down their human enemies. These Warrior exploits were admittedly religious to some extent in this cultural context, as they symbolized the king's victory over chaos and death.[106]

We find a nearly identical conception of sacred kingship in those urban centers that drew their primary inspiration from Mesopotamia—namely, the kingdoms of Asia Minor, Syria, and Palestine.[107] Among the Hittites of Asia Minor, especially after the Indo-Aryan incursion, there are hints that the king may have been considered divine.[108] He appears in relief sculptures with symbols of the Gods and the procreative powers, among them the winged sun disk and the Tree of Life. In Hittite literature he was given the title "image of God" and it was claimed he was descended from divine parents. But more usual epithets were "beloved of the God," "hero," and "the anointed one," all of which suggest his unique yet human nature.[109]

In pre-Hebraic Palestine mayor-kings ruled over a host of tiny city-states.[110] As in Mesopotamia, they appear to have been seen as servants and adopted sons of the high God, whom they knew as El Elyon.[111] In the great religious festivals the kings represented Ba'al, El's son. Temporarily at least, they thereby assumed a divine identity

The Hebrews originated, some biblical scholars believe, from among the loosely confederated tribes working as merchants and mercenaries in the lands between Egypt and Mesopotamia.[112] They assimilated elements of Egypt's culture during the Egyptian sojourn of the Jacob clans, and in their subsequent wanderings through Egyptian Palestine.[113] But they always showed a stronger affinity for Mesopotamian culture. Indeed, their legendary founder, Abraham, was said to have come from

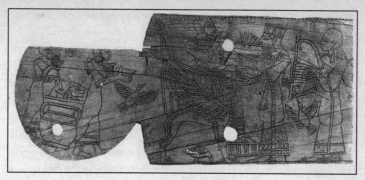

The Canaanite King in His Triumph:
Patron of Life and the Arts

the second millennium B.C. Babylonian kingdom.[114] Once the famous twelve tribes coalesced and occupied parts of Palestine, they felt the need for a king. Each tribe had been ruled over by a petty chief, or "judge," but military necessity impelled the election of a primary king.[115]

From the beginning it was clear that a Hebrew king was a mortal man, destined to remain in office only so long as the high God Yahweh and his spokesmen, the prophets, remained pleased with him.[116] Hebrew kings resembled their Mesopotamian counterparts—they were the acknowledged servants of the high God and the chief intermediary between God and people. Where a Hebrew king possessed power to influence the earth's fecundity and his people's welfare, it came largely from enforcement of and adherence to the laws of Yahweh.[117] Yahweh responded to moral rectitude and personal piety, not ceremonial magic or attempts at mystical identity with him.[118]

However, it does seem that elements of Canaanite kingship persisted in Palestine and influenced segments of the Hebrew people. Other sources corroborate biblical evidence that the northern kingdom of Israel incorporated the fertility rituals of Ba'al and his queen, Anath, into the religion of Yahweh. Yahweh was even called Elohim in the north, after the old Canaanite high God.[119]

There was another sense in which Hebrew traditions resemble divine kingship practices. The Hebrew law, the Torah, when upheld produced much the same effect as Ma'at and Dharma. The king's personal adherence to the Torah had at least the *near* magical effect of ensuring the fertility of nature and the well-being of his subjects.[120] In later years King Solomon, who permitted the worship of the old aboriginal Gods, was believed by the Hebrews to have been a great magician, capable of constellating Yahweh's powers at will.[121]

But for the most part, the Hebrew kings were in a very different relation with the King archetype than were the kings of Egypt, Asia, or the New World. What we see in the Hebrew kingship is a radical *disidentification* of the king's Ego from the archetype. The Hebrews knew the full archetype only in the guise of their sky-dwelling God.[122]

Yahweh is comparable to other King-Gods such as Indra, Zeus, and Ahura-Mazda.[123] He was regarded as the origin of the divine order under which all living things flourished. He was firm in his requirements that his "chosen people" adhere to his order, as expressed in the Torah. He was the source of fertility and good fortune. Through a gradual theological development, this former volcano God[124] developed, in the Hebrew imagination, into the sole creator of the universe.[125] He subsumed within himself, through the efforts of the biblical authors, the attributes and functions of many preceding Gods and Goddesses.[126] He loved and cared for all peoples because his sacred utterances had called all of them into being, not just the people of Israel.[127] At the same time his justice could be severe; he ruled his world with an iron hand. Yahweh was the source of enormous creative and destructive power.[128] Mere mortals could not behold him and live.[129]

Though Yahweh was at first suspicious of urban civilization,[130] the kings who reigned in his name were not. David and Solomon renovated and enlarged many of the former Canaanite cities, particularly Jerusalem. Yahweh's Ark of the Convenant was moved into Jerusalem, and because of this the city became for the Hebrews the center of the world.

The one important area in which Yahweh fell short of manifesting the archetypal King was in his relationship to feminine energies. Like a handful of other austere Gods (among them Persia's Ahura-Mazda), Yahweh had no queen. He did incorporate some of the traditionally defined "feminine" characteristics—relatedness, compassion, tenderness, mercy, the need to love and be loved. But Yahweh, and the Semitic high Gods who evolved from him (Allah and the Christian Trinity) ruled alone. We believe this aversion to accepting the feminine, and the women who embody it, has impoverished the entire experience of the divine in the Western religions. The cult of the Virgin Mary was one spirited popular attempt to redress the imbalance.

An odd thing happened shortly after the death of the Jewish prophet Jesus two thousand years ago. The early Christians transformed Jesus into the archetype of the King.[131] Never having known the man, they vested in him the structures and dynamics of the King-Gods from their non-Hebraic heritages.

Many early Christians came from religious backgrounds that included the sacred-king traditions of ancient Egypt, Greece, and Rome, as well as Hermetic influences, the Mystery Religions, and the Persian religions of Zoroastrianism and Mithraism.[132] The myths of these various faiths were replete with King-Gods, even where actual sacred kings were a thing of the distant past.[133]

Jesus was soon considered a God incarnate, born of a mortal woman divinely impregnated. Like Osiris in the Egyptian myths, he had been slain by his evil brother, called Satan by the early Christians. Again like Osiris, Jesus Christ had then been resurrected and had become the ruler of the dead. After his sacrifice, Jesus did just what the ancient pharaohs had done, ascending into the heavens and becoming one with the high God.[134]

According to Christian myth, Jesus was the creative Word of God (like the Word of the Egyptian God Ptah), the agent by whom the high God created the universe.[135] He became the teacher of a new kind of civilization, based on an inner balance. He thereby served, as had other law-giving, civilization-founding King-Gods and sacred kings, as the embodiment of cosmic order, and as the focal point from which that order radiated into the created world.[136] On earth he had been a great healer. He had had magical power over the forces of nature.[137] Like the Taoist emperors of China, he acted often through in-action.[138] By merely ordering his inner being he allowed his divine father to act through him. He had emptied himself of the fullness of his divine prerogatives, like Korea's Pak Hyŏkkŏse, and descended to this earthly plane in order to bring human beings the divine light by which they could live in harmony.[139] He had been the high priest, the supreme mediator, and the ultimate sacrifice.[140]

From a depth-psychological point of view, the Christological controversies of the first three centuries of our era[141] stemmed from attempts by theologians to understand the proper relationship between the human Ego and the archetype of the King. We can see an unconscious depth psychology at work. Those who argued Jesus was a God and not a man were, like the ancient Egyptians, *identifying* the human Ego with the King energy. Those who argued he was a man, not a God, were, like the Hebrews, *distancing* the Ego from the archetype.

In the end most theologians compromised with theories of co-inherence between the human and the divine. These early Christian thinkers unconsciously respected the psychological fact that the Ego and the archetype are two interdependent aspects of a total psychic system. The two are distinct from one another, with the Ego (Jesus Christ, the Son) subordinate to the archetype (God, the Father) but paradoxically essential to it, and sharing the same psychological "substance" with it.

An excellent film to watch in light of these issues is Martin Scorsese's *The Last Temptation of Christ.* Irrespective of any cinematic value the piece might have, it gives an excellent record of these issues. The basis of the film is that the man Jesus doubts his divine kingship, while his followers want him to accept it. Jesus can't shrug off the King projections his disciples try to give him, but he doubts the origin of his inspiration, the nature of his calling, and the necessity of his sacrifice.

Many men are dismayed by the idea of willing sacrifice. This important attribute of the King archetype strikes many as unnecessary, even masochistic. Jesus himself tries out this view in a long sequence at the end of the film, after being offered an easy way out of his crucifixion. Once he fully understands the consequences of evading his suffering, though, he chooses to go through with it—and so he is crucified. He constellates the *axis mundi*, and so makes of himself a conduit for pouring sacred energy into the profane world.

This is the intention behind the ritual and symbolic sacrifices we've examined. When the sacrificial king offers himself up, he takes upon himself the task of remaking the world, but only when he knows this is the only means he has to achieve this. A man who unconsciously sacrifices himself for his family is an ineffective sacrifice. He is unconsciously *identified* with the King. Here is the distinction between the masochist and the mature man. Jesus would *prefer* to avoid a painful death, but when he understands the circumstances that demand his death, he accepts it. He draws upon the King energy of stewardship—extending the bounds of his responsibility to where his responsibility truly ends.

Imagine for a moment if a man in our society were to do this. Imagine the oil-company executive who makes a concerted effort to clean up the environmental damage his company has caused—because he recognizes and accepts the extent to which his company is *responsible*. Imagine the husband who gives his wholehearted support to the realistic wishes and plans of his wife and children, not only because he is fond of them but because he has accepted his *responsibility* for them. What if a president were to make reparation for his mistakes, and the mistakes of his predecessors? Is such a scenario even imaginable? What if, instead of asking us to put on a brave face and forget these mistakes, he were to lead us in a national period of mourning?

If these possibilities seem outrageous, it is because of the extent to which we are used to projecting our King onto others. It is much easier to deny our responsibilities, when accepting them would so disrupt our habits of life. "Our company is ruining the city's water supply, I really wish the CEO would do something about it; I'd better not say anything though, it's none of my business." The man who is really accessing the King *makes* the social ills that trouble him his business. Most of us are so desperate to evade our social responsibilities, we'll go so far as to elect presidents who are the perfect image of our cowardliness, the Teflon Men who gladly accept the King projections a nation offers them, but who accept responsibility for little else, especially on the domestic front. And the cycle keeps turning on itself, because whenever we project our King onto a politician (or anyone else) we feel disempowered. "Why shouldn't I vote for him? I can't do anything to change it anyway."

What is truly amazing of course is what we *can* do, once we access and utilize our King energy. The spiritual systems of the world are designed to bring their worshipers in touch with this empowering energy, whether their leaders know it or not, because the energy has such a virtuous effect on those who access it. Note that "virtue" has the Latin root *vis*, meaning strength or power. The King's virtue is empowering. Hence Jesus of Nazareth, at least in part, makes an excellent paradigm of the King energy in the individuating male psyche. Hence also the enduring appeal of Ignatius Loyola's exercises. They provide their practitioners one kind of initiation into the mysteries of the King. (Unfortunately for Western women of recent centuries, the Christ paradigm is not really applicable to feminine individuation. For centuries we've neglected to affirm the Queen as an equally adequate image for feminine maturity and generativity. A rediscovery of the Queen image would greatly benefit our culture. After all, along with learning to access the generative *masculine*, one of the cardinal tasks now facing us is finding a way back to honoring the generative *feminine*, both *within* the male, the Anima, and without, in the world.)

CHRISTIAN KINGSHIP TRADITIONS

Throughout the European Middle Ages the Christian Church controlled the cultural, social, and ideological aspects of human life. It consequently formulated doctrines of kingship.[142] So far as the Church was concerned, Jesus Christ had been the only incarnation of the King energy. The mortal king was at most the specially chosen servant of God.[143] Still, pre-Christian ideas about the king's magical power to affect the fecundity of nature and the well-being of his subjects continued to play a part in the minds of average people.[144] Until fairly recent times, European kings were believed to have had the power to cure certain illnesses by the "laying on of hands."[145] By the late Middle Ages something very much like the ancient sacred kingship was on the rise. After the Renaissance era, Louis XIV of France could openly identify himself with the power of the sun.

Receiving the Crown:

The Mortal King and the Archetype

(the coronation of William II of Sicily, from Monreale Cathedral)

In Tudor England an interesting debate began which resulted in a doctrine of kingship called "The King's Two Bodies."[146] A legal question was raised over whether or not a reigning monarch could rightly claim ownership over properties his predecessor had secured. According to the theory the legal wrangling led to, the king had two bodies. One consisted of the mortal man temporarily invested with the monarchy. The other was the kingship itself, an ongoing legal entity transcending the individuals in whom it was vested. Here we see, once again, the struggle to understand the relationship between the Ego and the archetype. We can see in this strange world of dual beings the origins of the royal "we," as well as the custom of speaking to the king in the third person singular.[147] When we address a king as "Your Majesty," we pay our respects both to his own person and to the transcendent, majestic kingship he embodies.

Most national leaders are still treated with some reverence by the majority of their people. The old courtesies and protocols continue in song and ceremony even in thoroughly democratized societies. Their sacred significance is forgotten, but the pattern lives on. For example, in the United States, the president is often greeted at public appearances by the hymn "Hail to the Chief," in which he is compared to the "evergreen pine." This pine is another representation of the Tree of Life, a specific image of the *axis mundi* which can be traced at least as far back as ancient Assyria.[148] Though the United States avoided a monarchy, largely because of Washington's refusal to take the crown, U.S. presidents have ever since enjoyed appropriating the powers and trappings of kings. Franklin Roosevelt refused to relinquish his "throne." Richard Nixon tried to isolate his White House (which is, interestingly, an exact translation of the Egyptian word *pharaoh*) from the profane world. Like the Tibetan kings, he ostensibly at least let his ministers handle the government.

Ongoing Incarnation:
President Roosevelt

In many parts of the world today, the masses of humanity still invest their leaders with the attributes of sacred kingship. Iran is a case in point. Before his overthrow, the shah practiced ceremonies surviving from the time of the ancient Persians. After the Iranian revolution, the Ayatollah Khomeini stepped into the shah's shoes. He embodied the spiritual, administrative, and military aspects of the ancient kings. He proclaimed that it was his sacred responsibility to enforce the laws of Allah, revealed to Mohammed in the Koran. When he died his people beat their heads with their fists just as their ancient forebears had done. They cried out, "Our Father, why have you left us?"

In Latin America, though this seems to be changing rapidly now, a similar cult of the "great man" continues. Dictators there rule with the ancient prerogatives of benevolence and brute force. They defend the "sacred soil," as they call it, and the "sacred honor" of the military elites from whence they come. Wherever charismatic, inordinately powerful men rule by the wishes of the people, elements of sacred kingship survive. What is intriguing is the need so many people have to project an archetypal structure within *every* masculine psyche onto a single supposedly "generative man."

Many cultures besides those few we have examined have sacred kingship traditions of their own. Among them are other aboriginal cultures of the Americas, Africa, India, and Asia, and the kingdoms of Southeast Asia, of Sumatra, Java, Micronesia, and Hawaii.[149] The office of the "big man" in other cultures emphasizes ideals of manhood that draw on the same underlying archetype.[150]

This widespread phenomenon could be partly the result of cultural diffusion, the term for the transmission of ideas from one culture to another through direct or indirect contact. But this process cannot account for the near universality of the institution among peoples who have almost certainly had no contact with one another. Among the Maya, the institution of sacred kingship arose gradually, side by side with the emergence of higher civilization from an indigenous cultural matrix. This is typical of other societies. If cultural diffusion were primarily responsible we would expect a sudden and dramatic inception of kingship after contact with kingship societies. More probably cultural diffusion works as an elaborating impetus shaping a collective urge. An archetypal push, perhaps an inherited instinctual base (illustrated by the phenomenon of the Alpha Male) seems to be behind kingship traditions.

The more psychologically dangerous of the kingship traditions are those where the Ego is identified with the archetype. How-

individual psyche *can* still benefit from imaginally
ıg with the archetype. Personal neuroses and complexes
. be infused with the archetypal King's healing energy, and
ıs fullness of being. Premodern healing rituals often depend on
such a merger with the life-bearing Gods.[151]

In practice some distinction was usually drawn between a
mortal king and the God he was believed to be incarnating.
However, such a king faced the temptation, as does any modern
man with an ill-defined Ego, to identify completely with the
King energy. A disidentification of the Ego from the archetype,
as was emphasized in the Hebrew tradition, provides us with a
safer approach to the enormous power of the King.

Bear in mind that disidentification means *separation* but
not disavowal—the King energy must not be shunned. The
answer to the inherent dangers of power is not to *avoid* power.
Though the man who identifies with the King suffers a psycho-
sis, depression and aimlessness plague the man who represses
the inner King. In terms of a psychic geography, there is no
world (cosmos) without the King. Wherever he is he *makes* the
world, and the *axis mundi*. He is our means for traveling into
the sacred dimension. Without the King, the Warrior within
becomes a mercenary, fighting for pay and not for any worthwhile goal. Our Magician becomes a sophist without a King to
serve, able to argue any idea convincingly, and believing in
none. The Lover without a King becomes a promiscuous phi-
landerer. Or at the very least he will be unempathic and un-
caring in his expressions of love.

Some men are uncomfortable with the idea of showing that
they care for something. Caring seems to them to be dangerously "feminine." The danger they secretly fear is of being
overwhelmed by the feminine. Because they don't understand
that the feminine energy they fear is within their own Anima,
they believe it to be coming from the women in their lives—this
is why the mother, the wife, or the daughter can seem to be

threatening figures. But caring isn't limited to the feminine. Men like Gandhi, and the aptly named Martin Luther King, Jr., *cared* for their worlds. Theirs was an aggressive, masculine, potent caring, a caring powerful enough to remake the world. They are the examples of what a man can do when he responsibly stewards the numinous power of the King within.

THE KING IN HIS
FULLNESS

LIKE THE AVAILABLE CHANNELS A COMPUTER CHIP provides the electrical current that passes along it, the psyche holds certain hard-wired lines of force along which King energy can travel. The examined attributes and functions of historical sacred kings as well as those of the mythological King-Gods, in addition to Warrior, Magician, and Lover energies, reveal a fourfold pattern of King energy. This fourfold pattern has manifested in history precisely because of the four channels available to the King energy in the psyche.

Two of these lines of force center and concentrate the archetypal energy, building up a dynamo of numinous power, which the King releases both within the psyche and in the outer world. The very concentration of this energy effects transformation by its uniting of opposites at the Center and by its containment in the Transforming Vessel. We link these two characteristics of the archetypal King by seeing them as closely related aspects of one major form of King energy, Introverted Energy. Much like the hermetically sealed alchemist's crucible, which when heated transforms base material into fabulous riches, the King as Center and as Transforming Vessel changes unintegrated psychological contents into the gold of personal and potentially global creative transformation.

The other two lines of force within the magnetic field of the King in his fullness express Extroverted Energy. Here we see the archetype manifesting as Procreator and as order-producing Structurer.

While these four lines of force work together, it will be useful for us to distinguish their characteristics. But let us remember that they empower us, finally, as a *whole system* at the center of our psyches.

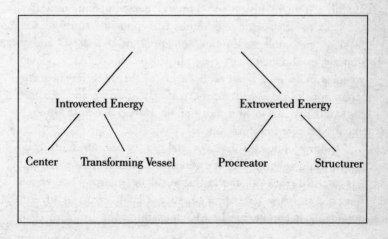

THE KING AS THE CENTER:
RECONCILER OF OPPOSITES

In myth and legend it is the king who constellates the Center of the world. He is the point in the world where sacred and profane energies meet in a dramatic exchange of Libido. The king is therefore the source of useful divine energy in the world. He is the Creator King-God, or the ancestral god-king, who founds and promulgates civilization. His Center is his phallic force, the *axis mundi*, which is variously represented as the Tree of Life, or World Tree; the Primordial Hill, sacred mountain, or pyramid; the city, temple, palace, or the throne he himself occupies. From his Center he can organize the chaos of the earth plane. The divine order, in the several forms we've examined— Ma'at, Dharma, Tao, and Torah—radiates from his Center and helps effect his organizational impulses.

The mortal king's successful incorporation of sacred energy in the profane world is *psychologically* a model for the Ego's attempt to make unconscious material conscious, thereby reconciling the opposites in the psyche. Where the Ego is successful, a tremendous potential energy is made actual and useful. Thus the Ego-King axis unites the opposites spiritual and physical, potential and actual, imagination and deed, and if properly established, can generate full selfhood. As a person becomes more integrated so does his world, both because his perceptions of the world are increasingly accurate and because the world reveals to him more of its essential nature through actually changed circumstances.

Uniting opposites involves making the infinite finite consistently and coherently.[1] We all know how enormously difficult it is to realize our dreams in the world we share. Whether the dream is an invention, an occupational goal, or a way of life, actualizing it can seem almost impossible. The problem is in

Uniter of Opposites:

Life and Death, Moon and Sun, Feminine and Masculine

(plaster cast of Richard I's second Great Seal)

part one of translation, of bringing personal, preverbal intuitions into words or forms that both we and others can grasp. This is the very problem sacred kings faced in trying to translate divine imperatives into human law.[2]

Communication along an axis between the opposites of mortal king and King-God typifies an Ego-archetypal axis of great importance to Jungian psychology. Although to Jungians, the Self at the Center of every psyche is a fully androgynous psychological

CENTER	PROCREATOR
Constellates the *axis mundi*	Incarnates Libido
Reconciles all polar opposites—spiritual and physical, God and man, life and death, light and darkness, good and evil	Manifests sexual and cultural erotic urges
Incorporates the sacred in the profane, the infinite in the finite, the potential in the actual, the unconscious in the conscious	Inspires subjects by beholding them, blessing them, and dispensing riches to them
TRANSFORMING VESSEL	STRUCTURER
Contains and concentrates divine spirit	Encourages education, and the expansion and ascent of Ego consciousness
Renders divine energy humanly usable Distributes a concentration of power to the created world	Translates divine order into technology, theology, philosophy
	Upholds divine order through human law
	Fortifies against inner and outer enemies—chaos and death

essence shared by both men and women, it is doubtful that such a Self can be constituted in the real world. More likely, any Self actually manifested by a human being will be predominantly either masculine or feminine.[3]

If this is true, the ultimate axis a man can realize *and still be a man* is an axis between his Ego and a masculine Self. This masculine Self can be known primarily through the Ego's appropriate accessing of the archetypal King. Since the fully manifested King experiences a passionate union with the Anima (a man's inner feminine sub-personality) as Queen,[4] a man can experience the deep Self approaching the Jungian exemplum, but his Self is likely to be *asymmetrically masculine*.

All pairs of psychologically dynamic opposites are reconciled in the tranquil but dynamic Self at the psyche's Center. The King is the agent by which these opposites are experienced. For example, life and death are united in the person of the sacred king. The resurrection of the dead king is one expression of this unity; the ritual slaying of one king and the installation of the next is another.[5] Behind such rituals is the wisdom that life must die before life can flourish. This is the thinking that sends John Barleycorn, the temporary King of Grain, out into the fields to die after the harvest.

There is a psychological truth to this thinking, that we must die to our old selves in order to be born anew.[6] In this dance of life and death, life is the victor. Saint Paul's Christ finally "swallows" death, ingesting it and using it for the purposes of a greater kingship: that of Christ Pantocrator, "Ruler of the Cosmos."[7]

Other King-Gods incorporated good and evil, just as Christ held life and death at once within his body. Yahweh in the biblical texts is the source of both good and evil, creation and destruction.[8] The Hindu deities transcend good and evil, by uniting the two in their own mysterious essences.[9]

We can read the Chinese symbol of the tao— —as a

visual image of these reconciled dialectics. Light and darkness, aggression and passivity, masculinity and femininity, good and evil—each polar opposite is intertwined with the other. At the exact point where one pole swells to its fullest expression there the seed of the other appears. The opposites are in dynamic union, each giving rise to the other, each interpretable only in terms of the other.

The same symbol could usefully represent the Ego and its Shadow. Since much of the personal Shadow carries values and insights that could contribute substantially to the Ego's experience of life, elements of the personal Shadow certainly need to be integrated. When they can be, they make for a greater psychic depth.[10] However, certain transpersonal aspects of the Shadow—what could be called the collective Shadow—cannot be integrated fully by any human Ego. Collective aspects of the Shadow express forces of radical destructiveness and death. Here is the point where the possibility of genuine, unmitigated evil arises.

Mystics from most spiritual traditions maintain that we cannot live intense, authentic lives without a consciousness of our own personal deaths.[11] So perhaps neither death nor forces of destruction should simplistically be viewed as evil. Only when life is experienced under the aspect of eternity can it be lived with genuine appreciation.

An Egyptian enthronement myth demonstrates the dependence of life and death, good and evil, upon each other.[12] Two cosmic antagonists, Horus and Set, were the sponsor Gods of Lower and Upper Egypt, respectively. It was the pharaoh who first harnessed the energy of their dialectic by uniting the two Egypts and wearing the double crown of Horus and Set. Though the two Gods were eternally antagonistic, their friction helped generate Ma'at in both the sacred and profane dimensions. The pharaoh was announced at his coronation as "The Two Lords"[13] because he had embodied and transcended the antagonism be-

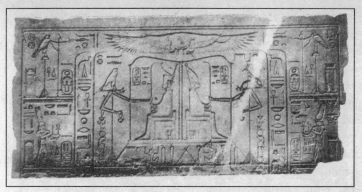

Horus and Set: Opposites United in the Sacred King

(Pharoah Senusert Enthroned as King of Upper and Lower Egypt,

nineteenth century B.C.E.)

tween Horus and Set. He offered his people an image of the essential conflict of the world, and an example for its resolution.

A king's marriage was as important a mythic union as his coronation.[14] In some societies, his marriage was literally to the land of his kingdom, as personified by the queen. In others the queen was seen as the representative of Mother Cosmos in her entirety. Underlying the various myths was the idea of the union of the opposites of masculine and feminine principles.[15] Without such union, subjects could hardly expect the Gods and Goddesses to yield up their bounties to the earth.

Most ancient mythologies harbored a very sexy set of Gods and Goddesses, often descended from an initial transsexual or bisexual creator. These second- or third-generation deities constituted sky, earth, air, water, fire, and so on, and it was they who were responsible for the daily maintenance of the world. In ancient Egyptian paintings, for example, Geb, God of the earth, was shown lying on his back, erect phallus pointing skyward toward Nut, Goddess of the heavens, who was arched languorously above him. Their happily-ever-after erotic interplay en-

Shiva and Parvati:
Masculine and Feminine United in the King's Lover Mode

sured the fructifying unity of earth and sky. The king and queen mirrored Deities such as these, and encouraged their eroticism by performing sympathetic sexual rituals on the earthly plane. In most societies a king without a queen was held to be sterile and his kingdom paid the price.[16]

The royal marriage expresses the masculine need for the feminine (and vice versa) in order to achieve fullness of being. In a good relationship with a woman, in a union that throws a man's masculine characteristics into sharp contrast with the feminine, a man can engender an intimate, enhancing relationship with his own Anima. In so doing he sets up an ever more stable Center, between his masculine and feminine poles. In our culture the Anima often gets split off and repressed. Feminine characteristics in a man are deemed highly suspect. But if a man consciously seeks to develop a relationship with his Anima at the same time that he seeks a deeper accessing of his masculine characteristics, he will find his masculinity affirmed and supported.

By acknowledging his feminine side a man raises his consciousness about complementary masculine structures, and can be inspired to achieve fullness of being *as a man.* As his sense of deeply grounded masculinity becomes more secure, he is free to claim his feminine qualities without fear of being overwhelmed by them. His capacity for creative expression will multiply exponentially.[17] His relationships with women in the outer world will likewise take a positive turn. Such a man, his masculinity reinforced by his inner feminine, can meet life with a centered sense of wholeness and compassion not often seen in our culture.

Reliquary of the Oracular Ancestral Kings:
The Archetype Contained in Order to Concentrate Its Power (Vona Vona)

THE KING AS
TRANSFORMING VESSEL

Saint Paul's Christ emptied himself of divine energy in order to take on human form and impart his Libido to the world. Once filled with his sacred essence, any man can become an equally sacred vessel. Other kings were more conservative of their divine energy and careful not to let it be improperly dissipated.

A king who was believed to be the Center was also naturally regarded as the locus of a tremendous energy. He too was a sacred vessel, a container of divine energy. Often this energy seemed so volatile the king had himself to be contained.[18]

By insulation and containment, subjects were shielded from their king's dangerous, unmitigated power. Also, when a king's energy was conserved within a single spot, it grew ever more concentrated and powerful. Through initiated priests and officers, by the appropriate rites and ceremonies, this concentrated power could be drawn off in its usable form for the good of the people.

This careful handling of the energy is reminiscent of nuclear power plant practices today. Reactor cores are carefully sealed off from the people who ultimately benefit from the energy produced. Direct exposure to this energy is fatal. The core is a reactive supply of concentrated nuclear material. Elaborate technology transforms this contained nuclear power into usable electricity. Any accidental exposure of nuclear material to the "profane" atmosphere results in widespread destruction of plant, animal, and human life—exactly what the ancients imagined the consequences of inappropriately released King energy would be.

Often subjects were not even permitted to look at their kings. In Iran, anyone who beheld the king's fiery crown would be blinded or driven mad by the sight. Yahweh had to turn his back to Moses on Mount Sinai so that Moses would not be destroyed.[19] Semele, a Greek woman, was not so lucky; a glimpse of Zeus reduced her to ashes.[20] Prince Arjuna was spared a similar fate before Krishna, by the use of a special protective preparation Krishna had supplied him. Even so, after seeing the majesty of his God, Arjuna had to beg Krishna to return to an anthropomorphic form, lest he lose his mind.[21]

Initiation served in other societies the same purpose as Arjuna's special preparation. Hebrew priests alone, through their schooling in the mysteries of the Torah, could manage touching the Ark of the Covenant as it was carried to Jerusalem. When once an ordinary foot soldier reached up to steady the precariously balanced Ark, he was instantly struck dead for his pains.[22]

Some traditions avoided these dangers by removing their kings from the everyday world. Taboos and rituals were employed to enable the king to conserve and concentrate his divine power, the energy of the archetypal King. The daily lives of many sacred kings were oppressively regulated, so much so that we know of instances in which the man selected to become the next vessel for the archetype's incarnation skipped town to avoid his coronation.[23] In Tibet, for example, the king was kept away from the outside world to avoid the diluting effects of lesser modes of reality. All his nominal administrative, military, even priestly functions were delegated to officers, who served for him in a way as stepdown transformers of his archetypal King energy. In parts of Africa the king was required to stay behind a veil or drawn curtain so that his divine communications would not for a moment be interrupted. From India to Central Mexico, taboos existed forbidding the king to touch his foot to the earth. The fear was that he would "ground out" and deplete the sacred charge.[24] This is the origin of the red carpet—it is a simple means of keeping royal feet off the ground. The incestuous marriages sanctioned by many royal lineages were a further method of keeping the vital essence concentrated and contained in the family.[25]

Another method of containing and concentrating the sacred energy was the construction of isolating rooms in the king's palaces and temples.[26] His inner sanctuary would often be protected by armed guards. Only the initiated or ritually purified could pass beyond them,[27] to the audience hall—and within this room the throne would be still more isolated—by being raised on a dais perhaps, or surrounded by a retaining wall.

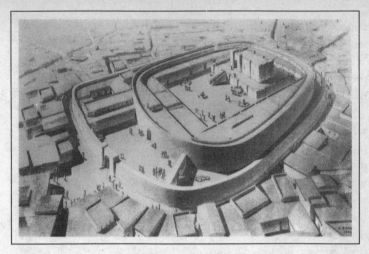

The Sacred Center Contained:

An Ancient "Generating Station"

(early dynastic temple at Khafajah, Mesopotamia)

The *psychological* truth supporting this degree of protection is that the archetypes are immensely powerful dynamic structures, deserving of careful handling. They must be accessed in a way that is life-enhancing rather than death-dealing. In their raw and uncontained forms the archetypes can easily overwhelm other psychological structures.[28] This is clearly the case in individual psychopathology. It is also true in the arena of world history, the sphere of the collective psyche. How many nations have been overwhelmed by the mass hysteria unleashed by the archetypal Warrior, for example, when Ego structures were not sufficiently strong! [29]

The Ego ultimately is the only psychological structure capable of transforming the energy of an archetype. A consolidated Ego, whose strength is augmented by a deepening and a broadening of its sphere of consciousness, is able both to develop individual Ego-archetypal axes *and* to balance one against the other. Ego structure is the psychological equivalent of the shielding and transformer systems noted in ancient ritual and in modern technology.

A properly functioning Ego-King axis gives a man the ability to keep a cognitive and emotional distance from the archetype, and to access and transform its energy in generative ways. The Ego's capacity to conceptualize the King as a circumscribed entity keeps the archetype's energy within bounds. This concentrates the energy of the archetype within the archetypal structure, and protects the rest of the psyche from being flooded by its expansive Libido.

THE KING AS PROCREATOR

Procreative energy constitutes the King's third line of force. Procreation is Libido in the process of incarnating itself. It is the process of a dynamic taking concrete form. Against enormous destructive potential massed against it, it is the force that is always saying "yes" to life, "yes" to the new, "yes" to creativity. It is the phallic thrust of creation, the divine urge to penetrate the profane and seed it with the sacred. It is the erotic urge that drives Gods and Goddesses to couple in order to generate earth, sky, sea, air, and all the forms of life therein. It is the force behind Yahweh's joyful command to his creatures to "be fruitful and multiply."[30]

Hindu iconography celebrates the procreative power of the King-Gods in their Lover mode.[31] From the passionate embraces of the Gods and Goddesses, the created world flows. Sculptures on the temple at Konarak depict hundreds of Gods and Goddesses in every conceivable sexual position, caressing, licking, sucking, kissing, penetrating and being penetrated; they are one great throbbing mass of Libido in stone. The message is that procreation is a central activity and perhaps the greatest joy of the spiritual dimension. Both the King-Gods and

Generator of Libido:
The King's Phallus Enshrined (Ellora Cave, India)

the sacred kings in the Near East were associated with such procreative images as the Tree of Life and the Waters of Life.[32] The Tree of Life here represents the *axis mundi* and the phallic generativity of the archetypal King. The Waters of Life were his semen.[33] Jesus said in his Procreator mode that he was the vine and we are the branches.[34] We are fruit therefore of the cosmic phallus. Through the Procreator the infinite is made finite, the possible made actual. The gleam in the father's eye takes flesh and the world moves forward.

At the most literal level, of course, procreation is the sexual event that results in offspring. It is an act of generativity

Through the Sacrifice of the Sacred King to the Tree of Life

(Christ crucified as a cluster of grapes)

that produces the next *generation*. The sacred king and queen were called upon to actualize the Gods' Procreator intentions. The heir of their union was concrete proof that the kingdom was flourishing. Guaranteeing an orderly dynastic succession, the crown prince assured uninterrupted economic, social, and political stability. He also assured that through him the life-giving energy of the archetypal King would be present for some time into the future.

But beyond the necessity of producing an heir, the king embodied the archetype as Procreator in a spiritual sense as well. In some ancient belief systems, the King-Gods actually imbued their subjects with souls.[35] The pharaoh imparted some of the eternal *ankh*, or life-force, to every Egyptian, drawing from his own limitless reserves of ka. He did this by beholding, blessing, and embracing his people. The sacred kings held their public audiences, when taboos did not prohibit them, as much *to see their subjects* as to be seen by them. Both sides drew power and identity from these meetings.

As psychoanalytic-self psychologists have pointed out, we become real to ourselves only insofar as our early care-givers are able to "mirror" us.[36] When a parent looks at a child, the child receives the look as a constituitive glance. The child feels real by virtue of being *seen*. Think of the four-year-old's repeated demands to have his every act *witnessed*. To the extent our parents can reflect back to us our real feelings, and affirm to us our importance by physically *touching* us and really *seeing* us, we are able to consolidate our identities. Having a sense of validated identity is essential to acquiring a sense of soul. A parent who has successfully imparted a soul to his child has experienced the ultimate act of parenting. This is the essence of what has historically been called blessing.

This process is one Gary Smalley and John Trent have examined in their book *The Blessing*.[37] In their comparative study of the phenomenon in ancient Hebrew culture and in modern times, Smalley and Trent outline the five aspects of blessing—meaningful touch, spoken blessing, attachment of high value to the other, picturing for the other a special future, and active commitment to the other to help realize that future.

A wonderful Egyptian painting from Tel el-Amarna illustrates elements of blessing in the context of sacred kingship. We see the pharaoh Akhenaten depicted standing in the upper window of a palace. In the courtyard below is his esteemed minister Ay, his arms outstretched to the king. Akhenaten is throwing the gold bracelets down to Ay, who catches and slips them one by one over his wrists. Akhenaten, the king-god, is blessing and valuing his minister. By showering such wealth upon him, Akhenaten gives Ay the means to picture a special future for himself, as well as to realize that future. The meaningful touch is offered by the sun disk hovering above Akhenaten's head, extending its rays like open hands.

Akhenaten was the incarnation of Horus, as was every pharaoh. The familiar hieroglyph of the Eye of Horus——is ubiquitous in Egyptian relics. The Eye of Horus created what it beheld, and so had a tremendous importance in Egyptian culture. Ay is being seen and created by his God. People crowded to public audiences in ancient Egypt because of the importance they attached to being seen by their pharaoh. It was for the people the most direct means available for being regenerated with a fresh infusion of ka. A similar thing happens today, when the British royals travel to America, for example, or the pope appears on his balcony at St. Peter's in Rome.

Think of some of the phrases we commonly use today. What does it mean to hold someone in "high regard"? Or think of what we mean when we say "That boy is the apple of his father's eye." Or the British epithet "damn your eyes"—why?—because whoever says that is being shamed by being witnessed. There is an undeniable power in the looks we receive in our

Blessing: Knowing and Honoring Others
(Akhenaten and Nefertiti showering Ay with gold,
Tel el Amarna, Egypt)

lives. When a mentor looks at you, his gaze is an act. He may
be supplying for you something you wish your parents had supplied. His look helps to create you.

Analysands will often report, in the midst of their course of
therapy, that they feel terrific for two or three days *after being
seen* by their therapist. Their depression lifts, and they feel vital
and capable. Then they fall back into their old patterns for the
rest of the week until the next appointment comes around.
Partly the temporary transformation is due to the transference
typical of this stage, but partly their vitality comes simply from
being witnessed.

Dr. Bernie Siegel is doing work with his cancer patients
based on the creative power of seeing. He has his patients go
home, find a private time and place, and look at themselves
standing naked before a mirror. He tells them to keep looking
until they find something about their bodies they can really

love. It doesn't have to be much to begin with—the shape of the nose, perhaps; the arch of the foot. He asks them to extend this beloved part of the body, taking as much time as necessary, until they can truly say they love their entire body.

This exercise is not useful only to cancer patients. Most of us use a mirror only to check to see that our mask isn't slipping, and that our hair is still in place. Try one day looking into your eyes in the mirror. Probably it will feel a little strange, and unfamiliar. Try giving yourself the kind of deep, compassionate look you'd give a loved one. You can see for yourself what kind of creative power resides in your eyes.

There is a further sense in which the king is the Procreator, a sense that seems odd indeed to us. Paradoxically, a king's sacrificial death, as well as his life of self-sacrifice, is procreative. His blood nourishes the earth as fertilizing semen. His sacrifices exist to provision the world.[38]

The psychological truth in this is that there can be no creation without self-sacrifice. The act of voluntarily dying to one's wider potential, in order to realize an actual (and therefore limited) goal, is what results in world building. We all know this. The choices we have to make in life are really acts of self-sacrifice. We must choose *this* option and not another. We sacrifice the potential for the sake of the actual.

Take for example the artist before a blank canvas. Until he dips his brush into the paint, the canvas offers him a pure white potential. Almost anything can happen. As soon as he begins to paint he has begun to sacrifice his options. The nearly infinite possibilities for subject matter, color, texture, and technique become finite. Limitless Libido is taking on finite form.

As he makes his choices, partly consciously, partly not, he experiences a sense of loss, because he does lose some of the vast, ecstatic, intuited imagery that inspired him. He selects against expressing everything. He sacrifices the whole of his creative Self for the purpose of realizing a fragment. Also, he allows the charge of creative life-force that has built up within him, demanding expression and release, to drain out of him. Here he is like the sacred king who touches his foot to the earth and loses his concentrated life-force to the material world.

And yet, not only has the artist provisioned the world and pushed forward the whole of creation, *he* has also been provided for. He is transfigured by a fresh upwelling of ecstatic life-force through the incomparable experience of empowerment that any successful creative achievement brings. Again like Saint Paul's Christ, or the East Asian Gods in the "myths of descent," he has emptied himself in order to re-create the world, and also like them, he has himself been filled and re-created. He has become in a sense his own Procreator and been born again.

The King-Gods of the ancient myths created the world. And through their incarnation or servant, the sacred king, the Gods continued to care for and to nurture not only human beings but all life and the ecosystem as a whole. The archetypal King in his Procreator mode is concerned about *all* living things and about a harmonious balance among them. This is the *ecological* sense of the Ma'at, Dharma, Tao, or Torah—the cosmic order the King-Gods and the sacred kings manifested. The sacred kings who embodied the archetype were always seen as the stewards of the *natural* order as well as the social. These kings were sometimes even referred to as the "Divine Gardener."

THE KING AS STRUCTURER

The archetype of the King provides the energy of the fourth line of force as a means to build things and put things in order. The sacred king who draws from this energy functions as a Structurer. He brings divine order to society through law and custom. He translates the tongue of the Gods into pictographs and runes, and thereby initiates written language.[39] Communicating with

The Divine Gardener and the Ecological Mission:

The King as Fructifier of the Earth

(the mace-head of Pharaoh "Scorpion")

The Sun-Lord:
The Archetype Imparting Masculine Consciousness
and Mediating the Divine Law
(Shamash enthroned, ninth century B.C.E.)

the minds of the Gods, he brings his people metaphysics and theology.[40] He expresses godly beauty by inventing the arts. Intuiting the hidden essences of things, he discovers science, architecture, engineering, technology, and architectural skills. He organizes the skilled trades, the merchants and craftsmen. He institutes hierarchical levels in his society, encouraging the division of labor and specialization in industry.[41] As the Aztecs said of Quetzalcoatl, "Truly it began with Him/Truly from Him it flowed/All art and knowledge."[42]

Succeeding kings take on the responsibility of sustaining the divinely instituted world order. Like Hammurabi, most ancient kings were the codifiers of laws. Each culture had a Moses. In order to implement their new laws, kings had to be able

135

administrators, repeating in miniature the King-God's administration of the universe. King and court paralleled the heavenly
court in which the Gods and Goddesses were the divine counterparts of the earthly councils of ministers.[43] The sacred king
was enjoined by the Gods to ensure peace and security for all of
his people. This he achieved as the supreme overseer of the
legal system and as the final court of appeal.

As ancient legal and prescriptive texts show, the early
systems of justice were often heavily weighted in favor of the
weak and the poor. Theoretically the kings protected the weak
against the strong. They were the special providers for widows
and orphans.[44]

In addition to protecting their own people, the sacred kings
were required to extend where possible the created order the
kingdom represented. They were also champions in the mythic
sphere in the Gods' cosmic war against chaos and death.[45] The
king's military campaigns were massive acts of sympathetic
magic designed to aid the Gods, so that when he most needed
it, the Gods would return the favor.[46]

Oracles and prophets lamented conditions on earth when a
lapse occurred in the continuity of a sacred kingship. In the
absence of a strong king in his Structurer mode, human moral
and ethical values, social cohesiveness, even the orderliness of
the natural world were experienced as breaking down. Neferrohu, an Egyptian scribe of the fifteenth century B.C.E., left us
this record of just such a catastrophe:

> Give heed, my heart, and weep for this land whence thou
> art sprung. . . . Ruined is this land, while none is con-
> cerned for it, none speaks, and none sheds tears. The sun
> is veiled and he shines not that the people may see. The
> river of Egypt is dry, one may cross it on foot. All good
> things have passed away, the land is prostrate in wretch-
> edness by reason of that food of the Bedouin who invade

the land. Enemies have arisen in Egypt, the Asiatics have descended into Egypt. . . . What never had happened has happened. . . . A man sits in his corner turning his back while one slays another. I will show thee a son as an enemy, a brother as a foe, and a man slaying his own father. Every mouth is filled with "Love me!" and all good things have passed away. . . . [47]

After this lamentation Neferrohu wishes for a sacred king to come who will restore order and drive the foreigners from the kingdom. Neferrohu proclaims a coming king whose characteristics and actions are not unlike those predicted a thousand years later for the Hebrew messiah. He writes:

There shall be a king of the South to come, whose name is Ameni. He is the son of a woman of Nubia. . . . He shall take the White Crown, he shall put on the Red Crown, uniting the double diadem; he shall pacify the Two Lands [Upper and Lower Egypt] with what they desire. . . . The people of his time shall rejoice, the son of man shall make his name forever and ever. Those who plotted evil and devised rebellion, they have stilled their mouths for fear of him. The Asiatics shall fall by his sword and the Libyans shall fall by his flame. . . . Righteousness [Ma'at] shall return to its place, unrighteousness shall be cast out. Let him rejoice who shall see it and who shall be serving the king.[48]

Ultimately the enemies of the archetypal King are on the mythic or spiritual levels of reality. Chaos is not the mere expression of randomness. Death is not simply the natural process of molecular descent from higher to lower levels of organization. Chaos and death are demons that directly threaten the divinely decreed world order. On high holy days sacred kings often assumed the roles of the Structurer Gods in dramatizations of the myths.[49] By performing in these dramas, they made immediate the life-and-death struggles between the King as Structurer and the demons of chaos and death.[50] Because the Structurer wins these struggles in the end, the sacred kings enacted and realized these happy endings for their own kingdoms.

This is not necessarily as archaic a practice as it may sound. In Shakespeare's England the Jacobean courtly masques provided the same function. Though prevented by decorum from speaking lines, the monarch and members of his royal family often appeared in these mini-dramas, richly costumed as Gods and Goddesses. The appearance of royalty would signal an end to the chaotic first scene of the masque, and banish the hags, satyrs, or witches who featured in this beginning. The royals restored proper order to the piece, and by implication to the kingdom. After a chorus in praise of the king, the court spent the rest of the night dancing.

Here is part of a speech from a masque by Ben Jonson in praise of King James:

> He is a god o'er kings, yet stoops he then
> Nearest a man when he doth govern men,
> To teach them by the sweetness of this sway,
> And not by force. . . .
> He makes it ever day and ever spring
> Where he doth shine, and quickens everything
> Like a new nature: so that, true to call
> Him by his title, is to say, He's all.[51]

King James's own son appeared in this particular masque. Presented on January 1, 1611, the masque concentrated the court's attention on the king's power to regenerate the year (he makes it "ever spring" despite the winter) and reign over chaos. The terrific expense of these masques (sets to this one were designed by none other than Inigo Jones) further underlined the

Exorcizing the Demons and Protecting the Realm
(Richard I fighting a lion, the personification of chaos and death,
sixteenth-century woodcut)

king's unlimited wealth and puissance. The entertainment assured the court that all would be well for at least another year.

The Structurer function of the archetype also helped the sacred kings order their own inner lives. As we have seen, this attention to inner harmony, whether it be channeled through Ma'at, Dharma, Tao, or Torah, brought to the outer world any successes the king had in his inner struggle. Since whatever occurred at his Center was transmitted to the outermost reaches of the kingdom, his own enlightenment amounted to kingdom-wide shifts in nature and society.[52]

In a sense the philosophers who posited ideas such as these believed themselves to live in a holographic universe. The whole was completely present in the king and the image the king projected was the image of the whole. In order to attain this level of personal development, the sacred kings, particularly of the Far East, became men of great learning. Even by doing only this they furthered the creation of the world, ultimately dependent upon Brahman or Buddha Consciousness for its definition and for its very being.[53]

This Structurer function of the King archetype signals his central role in the creation of consciousness. Consciousness, at least for the Ego, is a structured thing. A cohesive sense of personal identity is achieved optimally by a progressive expansion of Ego awareness, both of the total individual psychic system that a person is and of the outside world.[54] Usually human beings are conscious of only a limited number of either psychological contents or of outer world phenomena. The purpose of conventional education is to widen the scope of consciousness to include more and more data about the world around us. The pursuit of self-reflective disciplines, such as psychology or the spiritual traditions, deepens Ego awareness of the structures and dynamics of the psyche.

The minimal degree of Ego consciousness that satisfies most people demands the splitting off and repressing of enormous amounts of psychological material. People have been taught to disapprove of much of this material. But life circumstances, inner neuroses, relationships that offer great joy or pain, all conspire to expand awareness. When the Ego confronts and accesses previously unwanted, uncomfortable psychic material, the Ego builds for itself a more cohesive, structured, and open-ended Ego consciousness.[55]

Ego consciousness seems to depend upon the capacity to differentiate one thing from another and to make value distinctions between them. This idea is related to the "masculine" principle of discernment. Though not an exclusively male preserve, the mythic image of discrimination is of the *sword* that cuts through confusion.

When confronted with the impossibly tangled Gordian knot, one no man had yet been able to untie, Alexander, discerning the intellectual dishonesty of the knot's design, took his sword and simply cut the knot in two.[56] Solomon was able to decide to which of two mothers he should award a disputed baby by offering to take a sword and cut the baby in two.[57] The baby's true mother of course forsook her rights to the child, preferring it should live at all costs. By this Solomon recognized her as the true mother, and restored the child to her.

The ancients called this masculine principle the "sword of gnosis." By distinguishing between light and darkness, good and evil, and other polar opposites, discrimination provides us with *gnosis,* or insightful knowledge. In many of the Near Eastern myths of creation the Creator God can make the ordered world only by distinguishing between finite entities. Ptah, for example, made the Egyptian world by speaking the names of things.[58] He drew up names from the creative abyss of his own mind, where all things were undifferentiated, only because he had achieved a level of consciousness in which he could imagine definite things.

Christian thinkers developed a similar theology of the

logos, or the Word.[59] This builds on the Genesis story, wherein things are spoken of, and thereby created. In the Babylonian creation epic, Marduk *literally* wields the sword of gnosis when he slays Tiamat, the dragon of chaos.[60] With one half of her divided body he makes the oceans; the other he uses for the sky. He carves up her consort Kingu as well, into the earth and all the earth's creatures.

Other structures rising from formlessness emulate the emergent nature of consciousness. Egyptian mythology tells of the primordial hill rising from the ocean, just as the Ego structure arises out of an undifferentiated consciousness. The hill expanded quickly, lifting more and more land up from out of the cosmic depths. Similarly the growth of Ego structure depends on the process of making more and more unconscious material conscious, and raising implicit structures of personality into the explicit light of awareness. The sacred king imitates this by building his pyramid, ziggurat, or dais; and from his raised vantage point he calls his people into greater consciousness and on into the adventures of civilization.

Mount Sinai, Mount Zion, Mount Meru, Mount Hara-berezaiti were all sites of revelation. These summits represented the process of ascent involved in raising a civilization. Where a sacred mountain was unavailable, pyramids or ziggurats were erected as their artificial echoes.[61] Atop the stepped pyramids the Maya's god-king communed with his ancestors.[62] In the small blue-tiled temples at the ziggurat's summit, Shamash dictated his laws to the Mesopotamian kings. Moses ascended Mount Sinai for the Hebrews, where he received the tablets of the law straight from Yahweh's fiery intellect. Christian mythology states that Jesus was transfigured on the top of a high hill, and he delivered his definitive sermon on a mount.

The pyramids and ziggurats were conceived as staircases. Their levels stood at once for the different planes of reality and for the steps to enlightenment. Even the smooth-sided Egyptian pyramids were referred to in contemporary texts as stairways, meant to aid the pharaoh's ascension to the heavens. The sloping sides represented the sun's slanting rays, and the golden capstone also was an image of the sun, helping to draw the pharaoh's soul up into the mind of God.[63]

Why is consciousness depicted as ascending? Why were these enormous structures raised to illustrate and facilitate consciousness raising? Because this is true to our experience of Ego consciousness in relation to the unconscious. We know that it takes tremendous effort to become conscious. To do this we must build psychological structures. Our sense is that the unconscious, while not inferior to the Ego, is still somehow underneath it. The ultimate literal source of light, the sun, is always above us. Since consciousness has universally been associated with light (perhaps because our primary discerning organ is the eye?), we must look up in order to be conscious.

Almost universally the sun has been deified.[64] This is sensible, as all life depends upon the sun. Ancient peoples believed an unimaginably self-ordered and enlightened consciousness had created the world, and for an image of this they looked first to the sun. The sun Gods rose to prominence over the widespread chthonic, underworld Gods, and the remnants of the earth Goddess religions of even earlier times, during the era when the great urban civilizations first appeared.[65]

These sun Gods triumphed over an essentially *feminine* unconsciousness. This fits well with the insights psychology offers in understanding the development of the masculine Self.[66] "Chaotic" feminine unconsciousness predates the emergence of masculine Ego structures. In fact, recent brain-structure research suggests that the genetically male fetus begins with an essentially female brain. Only after the male genitals form and testosterone is released in the fetus does the brain *structure* itself in a typically masculine configuration. The underlying, primal feminine matrix, which does, in fact, express more *dif-*

Where the Light Is:
Ascending the Mountain of Masculine Consciousness
(Naram-Sin's stela of victory, Mesopotamia)

fuse consciousness, is superseded by the burgeoning masculine capacity for *focused* consciousness, for a more structured and specialized way of postnatal perceiving, feeling, thinking, and behaving. As we've seen, Marduk defeats a chaotic feminine sea dragon. The association of the watery abyss with the feminine reflects the briny amniotic fluid of the womb where we all have our beginning. Ocean and mother are intuitively linked. In the early stages of development, even after we are born, we are for a time quite largely psychologically one with our mothers. It is with the utmost difficulty that we learn we are separate from her.[67]

Most of us never do learn this completely. This struggle to achieve a separate identity is most urgent for a boy, since his gender identity depends on the separation.[68] The child in every man longs to return to the womb, a place where his every need was attended to. Utter passivity was possible in exchange for an absence of Self. Anyone fearing a loss of Self might come to view the realm of the feminine with hostility.[69] But masculine consciousness is won only to the degree that the boy and the man can break definitely with the "seductive" power of his mother. He must be wary that her power doesn't draw him back into a regressive merger with her, back into a time before "he" existed. The burning light of the sun draws his masculine Ego up like oxygen from the darkness of that first watery unconscious nirvana.

The circuit diagram necessary for ascending into a masculine consciousness is the archetypal King. He is the Center of dynamic energy, transformed and made useful by his Procreator and Structurer aspects. His interests lie in his generativity, consciousness raising, and world building; he is particularly discerning and independent. Such is the fully manifested archetypal King—the King in his fullness—as expressed in myth and history. He consolidates the functions of the other mature masculine archetypes. The Warrior aids him in setting, defending, and extending boundaries. The Magician helps order his thought, and provides ideas on how to materialize them. Both the Magician and the Warrior help develop the psychospiritual machinery a man needs before the King can incarnate within him. And the Lover ensures that incarnation will be life-enhancing and joyful.

GENERATIVE MAN:
THE CHALLENGE
OF KINGSHIP FOR
CONTEMPORARY MAN

T HE QUALITIES MOST CULTURES IDENTIFY AS MASCU-
line in most historical epochs are remarkably consistent.[1]
David Gilmore cites in his *Manhood in the Making* cultures that
include those of North America and the Mediterranean world,
past and present, societies of South and East Asia, of Truk
Island in the South Pacific, the Mehinaku Indians of South
America, the Samburu of Africa, the Sambia of New Guinea,
and many others.

He finds in nearly all of them common understandings of
what constitutes manhood. The "big men" of New Guinea, the
"muy hombres" of Spain, and the "worthy men" of the Samburu

are all protectors, providers, and procreators. They manifest a selfless capacity for hard work, risk taking, courage, and endurance. Mature men embrace these roles in order to nurture their families and build their communities. They are community bulwarks against natural and human foes. Where able to accumulate wealth, they share it liberally. They are expected to be energetically sexual and to foster the next generation. While there are local emphases on one or another of the different functions of this transcultural understanding of manhood—*protector, provider, or procreator*—Gilmore notes that the pattern is consistent.[2]

The evidence from this new anthropology, as well as from other fields of study, makes plausible, even compelling, the idea that these traits of manhood are a transcultural expression of the archetypes of mature masculinity and, ultimately, of the incarnated King. Each of the four foundational archetypes powers the tripartite engine of Gilmore's manhood. He largely stresses characteristics we assign to the King, the Warrior, and the Lover. He misses the Magician. Though he recognizes man as hunter, worker, provider, and creator, for the most part he neglects man as thinker and ritual elder. We speculate that because Gilmore himself is a thinker and unconsciously a "ritual elder," pointing out the enlightened way to other men, his oversight is in missing his own dominant characteristics. We are all more or less subject to blind spots, which, in fact, hold the keys to our personality styles, interests, and motivations.

From Gilmore we can take a transcultural perspective concerning the ideal mature masculine Self, one we'll be calling Generative Man. A generative man may be communist or capitalist, industrialist or peasant. He may be an animal-rights advocate or a whale hunter, and is as much a poet as a soldier. While a man's life-style and work, under the best of circumstances, will reflect his generativity, Generative Man is the *foundational aspect* of every man in every culture and the closest parallel modern psychoanalysis has offered for the archetypal King.

Generative Man is a term the psychoanalyst Erik Erikson coined.[3] In our view, Gilmore's manhood and Erikson's Generative Man are two similar ways of viewing the King. The man appropriately accessing the King *is* the protector, provider, and procreator for his people and his world, whoever and wherever they may be.

Generativity is the true basis for mature human being. Besides procreation in the biological sense, generativity includes all the products of the human imagination—cultural, religious, technological, and ecological. For Erikson as for Jung, there is no inherent conflict between the instinctual drives in human beings and their psychological and spiritual aspirations. The so-called higher functions of human being arise out of our animal roots. Erikson calls the archetypes "action patterns,"[4] and when they are not distorted by psychopathology of one kind or another, their push is always toward generativity.

According to Don Browning's analysis of Erikson, Generative Man's virtues are *love*, *care*, and *wisdom*. As Browning says, "The basic trust and hope of the generative man . . . gives him the trust not only to continue his own existence but to share in the generation of succeeding generations and to help care for and sustain their lives with hope."[5]

All the risks taken by a mature man, all the wealth he accumulates, are finally designed to care for and sustain his family and community. Ultimately, this caring and sustenance are intended for his children, the world's inheritors.

Trust and hope are products of *strength* and *maturity*. Out of strength and maturity, Generative Man can draw upon inner resources of *autonomy* and *will*. Out of his autonomy and will, he desires and has the capacity for intimate relationships. In personal relationships, as far as the social hierarchy will allow, he beholds the true worth of others. He provides what Erikson calls "a confirming face."[6] In other words, he mirrors and blesses. This is certainly the case in the male-bonded egalitarian brotherhoods Gilmore examines. For Erikson, Generative Man's relationships are not only intimate but societal as well—he has the capacity and desire to make meaningful contributions to the community.

All these qualities bring a generative man a viable identity. This identity incorporates flexibility with integrity as well as with a consolidated style of fidelity. Out of this consolidated Self, a generative man is able to make commitments to his family, to his society, and ultimately to his God. His vision is of a Transpersonal Other whose coherence derives in part from his own integrity.

The initiated men of any society have placed their personal concerns beneath those of the larger social groups; and the social groups are subordinated to a divine reality. To Gilmore's way of thinking, manhood can be either tribalistic or universal in its general outlook and in its visioning of its own tasks and duties. Real men, for him, can function with a variety of definitions of the greater good, from the most parochial to the most expansive. However, Erikson goes a step beyond Gilmore here. Erikson claims that Generative Man must be a universalist. He must nurture his own progeny, culture, and religion, as well as the larger world of all human societies, and the environment as an ecological whole. Generative Man, for Erikson, balances the good of society with the good of the planet by honoring both technology and nature. As Browning says, "To generate and maintain a world, but in such a way as to include and yet transcend one's own issue, one's own family, tribe, nation and race—this is the essence of the generative man . . ."[7]

A man who has accessed the King properly demonstrates Gilmore's "manhood," and Erikson's Generative Man. The King calls *every* man into an Ego-archetypal axial relationship. *Men who can achieve such a relationship are modern-day embodiments of sacred kingship.* When the Ego is in the proper alignment with the King it achieves the humility of the creature before its transpersonal source, its God. At the same time the Ego comes to realize that God is within. "If you knew me, you would know my Father also,"[8] said Jesus. Jesus' statement illustrates an Ego in an integral relationship with the inner King.

Let us portray an ideal generative man. Though our portrait may have a somewhat culture-specific coloring, the underlying manhood structures remain transcultural. No man can fully embody all of these qualities. However, psychologists often will describe at length what is *wrong* with us without providing us with an image of what it would be like to be healthy and whole. We'd like to address this imbalance here, for "without a vision the people perish."[9]

THE GENERATIVE MAN:
A VISION FOR US

A generative man, drawing on the characteristics of the archetypal King, accesses the Center, Transformer, Procreator, and Structurer functions in an integrated way.

He is creative himself, and he welcomes creativity in others. He provides a safe, containing space where the people around him can flourish. He offers encouragement by taking care to really *see* others. In beholding his fellows he mirrors and affirms them. [10] He confirms their individuality and the reality of their suffering and their joy. He is conscious of and sensitive to their underlying feelings and motives. He blesses their lives by sanctifying the fruits of their inner and outer labors.

Because he is himself secure and centered, the generative man can allow others to be themselves. [11] He does not experience them as extensions of himself, but recognizes when he is confusing his own motives and values, his own hopes or fears, with those of others. He is not easily thrown off balance by others. Even hostile and aggressive people cannot easily get to him. His integrity is such that sarcasm, innuendo, accusation, and confrontation have little effect upon him. He can manage in most situations to defend his legitimate personal boundaries firmly, and without hostility.[12] Yet when a wrathful response is called for, he is able to act aggressively. There are situations that present clear and present dangers to us.[13] The generative man, drawing upon his Warrior-King reserves, responds with vigor in these situations to neutralize his foes.

A generative man seeks to free himself of envy.[14] Possessing all the power he needs for his own life, he can dispense to those who need and deserve it the affirming energy of admiration. He confers deserved riches, symbolic and material, upon members of his family, his friends, his business associates, and others. Rather than belittle others he supports them in their attempts to contribute something of value to society.

In a leadership role the generative man evaluates his subordinates' ideas and performances objectively and with compassion. If others have good ideas, he celebrates them, implements them, and gives credit where credit is due. At home, he lavishes deserved praise upon his children when they come to him for mirroring. But he never exaggerates his praise.[15] He speaks the truth, and the truth he speaks gives every member of his family a firm basis for self-evaluation and self-affirmation. His truthful words and actions help others feel their own reality and get a sense of their own authentic being. He deflates grandiosity and enables others to discover their *realistic greatness*.[16]

A generative man may be a mediator between the archetypal King and his fellow human beings. He may be further along than others in accessing the King and the other mature masculine archetypes without being overwhelmed by them. He is a seasoned veteran of the energy exchange between Ego consciousness and the depths of the unconscious. He is familiar with the inner landscape we all share, its dangers and pleasures, its angels and demons, its illusions and truths. With the wisdom of this familiarity, the generative man can help others in their efforts to integrate. [17] He can reflect back to others what he hears their inner adversaries and allies saying, because at one time or another he's heard the same voices himself. [18]

A faithful steward of the creative life-force, a generative man never engages in wanton destruction. He is not indifferent to the plight of the oppressed. [19] He is vitally concerned about the rights, safety, health, and material prosperity of all human beings. Beyond this he is interested in the welfare of the eco-system as a whole.

Though he may be a master at utilizing the physical environment for the benefit of his family, his nation, or all human-kind, he honors both technology *and* the environment in a balanced way. He encourages the harmonious interaction between society and nature. He is neither the enemy of science and industry nor an irresponsible dumper of toxic wastes. He seeks a middle path which is responsible to immediate and to long-range human needs, and to his planetary home. [20]

The generative man vigorously pursues the extension of the created order against the forces of destruction and death. There are many facets of these forces—drugs, racism, classism, nationalism, religionism, poverty, child abuse, spouse abuse, petty quarreling, ignorance, egoistic power-grabbing, environmental pollution, political and economic depression—and all are expressions of human chaos. Their ultimate effect is always the destruction of global well-being. A generative man is concerned with law and order wherever that law and order contribute to the flourishing of human beings. He is a protector of the weak and disempowered. He does what he can in order to assure justice and equality of opportunity for all people.

The man who adequately can access the archetypal King is a reconciler of opposites. He listens for what truths are spoken on all sides of a dispute. He looks beneath the surface arguments to the fear and anguish of the child within.[21] He addresses this deeper reality when he speaks to each of the opposing sides. While he prefers diplomatic solutions, where destructive impulses need subduing he acts swiftly and decisively to reestablish order out of his own sense of integrity. Even when others grumble about his severity they know that he is just. Everyone knows the difference between men in leadership positions who are firm because they are genuinely interested in our welfare, and men who are severe out of their own grandiosity. A generative man is able to help us subdue our own self-destructiveness. And for this we deeply appreciate him.

Self-sacrifice is an inescapable part of world building, something this man realizes. The generative man gives his life's blood for the people and causes entrusted to him. His hard work and personal sacrifice provision others and advance the generativity of the world. He spends as much of his life energy as he can to help others build their worlds. At the same time he is no martyr or masochist. He cares for his own welfare, only choosing to sacrifice himself because of his sense of an abundant and replenishable self-worth. He volunteers in causes that awaken both his compassion and his just anger. In these and other ways a generative man provisions the world.

Like the sacred kings of the Far East, the generative man works toward harmony and order in his own inner life. He views setting his own house in order as a prerequisite for helping others order their own lives. He is relentlessly honest with himself about his failings. He takes his share of responsibility when things go badly, but no more and no less than his share. Out of this empowering stance he is able to do something positive and concrete about the problem that confronts him. He may be involved in some form of psychotherapeutic process.

He knows that where his own integrity is at stake, one way or another he must work to develop his own psychological and spiritual life.[22] He is open to criticisms for he realizes that they will usually hold some truths. He is not, however, a misguided moral perfectionist. Rather he urgently engages himself in a quest for wholeness and moral seriousness.[23]

Out of his deep loyalty to himself the generative man is able to be loyal to others—his family and friends, his company, any voluntary organizations he may be fostering, his community and his nation, and ultimately his world. These loyalties may at times be at odds with each other and set up intense conflicts within him. To the extent, however, that a man can be generative, his loyalty will be to the greatest good for the greatest number. His loyalty in the end will be to a Transpersonal Other[24] that is deeply compatible with his own sense of self.

Finally, the generative man has achieved a rich masculine identity both by building his inner masculine structures and by valuing his inner feminine characteristics. He has come to know the mystery that his masculinity is enhanced to the extent that he is appreciative of his Anima. He has experienced *within himself* the sacred marriage of the King with his Queen. Full generativity, he realizes, in psychospiritual affairs just as surely as in biological ones, is possible only where the masculine and feminine energies are united.[25] He is almost certainly sexually active and eager for intimate relationship with a partner as capable of intimacy as he is.[26] Together they may generate and nurture children; if not, their energies combine in more subtle but still tangibly creative ways.

Protector, provider, procreator, a generative man is a Center for world building, an *axis mundi* around which others may rally. At his Center he is unassailable. He provides stability to his inner world, and to others who come to him looking for order in themselves. His own opposite impulses are reconciled at his Center, and through his experience of this he helps others to do the same. As a Transformer he makes usable the creative life-force he carries within him. Others draw from him a sense of their own empowerment. He may be a Procreator in the specific sense of fathering children he cares for and teaches. Certainly he is a Procreator in the broad sense of initiating creative advance in the world he has been given to steward. And he is a Structurer, establishing calm in the midst of chaos, and facilitating order through determined action. He is committed to the preservation and the extension of a civilized, yet vigorously instinctual way of life. In these ways he incarnates the potential in the actual, the sacred in the profane. He is an image of mature masculinity toward which we may all strive.

PART 3

MALFUNCTIONS: THE SHADOW KING

Beneath the Tyrant:

The Weak and Weary One (Sesostris III, nineteenth century B.C.E.)

THE SHADOW KING
AS THE TYRANT
USURPER

W HENEVER A MAN NEGLECTS THE THRONE OFFERED
him by the archetypal King in his psyche, he leaves that
throne open to a usurper. In the *usurpation syndrome* the usurper's own Ego takes over as the King. As a result of the inrush of
archetypal energy the Ego becomes bloated and distended. The
Ego becomes the captive of the Tyrant side of the archetypal
King's Shadow. It suffers from something akin to radiation sick-
ness because it has not kept a safe distance from the archetype's
power in an appropriate Ego-archetypal axis configuration.

The usurpation syndrome is the result. The *abdication
syndrome* reflects the *other* pole of the King's Shadow system,

the Weakling. The abdication syndrome results when a man projects the archetypal King onto someone else, rather than integrating the energy into himself. It is interesting to note that every abdicated king needs at least one usurping king, and every usurper must find willing abdicators. Within this bipolar Shadow arrangement, each pole is dependent upon the other. Where a man is possessed by the Weakling King, he carries a wound the exact size and shape of the Tyrant's sword.[1] Such men always have tyrants in their lives whom they hate and fear. The man possessed by the Tyrant has a wounded vulnerability that causes him to hate and fear the weak men in his life, because these men remind him of his own secret underlying weakness. In their bipolar dysfunctional system, Tyrant and Weakling—usurper and abdicator—*need* each other to remind themselves of their other half.

The Ego that is possessed by one of the poles, and feels identified with it, experiences its *personal* Shadow as the archetypal Shadow in its *opposite* polar form.[2] In fact, the kernel around which the personal Shadow complex organizes is usually archetypally based.[3] Under conditions of heightened stress, the Ego may be drawn to the charge of the opposite pole and suddenly reverse its characteristic state. An Ego possessed by the Shadow King oscillates between overinflation by the "positive" charge of the Tyrant and radical deflation by the Weakling's "negative" charge. Depth psychologists call this Ego experience positive inflation and negative inflation.[4] A man whose Ego is caught between these alternating charges cannot be generative.

Ego structures are essential to optimal psychological functioning. Consolidated Ego structure enables us to balance the demands of archetypal forces in our inner lives with competing demands in our outer lives. At its best, an Ego processes data in terms of personally established norms, prioritizes it, then acts upon it.[5] Optimally a man's Ego determines how he will act in any life situation.

As we've suggested, this is often not the case. Far more often than we like to admit, the Ego is possessed by one or more complexes and by the archetypal forces behind them. A man may believe he is acting with free will, but close examination reveals that he has acted under inner compulsion.[6]

We are all familiar with the phrase "the male Ego." "Oh, I wounded his male Ego," we hear someone say dismissively, or "You're just letting your male Ego do the talking." There is such a thing as a *healthy* male Ego, but in popular usage "male Ego" equals "macho arrogance." In this way "Ego" is commonly used as a negative term since there are far more *un*healthy than healthy Egos (of either sex) abroad in the world.

The ancients called forces that result in compulsive, emotionally charged behaviors "demons," and they recognized the power of "demonic possession" to ruin our lives.[7] They worried most about a particular possession, called "hubris"[8] by the Greeks, and "vainglory"[9] by the biblical authors. Hubris is an overweening pride and arrogance that gives a man pretensions to godhood.[10] Such a possessed man deludes himself into believing he is invulnerable, with an exaggerated store of power, competence, and knowledge. Carried away by these delusions, he sets himself up for a fall. The greater the hubris, the farther the fall.

Greek tragedy is full of such stories, many of them about kings. Pentheus was one; he tried to flout the designs of the God Dionysus.[11] After mocking and imprisoning the God and his followers, Pentheus was torn to pieces by his God-possessed mother. King Agamemnon sacrificed his daughter for the sake of conquest and was struck down upon his return by his wife and her lover.[12] King Midas wished that everything he touched might turn to gold. After even his food turned to gold, Midas realized the consequences of his greedy pride.[13]

Sophocles, the ancient Greek dramatist, tells of King Creon of Thebes in his tragedy *Antigone*. Creon brings disaster upon himself and his family by defying the will of the Gods.[14]

He has given the order that the body of Polyneices, his nephew and a traitor to the state, should not be buried. Anyone attempting to bury him faces a death sentence. The body lies in a field outside the city walls, just where his brother slew him. Polyneices's sister Antigone defies Creon's order and buries her brother. The citizens of Thebes support her, though they are afraid of Creon. Even Creon's son Haemon (who is engaged to marry Antigone) speaks against his father. Creon, mad with rage at Antigone's, Haemon's, and his city's defiance, orders Antigone buried alive in a rock-cut tomb. There she hangs herself. Haemon breaks into the tomb, finds her dead, and falls on his sword. When Creon's wife hears of Haemon's act, she too kills herself. Creon, the once cruel, self-righteous tyrant, ends a broken man. Sophocles's play concludes with this sobering moral:

> Our happiness depends
> on wisdom all the way.
> The gods must have their due.
> Great words by men of pride
> bring greater blows upon them.
> So wisdom comes to the old.[15]

Within the Hebrew tradition, divine justice was meted out to the kings of Israel and Judah by an angry and jealous God who tolerated no human pride or ambition. The Bible tells us again and again of the fall of proud men.[16] The whole of human history can be read as a parable of the effects of pride. Adam and Eve's expulsion from the Garden of Eden results, in this interpretation, from their sin of pride. Their decision to eat the forbidden fruit was their inflated attempt to gain godlike powers of secret knowledge and immortality.

Satan's fall from heaven can also be read in this way.[17] In the most prevalent version of the myth, Satan is at first the greatest of God's archangels. He comes to resent God's authority and power. He foments rebellion among the hosts of heaven, and moves to overthrow the Creator. Satan seizes God's throne and proclaims himself the true ruler of the cosmos. God manages to reclaim his throne, then hurls Satan and his collaborators from the highest heaven to the deepest hell.

From a Jungian perspective, these stories are recounting the inflated Ego's delusional attempts to assert its own godhood, followed by its inevitably violent deflation.[18] As tragically as many of these stories end, the goal of the deflating dynamic is not to *destroy* the Ego, but rather to *restore* to it a realistic relationship with the archetype of the King. Remember the final line of *Antigone*—"So wisdom comes to the old." Creon's tragedy brings him wisdom, and humility. He pays what may seem a terrible price for his wisdom, but the price is in keeping with the scale of his arrogance. If a man is not humble in his dealings with archetypal energies, he will suffer.

As Creon's story demonstrates, the tyrant visits his personal disasters upon those around him as well; often a whole kingdom suffers with him. We need only glance through the pages of any world history to see the truth of this. Assurbanipal, Rameses II, Nero, Caligula, Genghis Khan, Hitler, and Stalin—the Ego inflation of Shadow Kings leads them often to be fanatically destructive. In modern Iran, the Ayatollah Khomeini condemned an entire generation of young men to the horrors of holy war. And those horrors were not limited to the economic hardships of Iran and Iraq, nor to the enormous casualties sustained by combatants and civilians alike. The devastation wreaked upon both nations shows up afterward in the psychological scars of millions of human beings caught in the grip of relentless grief and hatred.

So also with the Gulf War, which the apparently Tyrant-possessed Saddam Hussein launched against Kuwait. Besides his interest in Kuwait's oil and revenues, Saddam Hussein doubtless felt that a quick, effortless victory would restore his nation's wounded pride and prop up his tyrannical regime as well as his own grandiose claims to uniqueness. The carnage and desolation wrought by the Coalition's defeat of Iraq once again demonstrate the consequences that sooner or later overtake tyrants and all those around them. Doubtless this chain of invasion and counterinvasion in the Middle East will leave the region destabilized for years to come. We can hope that all sides will take to heart the lessons offered by this chaotic situation, and our nations will be able to avoid a Tyrant-induced tragedy on a *truly* horrific scale.

As we look elsewhere around our contemporary world, it is all too easy to find similar material and psychological ruin instigated by men possessed by the inflated Shadow King as Tyrant. No matter how holy their cause, these men can be judged by the ruined lives they leave in their wake. When Chinese students made a bid for greater freedom of expression, they looked to their leaders for blessing. But instead of being valued for their creativity and self-affirmation, the students were first rejected, then scolded, then mowed down in the streets. Beyond their loyalty to an outmoded Communist ideal, the personal Egos of a few old men had clearly become inflated by King energy. Their brutal actions were recorded for all the world to see. These men could have set aside their Tyrant-possessed Egos and helped the Chinese people move toward greater individual expression and democracy. They could have seen that the era of the "great man" was coming to an end in China. They could have realized that a process was under way leading every Chinese man and woman to the *inner* source of creative world making. By reacting tyrannically the Chinese leaders assured a major setback for their nation and their own eventual downfall.

This destructive dynamic of the Tyrant-possessed Ego is not hard to see in our own work lives. The boss who habitually bullies, upbraids, or sexually harasses his subordinates is destroying at the same time, in all likelihood, his own health and

The Tyrant King Throttling His Subjects

(the Belgian king, Leopold, as a serpent crushing the people of the Congo,

a *Punch* cartoon)

maybe his career. He undermines his employees' sense of self-worth. If his sphere of influence is wide enough, the office, department, corporation, and even the community at large will also suffer irreparable damage.

We have many examples of wholesale self-destruction in the corporate world. The S and L and banking crises, Chicago's Commodities Exchange scandal, Wall Street's insider trading fracas, the downfall of International Harvester, and the life-and-death struggle of Eastern Airlines are all typical of tyrannical business behavior. Arrogant and paranoid union leaders held International Harvester in a lengthy strike, eventually bankrupting the company and losing the union members their jobs—permanently. At Eastern Airlines, tyrant kings in both union and management circles decimated this once flourishing, prestigious enterprise. The man possessed by the Tyrant has no real conception of service to anyone or anything besides himself. Like Creon, these men learn the hard way that "great words of pride bring greater blows upon them." Unfortunately, these blows fall just as heavily on those around them.

This is very clear when we see the tyrant in a family setting. Take for example the husband who humiliates his wife in front of the children. He may also routinely ridicule his "clumsy" children, ensuring that their self-esteem is too damaged for them ever to mature. This is the man who, after watching his son struggling to build a doghouse, grabs the saw and hammer from the boy and snaps, "Let me do it. Can't you do anything right?"

And the kinds of tragedy this man calls down on his head? A divorce, perhaps; and as hard as it may be on his wife and himself, it will be all the harder on their children. Where divorce isn't pursued, his reward will be a hateful marriage—to a wife frightened into silence or angered into provoking endless arguments. If his children don't grow up to hate him, the tyrant may be forced to witness an even more horrible result: his children repeating his tyranny with their *own* children. His only legacy is a store of misery handed down from generation to generation.

Joseph Campbell used to tell a story about a family tyrant he overheard in a restaurant.[19] The father was trying to get his son to drink his tomato juice. The boy refused, saying, "I won't drink it! I hate tomato juice!" The mother said, "Don't make him drink the tomato juice if he doesn't want to." And the Tyrant-possessed father replied, "He can't go through life thinking he can do whatever he wants. Look at me! I've never done anything I wanted to do!"

Campbell used the story to illustrate what he called the "Tyrant Holdfast,"[20] the bitter man who is envious of the young, the spontaneous, and the honest, those who are experiencing life directly and seeking its joys. The tyrant has likely never "followed his bliss." Campbell talked of an individual's bliss being the call to live, grow, and consolidate an authentic identity. Your bliss is to be found where your greatest talents and interests lie. The tyrant has ignored his life's work, so he cannot bear to watch another follow *his* bliss, and enjoy a generative life.

Men possessed by the Tyrant are off-center. Their reactions to criticism, overt or implied, are exaggerated. They fragment easily under pressure. At the board meeting, if a junior executive dares to offer his own innovative plan, the tyrant will come apart at the seams. He may conclude a slow boil with a display of fist-pounding infantilism. If his style is more covert, he may, like a sleepy-eyed serpent, sink his deadly fangs smoothly and subtly into his subordinate's neck.

A tyrant will always be, to some degree, defensive and paranoid.[21] He looks for challenges to his authority everywhere, in the slightest indications of impatience or disapproval from those around him. He may set up office spy systems and make it a point to eavesdrop on the secretaries during coffee breaks.

Any young man who takes initiative he interprets as being threatening. More likely this young employee is only doing what he was hired by the tyrant to do.

Tyrants are envious. Unsure of their own capacities, and their own masculine identities, their wrath knows no bounds. They envy new life and creativity wherever they encounter it. In the New Testament King Herod sends out his armies to slaughter the newborns as soon as he learns of the birth of the Christ Child.

Tyrants are also greedy. They believe what's theirs is theirs and what's yours is theirs as well. Once again the scandalous individuals from the high-finance industry come to mind. Also typical are the Latin American revolutionaries who stockpile millions of public-relief dollars in private Swiss bank accounts. These tyrants are quite willing to fly in the face of the idealized images they paint of themselves. Like Ferdinand Marcos, they build palaces and personal fortunes out of money wrung from their impoverished people.

A man who is Tyrant-possessed is as abusive of nature as he is of other human beings. Buffalo Bill Cody and his kind rampaged across the North American plains, all but wiping out the indigenous bison herds. These men were examples of the inflated male Ego's total disrespect for other life forms. The Ego-aggrandizing big-game hunters of the last century demonstrate destructive Tyrant attributes. The Exxon executives who have shown so little inclination to do a thorough cleanup of the Alaskan coast after the *Exxon Valdez* accident, the men who are in charge of toxic-waste dumping, and the CEOs who refuse to cut the hazardous emissions from their industrial facilities are all *destroying* the created world rather than building it. They are violating the ecosphere, and we will all pay for it. They will have to pay finally as well, although their fond belief is that they will escape the reckoning.

The Tyrant-possessed Ego arises out of the natural grandiosity of childhood.[22] In the first few months of life we are not able to distinguish between ourselves and the world around us, so in a sense we all begin as grandiose little beings. We have to be taught over a period of time that others are distinct from us and do not exist to serve our needs. This is a painful teaching under the best of circumstances, and one we seldom fully accept. We have to allow those who raise us to set the initial boundaries that define who we are. While we are learning that we are not the center of the universe, we need to have our personal worth vigorously confirmed. We need to be affirmed and celebrated for who we are. If these two dynamics are in place a child can begin to build an Ego structure, which develops his sense of legitimacy and autonomy, allowing him to more or less willingly exchange grandiosity for realistic greatness. The developing Ego can then be taught to distinguish between itself and the moods, complexes, and archetypes which are behind it.

The process in a boy's childhood of incarnating his mythic potential in the actual world of hurly-burly and competition is made possible by the Ego-Hero configuration. The Hero is the culminating archetypal influence of boyhood.[23] Where the boy's Ego is appropriately accessing the Hero, he is empowered to differentiate himself from the universe, from the complexes and archetypal energies within him, and finally and especially from his mother and father. It enables the boy to "slay" the internalized parental opinions, values, and controls, and break free of their domination. Once this is done, the Ego must pass beyond the heroic stage, the last stage of legitimate grandiosity, to a condition of true humility. It must offer its loyalty to the Transpersonal Other in its form as the archetypal King and Queen.[24] The entire process, if all goes well, consolidates an emergent Ego-King axis and leads to mature selfhood.

If this process goes awry through parental abuse, shaming, or neglect, the child goes into a kind of shock. The original grandiosity is split off and left behind intact and untransmuted, and defensive narcissistic rage is triggered. In this wounded condition the fragile Ego is a sitting duck for possession by the various archetypal Shadow systems. One or more of a host of personality disorders may be set in motion. These pathologies may reach clinical proportions. The usurpation syndrome may take over the Ego and manifest in any of a number of rage disorders. These leave the individual narcissistic, histrionic, aggressively antisocial, or paranoid.[25] If a more passive temperament develops, an individual may become dependent, passive-aggressive, or schizoid.[26] These latter disorders characterize the abdication syndrome.

The two syndromes actually manifest together as a single bipolar Shadow system. The crippled Ego oscillates between the two poles, though it usually tends to prefer one pole or another. But a tyrant's bluster is his attempt to hide the fact that underneath he's a weakling, as so much of world history bears out.

THE SHADOW KING
AS THE WEAKLING
ABDICATOR

A MAN WHO PROJECTS THE ARCHETYPAL KING ONTO another—whether a sacred king, a politician, a religious leader, a boss, a teacher, an analyst, or a father—exemplifies what we call the *abdication syndrome*. He abdicates from the throne his own psyche has prepared for him. He becomes possessed by the Weakling King, allowing any forceful personality that comes along to bully and control him.

Legend and history abound with stories of weakling kings. One of the most famous is the Egyptian pharaoh Akhenaten.[1] He was apparently a creative theologian and a man of great personal integrity. Perhaps he was more suited for poetry or

The Weak King, Mortally Wounded:
Arthur on His Voyage to Avalon

mysticism than a throne. Akhenaten aroused the ire of his own people by foisting revolutionary ideas upon them. He let the empire of his ancestors slip through his fingers. When his loyal Palestinian city-states urgently petitioned him for military aid to repel an invasion of fierce nomadic tribes, he did nothing. During his rule he allowed an orderly system of government to dissolve. He was unable to think strategically in his political battles with the Egyptian priesthood. He managed to die young without an heir.

Our modern age has produced its share of rivals for Akhenaten. On the eve of World War II, Great Britain's Prime Minister Neville Chamberlain engaged in catastrophic wishful thinking about Adolf Hitler and his intentions. He never grasped what a serious threat Hitler represented. Chamberlain impotently maneuvered to appease the tyrant's fury while Hitler carved up the nations of Europe.

In our own recent history we've seen the Weakling typified by Jimmy Carter. Emblematic of his weak thinking was his absurd attempt to dramatize energy conservation by not lighting the national Christmas tree, an ancient symbol of eternal life and ongoing vigor. Of more consequence was his impotent reaction to the Iran hostage crisis, and his failed desert rescue attempt. Similarly, John Kennedy's weakness during the Bay of Pigs operation cost the lives of hundreds of freedom fighters.

Anglo-Saxon legend gives us the example of King Arthur and his Knights of the Round Table.[2] Arthur, for all his good intentions, could not steward the ideal Camelot he had built. He turned a blind eye to Lancelot's interest in his own queen. Arthur's neglect of Guinevere was a topic of national concern, not only because of her adultery but because the royal couple never produced an heir. Arthur's only son was the bastard Mordred. After alienating his people, his inaction and indecision brought ruin upon himself and his kingdom. In the end he lost his queen and his best friend, he killed his son, and his knightly order was left as decimated as his nation.

In medieval times kingship ideals were of such concern to the Church that clerics produced a number of treatises on the topic. These were designed to aid monarchs in assessing and improving their performances.[3] We can get a clear picture of the Shadow King as Weakling from these treatises simply by converting attributes ascribed to the ideal king into their opposite characteristics.[4]

The weakling's principal flaws, from a medieval point of view, were sloth and lethargy.[5] This accounts for his lack of interest in or control over the justice system, the military, and the anarchic elements abroad in his kingdom. He didn't have the will to take up his fatherly duties to nurture and support his people. His self-indulgence was born of laziness; it takes considerable effort to build an Ego structure that makes possible service to others, and he took none.

We all know modern men who fit this pattern. There is the case of a CEO of a peer-group counseling agency in the Chicago area. The agency was mandated to set up teen peer-groups in the public schools, and through them to tackle such problems as teenage pregnancy, truancy, and other more serious delinquent behaviors. This was a task that required as much energy and transpersonal commitment as any individual could have mustered. The man who was promoted to lead the agency came from the ranks of the group leaders. Once he had secured this advantageous position, he manifested all the signs of the weakling. He finagled a considerable salary out of the board. He squandered the agency's money on luxurious leather office furniture. Besides frequently not reaching the office until after 11:00 A.M., he left as often by 2:00 P.M. What little time he was in the office he spent reading the paper, or setting up liaisons with various women, despite the fact that he was married. He demanded his sexually harassed secretary help set up his dates.

THE WEAKLING DID *NOT:*	Keep the peace
	Render justice himself, or ensure justice was delivered by his appointees
	Apply law impartially
	Get good advice
	Produce an heir to the throne
	Set a good example
	Aid the poor
	Master military science and strategy
	Strengthen the faith
	Show restraint in his personal conduct
	Promote the intelligence and education of his people
	Show mercy to his enemies when they were in a suppliant position
	Dispense deserved riches to his people
	Preserve the people's personal freedoms
THE WEAKLING *DID:*	Allow anarchy to reign in his kingdom
	Place himself above the law
	Alienate his people
THE WEAKLING WAS *NOT:*	Diligent
	Sober
	Faithful
THE WEAKLING *WAS:*	Ignorant
	Greedy
	Unchaste

Though entrusted with overseeing the work of the group leaders, he seldom troubled to do this. As a result, this potentially valuable project drifted into anarchy and disrepute.

Another example is of a successful car-dealership owner who retired early to luxurious living in Florida. He left the company in the incapable hands of his son. The son conducted himself in much the same way as the CEO above. He spent little time in his office. When he did work the deals, he was frequently moved by petty vindictiveness and rage. As a result, business suffered and the dealership began to fall victim to its competitors. Both the lazy, self-indulgent owner and his incompetent son showed symptoms of possession by the Weakling King.

There was a young man who for years pursued a woman older and considerably more mature than he. She had three teenage children. Against her better judgment she finally agreed to marry the young man. He had succeeded in convincing her that his love was sincere and constant, that he was committed to the kids, and that he regarded marriage as a great adventure which they could all share.

As soon as she said yes to his proposal a strange thing happened. He seemed suddenly unsure of himself. He dragged his feet with his share of the wedding preparations. On the wedding day he was visibly uneasy and unhappy. Within three weeks of the ceremony he began to have panic attacks. Several months later he was gone.

During this briefest of marriages the man agreed to a host of circumstances that caused him a great deal of discomfort. He had moved into a house his wife had established with her children rather than moving them to a new place where they could start life together as a family. He didn't hold a steady job and relied on his wife's income. Unable to command the children's respect, he couldn't discipline them. In fact, he often acted like just one more kid around the house. He never made his own

The Original Axis Mundi/Tree of Life

(Gombi)

Quadrated Majesty: Lord of the Four Quarters

(Brahman in His four aspects)

Osiris: The Archetype Enforcing Ma'at in the Otherworld

(from the Hunefer papyrus, 1317–1301 B.C.E.)

King Dasharatha Enthroned in Splendor

Veiled Effulgence (sixteenth-century Persian miniature of Mohammed and his
son-in-law, faces veiled to dim their blinding light)

Emperor Yung-lo: Bringing the Tao to His People

(Ming dynasty)

Solomon and Sheba:
King and Queen in Celebration
(thirteenth century,
Canterbury Cathedral)

The Sacred King as Mediator
Between the Human
and the Divine
(Maya mural from Bonampak)

Hearing the Words of the Sun: Hammurabi Receives the Law from Shamash
(from the Stela of the Law, 1792–1750 B.C.E.)

Combatting the Demons of Chaos and Death: The King in His Warrior Mode
(Rameses II at Kadesh)

The Tyrant:
Narcissism in the Flesh
(Joseph before Pharaoh)

The Supreme Lord: Dancing the Four Quarters
(Krishna as Cosmic Lord)

Centered Majesty: King Khaf-Re
(Old Kingdom of Egypt, circa 2550 B.C.E.)

boundaries known. He never stood his ground on any issue. Cooperating with his own disempowerment, he abdicated his personal throne and remained a frustrated "prince." In the end he felt impelled to desert his chaotic kingdom entirely.

The moody man, the listless man, the man who is apathetic, irritated, anxious, and depressed, the man who is basically naïve about what life requires of him—he is possessed by the Weakling King. When he isn't overcome with malaise, he's coldly withdrawn. He is the man who, rather than stand up for himself, will retreat into a corner and sulk. He is paralyzed when his boss reprimands him. Though he could either challenge his boss or accept the reprimand and resolve to try harder, the man under the power of the Weakling does nothing but reproach himself and nurse his resentments. His wife, his children, his friends and associates, all bear the brunt of his irritable disconsolation.

Such men are out of touch with the archetypal King in his fullness. Unlike the man possessed by the *Tyrant,* the man in the grip of the *Weakling* doesn't *feel* his split-off and repressed grandiosity. Only under pressure will the weak Ego suddenly jump to the active pole of the Tyrant. At such times self-indulgent moodiness will suddenly arc into displays of righteous indignation.

When the CEO above was finally challenged by his secretary about his irresponsible behaviors and his sexual advances, he exploded in a fit of rage. The lazy man was suddenly a wrathful dictator. He fired her on the spot. When she filed a sexual-harassment suit against him, he set out to get her with the maniacal fury of the possessed. When the son of the car dealer was finally taken to task by his best salespeople, he erupted in a fit of self-righteousness. "How dare you criticize me! You people can't even sell cars, much less run a business!" The sales force quit the dealership and left the tyrant powerless. When the wife confronted her husband about his desertion, he blamed her for everything. Scratch a tyrant and you'll find a weakling. Pressure a weakling and you'll find a tyrant.

Anyone who is out of touch with the archetype can be sure he is projecting it onto someone else.[6] We need to look around and ask ourselves who the tyrants are in our lives. We are often unwilling to access our inner King because we would then have to assume the sacred king's responsibilities for creatively ordering our lives. *We* would have to put our houses in order *ourselves*, rather than waiting for others to do our work. In addition, we would have to forsake the pleasures of cynicism. Abdicating kings love to knock the efforts of others. As long as we are not responsible for making things better, we can be as depreciating, as hostile and envious as we like. There is always someone else, someone we've given our power to, we can blame for what's wrong in our lives. Projection gets us off the hook, or so we imagine!

The problem is that when we do not experience the King's power ourselves, not only do we become profoundly dissatisfied with ourselves, we become weak. We lose the capacity to take initiative, to stand up for ourselves, to protect, provide, and procreate. With the responsibility we give up the joy of experiencing an integrated, autonomous sense of self. Those we cast as our tyrants fill the power vacuum our own abdication has left. Strangely enough, those tyrants are unable to be generative when *we* are not. The power we have given them is tainted. The weakling and the tyrant, possessed by their archetypal counterparts, are locked in a relationship of mutual destruction, with a world around them as desolate as their lives.

PART 4

ACCESSING THE KING WITHIN

HISTORICAL PATTERNS
OF ACCESSING THE KING

S ACRED KINGSHIP, IN ITS LITERAL HISTORIC FORMS AS
well as in its modern equivalents, can be a mixed blessing.
Societies that have a single individual embodying the archetypal King are at their inception exceedingly stable and creative. Since only one man's Ego *really* matters, the clash of
competing Egos is minimized. Everyone knows his place in the
pecking order. As long as the pecking order isn't overly oppressive, these societal systems allow individual efforts to be directed toward transpersonal rather than egoistic goals.

Sacred kingships are most creatively successful in their
early phases. Because a new king often brings to his society law

and order, safety from external threat, and relative freedom from want, he establishes also the necessary material and psychological conditions for cultural advance. And in a new society, as with any structure yet to be rigidified, individuals are in a unique position to make significant contributions to the culture.[1] Since advances in any field are made primarily by individuals (albeit in a supportive context), and individuals in sacred kingships are relatively unencumbered by egoistic competition, these first ancient monarchies were historically the most creative societies known to humankind before the modern era.

Perhaps also the archetypal basis of kingship provides people a psychospiritual anchor for individual and collective aspirations. The king becomes a basis for his people's projection of what the incarnated Self might be like. Outside of kingships the common man can find it difficult to know what is expected of him. With the king's image in mind, he has a very concrete idea of what he needs to do to actualize himself.

At first, this kind of projection provides security and comfort; from this solid base people gain a certain freedom from chaos, enabling them to be for a time joyfully creative. The downside of this is that large-scale projection of the archetypal King onto a single person eventually robs people of their individuality. At first people are thrilled by the security, but finally they are afraid to change anything that might threaten that security. Creativity is nothing if not change.

In Egypt, after an initial burst of creativity in engineering, mathematics, theology, literature, and the arts, artistic canons became rigid and few novel scientific or philosophic achievements emerged.[2] Culture remained more or less static thereafter for three thousand years. The same is true of other ancient kingship societies from the Maya to the Chinese. The initial inspiration of large-scale projection turns into a passivity of abdication, preparing the Tyrant's way. Mircea Eliade has noted the pervasive fear of history and individual responsibility to be found in tradition-bound societies.[3] The vast majority of people regard themselves as essentially slaves of the Gods, as in Mesopotamia,[4] of God-men, as in Egypt, or of a particular tyrant, as in so many modern societies. This leads to a kind of collective kindergarten atmosphere,[5] in which the divine or semi-divine enslaver is expected to make all the decisions about what to do and how to do it.

With a loss of initiative and personal identity there is no possibility of attaining maturity.[6] Authentic maturity requires introspection and self-adopted responsibility. Where individuals project their King onto their ruler, they lose access to the corresponding collective aspects of their own psyches. This in turn restricts the collective consciousness available to a society and guarantees that the society will never mature.

Despite our innate longing, a single leader cannot be generative when his people abdicate their own selves. And instead of inspiring people to develop themselves, most historical leaders have done the opposite. Facing the power vacuum left by an abdicated populace, leaders have tended—benevolently or not—to try to control more and more of the details of living, assuming that if they don't, nobody will. Hitler's staff generals were often irritated by how little he left them to do. Russia's tsar was responsible for every tiny bureaucratic decision involved in governing his nations of millions. No government official under him had authority to make decisions—their only real (and easily corruptible) power lay in suggesting or blocking an audience with the tsar.

By refusing to own the power of our inner King, history shows, we ease the way for the brutal repression of dissent, the establishment of inflexible cultural and religious canons, and the pursuit of devastating wars of national conquest. Whole civilizations have been undermined as a consequence. An abdicated populace enables the usurping few to subject any human being they may choose to unequal opportunity, unjust imprisonment, dislocation, unemployment, torture, rape, and whole populations to genocide.

Rituals of initiation can be an important psychological aid to maturity. However, it is often true that kingship societies use rites of passage to encourage conformity to an impersonal ideal of manhood.[7] There is then no encouragement offered a man toward his development of a perosnal masculine identity. There is *only* commitment to an impersonal other who takes little or no account of individual Egos. Where personal psychological growth is curtailed, no generative man can emerge.[8] Conformity, because it limits maturation, leads to cultural stagnation.

Egyptian scribes and artists were subjected to extended periods of apprenticeship. Rote memorization of traditional theories and techniques was believed to be the only method of tapping into Ma'at.[9] Innovation and experimentation were condemned as the chaotic way of Set. Initially profound insights into the meaning of human life were catalogued and passed along as clichéd, moralistic aphorisms.

Despite all the negative consequences of sacred kingships, a breakdown of these systems was equally disastrous. As we look around our contemporary societies we see striking parallels to the conditions ancients associated with these breakdowns. We heard the lament of one such ancient, the Egyptian Neferrohu (quoted in Chapter 4), during the long interregnum his chronicle describes. To some degree we still seem to need to project our inner King upon our leaders. To what extent are we aware of our inner lives even now? We might ask ourselves whether we behave as abdicators or usurpers in our relationships with others. What of the chaos and violence we see in the world around us? Are we currently living through an extended collective *psychological* interregnum, between the institution of sacred kingship and the internalization by every man of the archetype of the King?

DEMOCRACY AND THE
INTERNALIZATION OF THE KING

In a world in which the great masses of men more or less abdicated their inner thrones and responsibilities, one lone city remembered a more ancient way of life. In the Athens of the late sixth century B.C. the rule of the people was reinvented.[10] At that time Athenian democratic suffrage was limited to free male citizens. This consciously or unconsciously reflected a tribal past in which adult males held collective masculine power. In effect, these men shared the archetypal King among themselves.

Anthropology and archaeology suggest that most preliterate and early urban peoples were more or less democratic in this way. We cannot be sure whether the distant ancestors of the Dorian Greeks were, but it would seem likely. In North American Indian culture, and in Africa among the rain kings, leaders ruled in concert with a council of male elders. The Hebrews (and to a lesser extent other Semite and Indo-Aryan tribes) were able to disassociate the king from the King archetype. But the Athenians were the first recorded civilization to radically internalize the archetype, and to dispense with a king altogether.

Of course, there was none of the *conscious* internalization modern depth psychology encourages. But Greek philosophical developments resulted in a widespread realization that Gods are, in part, projections of the psyche, and that ultimately what fuels the projections is the God energy *within* the psyche.[11] Pre-Socratic philosophers transformed Gods into natural laws and processes, including psychological ones, which were expressions of a supreme Deity.[12] As Plato reconstructed the dialogues and speeches of Socrates, Socrates believed in a King-God.[13] But he also spoke of *daemones*, entities that could be found both within the psyche and in the outer world in the various levels of cosmic reality. Hermetic and Gnostic traditions in the later Hellenistic Age elaborated upon the idea of an internalized God.[14]

The birth of democracy in Athens went hand in hand with these philosophical speculations. This is not to say that for the Greeks Zeus, or other Deity constructs, ceased to exist as Gods in the external world. Rather the Greeks realized that the inner and outer worlds may be the same reality viewed from opposite perspectives.[15] Furthermore, the human Ego was never identified with the indwelling God. Socrates was quite clear that he served an inner spirit, one that prompted him to give up the life of the Ego for the pursuit of truth.[16] The Gnostics believed the God they contacted dwelt in the pleroma, a region strikingly similar to the modern conception of the unconscious. At the same time they experienced themselves as sacred vessels containing this God. Thus the King-God was both other and within.[17]

A parallel development took place among the Jews of the Roman Empire. If we take the Gospels to be a metaphorical history, we see the man Jesus taking the role of sacred king upon himself. He proclaimed himself the son of the King-God. He is reported to have had magical power over nature. He allowed himself to be thought of as a messianic savior, come from heaven to restore the essence of the Torah. He even sacrificed his life to bring the world into harmony with the sacred order of the Kingdom of God.[18]

Jesus exhibited in his life and teachings a paradigm of the Ego-archetypal axis. When he said, "If you knew me, you would know my Father also,"[19] he might have been implying an Ego-archetypal merger. But he also said, "I have come down from heaven, not to do my own will, but the will of him who sent me,"[20] which disidentified his Ego from the archetype. The message of the Garden of Gethsemane story is that he had a human Ego struggling to face its imminent death, but that he was also a vessel filled with divinity.[21]

Where the Kingdom of God is, presumably God is as well. Jesus said unequivocally, "The kingdom of God is not coming with signs to be observed; nor will they say, 'Lo, here it is!' or 'There!' for behold, the kingdom of God is in the midst of you."[22] Again, he insisted, "I am in my Father, and you in me, and I in you."[23]

Christian Gnostics blended Hellenistic philosophy with a mystical interpretation of these and other sayings of Jesus. They proclaimed that God was within every person as a light from an unfailing eternal light which would continue forever as the source of life.[24] The Gnostics, like the Athenians, governed their societies democratically.[25] Nobody could be king if *everybody* was one already.

This idea of the inner King was at the heart of various medieval heresies.[26] Protestantism incorporated the idea into its doctrine of a "priesthood of all believers."[27] This doctrine was wedded to the memory of Athenian democracy to provide the psychological and spiritual basis for the American Declaration of Independence and the Constitution.[28] Huey Long's democratic ideal of "every man a king" is the sociopolitical expression of the psychological truth that there *is* a King within every man.

MODERN CULTURE AND THE
REPRESSION OF THE INNER KING

Whether the men of a premodern society internalized the archetypal King as an inner Deity, or projected him onto a sacred king or a sky-dwelling King-God, the archetype was an experienced reality. This changed with the onset of modernity. Though there are antecedents, we locate the beginning of the modern era primarily with the eighteenth century French Enlightenment.[29] Characterized in broad terms by rationalism and materialistic reductionism, the Enlightenment is still impacting world cultures.

Rationalism is the Ego's domain, and in theory excludes intuitive or emotional modes of thought. According to modernity, rationalism is the highest expression of human being. Anyone interested in mystery or alternative modes of reality is called "superstitious" or "obscurantist." Materialistic reductionism is the doctrine that there is no reality besides what can be perceived by the senses or the various instruments of science. Science is the great faith of the modern era; we believe the universe to be a vast machine, and the unknown is "mysterious" only because we have yet to invent instruments to explain it to us.

The fruits of this "faith" are impressive. Rapid advances in the fields of technology and theoretical and applied science have supported the concurrent developments of rationalist politics, industrialized economies, and materialistic consumerism. Demythologization[30] characterizes thought in the religious sphere. Sacred myths are regarded now as prescientific attempts to explain natural processes. Myths are said to represent wishful thinking in response to the harsh realities of socioeconomic forces in a mechanical universe.

Rationalism is of course *irrational*, in the assumption that only a particular mode of Ego consciousness is valid. Our modern era has been aptly described as a cramp in the Left Brain. Even the materialistic perspective on brain functioning demonstrates that modernity neglects most of the nervous system—the Left Brain's logical, linear thought processes are prized, but the Right Brain's feeling-inflected cognition is not. Nor are the more instinctual impulses and behaviors that arise in the deeper layers of the brain, nervous system, and body. Right Brain cognition leads us to very different conclusions about the nature of reality than does the Left Brain's rationalism. Ironically, even thinkers on the rationalist frontier—Kant, Einstein, and

Heisenberg, for example—made discoveries that directly contradict the rationalist doctrines of modernity.[31] Unfortunately, society at large has yet to catch up to its leading intellectuals.

We suffer serious consequences from the stubborn rationalism of our times. Jung observed long ago that without an adequate spirituality, with a supra-rational experience of a transpersonal other at its center, a psychic vacuum is created, which the unconscious fills with inferior psychic contents. According to our view, the central content of a male psyche is the masculine Self. This is represented to the male Ego largely as the archetypal King. Since agnostic modernity withholds the masculine Self from the Ego, the missing King-God in the unconscious is replaced by inadequate, ultimately dysfunctional objects of transpersonal commitment. We try to make lesser Gods suffice for the masculine Self.[32] Our minor deities include the State, the Party, the People, the Company, and Science. While these things are important, they cannot substitute for the God within. They are not reliable suppliers of Libido. The State becomes oppressive, the Party corrupt; the People prove to be fickle; the Company rarely rewards our loyalty, and the faith we have in Science's tangible materialism is undermined by the very discoveries of Science.

The modern age is an age of regicide. One of rationalism's immediate products was the guillotine. While undoubtedly the French Revolution was an inevitable political corrective, what does it mean when a people beheads its king? For this is the script we are still playing today. The French Revolution was partly inspired by the American model, and because the culmination of theirs was so extreme it provided inspiration in turn to the anarchists and socialists of nineteenth- and twentieth-century Europe. When for a short time the Russian revolutionaries felt their successes slipping, they too committed regicide to absolutely confirm the process they had begun.

There are few monarchs left today who do not serve largely a symbolic function. Those modern dictators who try to set themselves up as kings have to build up a brutal military to maintain their position, though ironically the same troops are often behind the coup d'état that secures the dictator's eventual downfall. A global instinct for regicide is in some sense rich with possibilities. No longer do masses of people need to feel enslaved by powers beyond their control. Once the masses reject the absolute power of the State, they make room for themselves to take power as individuals.

Unfortunately, at this period in history our instinct is to take power away from our leaders and then avoid it ourselves. Once the king is beheaded, and the people have visceral proof that such a thing can happen, they can begin to see the King that is within them. But the archetype of the King is so psychoactive, so incredibly loaded with power, it scares people. When an energy scares us we try to disassociate ourselves from it. This is why individuation is in Jung's view a *moral struggle*.

The archetypes are imperialistic. They do not want to share the psyche and be balanced one against the other. Each wants complete hegemony. But we do not want to *be* an archetype. Maturity is getting to a place of strength where none of the archetypes can take us against our wills and possess us. We don't want to let go of any of them either. The archetypal energy we can hold on to will be a *source* for everything we do. And because the source is in the collective psyche, it will never run dry. There is never a need to be sparing with this energy, because if used properly it is inexhaustible.

A mortal man cannot hold the projection of the King for long. There are plenty of men who love trying. They find thousands of others willing to give their power away, and all that power can be deeply seductive. The man who accepts all the power he's offered lights up like a target. In our regicidal era, sooner or later someone will come along and say, "There's a king. Let's kill him." But until this happens, he starts to believe he *is* the archetype. After all, he's glowing with the archetype's energy, he's lit up like a Christmas tree, and everyone around him confirms his radiance.

Archetypes are not human, and can do nothing wrong. They cannot be destroyed. So the man who is possessed by the archetype starts to believe he is invulnerable too. Maybe he gets the idea to run for office. This goes well, so he thinks, why not run for president? Everyone around him tells him what a great idea this is, what a great job he's doing, so he lights up. And when rumors are spread about his extramarital affairs, he holds a press conference. "Why don't you put a tail on me," he dares the reporters. At this moment in time he's almost too bright to look at. Pretty soon afterward, of course, he's over his inflation, because the press never tail an archetype. They follow a real flesh-and-blood man home and take pictures of the woman who comes to stay the weekend.

Or maybe you're a little more careful to conceal your affairs, because everyone thinks your wife is a national treasure and you like the light that casts on you. But you nickname your administration Camelot, and you ignore what your faithful Secret Service men tell you about your relative popularity in Texas. That's what you've come here to address. You can ride around Dallas with your car top down; you've faced danger before and won on your own terms. The people *need* to be seen by you. And anyway, nobody can kill an archetype.

Archetypal dynamics must not be taken lightly. If we let him, the King will take us over, as a magnet takes over iron filings. On the other hand, we cannot repudiate him because he is the archetype that (properly accessed) regulates the other three archetypes of the mature masculine. Without the King the Ego has no access to life-sustaining Libido.

But this isn't the worst of it. When the Ego ignores the archetype, an ominous dynamic is set in motion. The archetypes manifest to the Ego in their destructive bipolar Shadow forms, disrupting personal life and wreaking devastation in the world. A borderline personality is an extreme example of a psyche that holds a lot of archetypal energies without a King to keep them in order. The Gods must have their due. Without it they become hostile, reminding us of their presence in unpleasant, even life-threatening ways. Just before the outbreak of World War II, Jung became fascinated by an uprush of archetypal material he noted in the collective unconscious of the German people. Jung believed the Nazi movement drew upon attributes of Wotan, the Teutonic god of storm and wrath. Citing the "return of the repressed" phenomenon typical of psychotic patients, Jung theorized that Wotan had returned through the collective unconscious of the Nazis because they had repressed their spirituality. A transpersonal commitment to death and destruction replaced the God-image in the German unconscious. Jung believed the God-image was the only psychologically adequate Transpersonal Other. The Nazis suffered its absence, and made millions suffer with them.

Ego inflation occurs in the absence of such a Transpersonal Other. Our modern era itself represents this inflation by its exclusive reverence for rationalism and materialism. Without a spiritual dimension the Ego loses the ability to orient itself generatively in the context of a larger reality. To be generative, as we've noted, the Ego must be engaged in an Ego-archetypal axis. Whatever is unconscious to us possesses us.[33] If we wish to differentiate ourselves from our possessors we must first become conscious of them. Becoming conscious of the archetypal King within, we can realize the Ego-King axis while at the same time differentiating ourselves from the archetype. We thereby avoid becoming inflated by it.

Jung believed inflated Egos have perpetrated most of the horrors of history. The present catastrophic world situation is certainly a legacy of Ego inflation.[34] Jung felt that the collective unconscious has retaliated against the Ego's "god almightiness"[35] by the development of the atom bomb. The collective human Self, impersonal nature in psychological form,[36] used the Ego's own rational dynamics to bring the unspeakable into being, dramatizing the absurdity of the Ego's inflated arrogance.

THE POSTMODERN
RETURN OF THE KING

We are now moving in a postmodern era, one which is recovering a sense of hidden, divine, and in psychological language, archetypal heights and depths. Rationalism and modernity are collapsing under their own *ir*rational weight. And that collapse has prepared the way for the return of the King.

The first serious crack in rationalism's facade appeared after Einstein published his Theory of Relativity. Though this theory is the better part of a century old, modernity lingers on because the world of subatomic physics is so intellectually challenging popularizers are still having difficulty explaining the meaning of the work Einstein and his colleagues have left us.[37] The atom bomb, of course, is one direct application of the work—rationalism's apocalyptic achievement is based upon discoveries that undercut the certainties of rationalism.

Among the most disconcerting discoveries was that our apparently solid world is mostly made of empty space. Atoms can be described as akin to mini solar systems, in which subatomic particles are relatively just as small and far apart from one another as are the planets of our solar system. Furthermore, the major subatomic components, the electron, proton, and neutron, can be broken down into even smaller components, which can themselves be broken down, and so on in an apparently endless regression.

These particles exhibit extremely bizarre characteristics. They seem to be able to travel backward in time.[38] They seem capable of localizing in two places at once, without ever having divided.[39] These tiniest of particles may not even *be* particles. They also behave as if they are waves of radiant energy. They appear to spontaneously arise from and subside into a mysterious, underlying energy grid, an invisible matrix which may permeate what we have considered to be the void of empty space.[40] Subatomic particles seem to be transient, granular concentrations of this underlying energy field.[41] This makes the void fairly dance with energy, whatever *energy* may be. Many have noted how the new physicists have had to resort to the allusive, spiritual language of mystics to explain their concepts.[42]

Physicists working with astronomers are inventing a new "mystical" cosmology. These new theories are fundamentally challenging to modernity's assumptions about the nature of reality. According to the prevalent Big Bang theory, this immense universe was once packed into a tiny point smaller than an atom's nucleus.[43] Within this unimaginable density the four major energic forces that drive and shape our universe were combined in one single undifferentiated force.

Max Planck worked calculations back to chart the universe's course to within 10^{-43} of a second after the Big Bang.[44] Before this time, he proposed what we now designate as the Planck Era in which time and space as we know them did not exist. Recent theorists have enjoyed speculating about the Planck Era.[45] They imagine a kind of foam that throws up bubbles, most of which fall back into the Planck Era. Those that escape explode into universes, each of which generates its own unique space-time. Our universe is one such expanding bubble.[46] Each bubble contains in miniature the inherent structures of the universe it will become. Astronomers have now collected sufficient data to map galaxy distributions—and they have found that galaxies are distributed in vast strings and clumps. This is in accord with the uneven quality physicists believe to have been implicit in our tiny Planck Era bubble.[47]

As if these discoveries weren't enough to confound the rationalist Ego, biologists have begun to explore the unseen dimension from which biological forms and processes derive.[48] Just as there is an implicit grid along which mineral crystals form in explicit detail, biological phenomena seem to arise as explications of a mysterious implicate order. Adolf Portmann postulates hidden "operators," or structural forms, explaining: "Formation and new formation in the realm of living organisms are not a production of order out of a disordered chaos, they are the production of order out of an already given, ordered structure."[49] Portmann has spoken of an invisible "abyss of mystery" in which these structural forms are implicit, an "immense, unknown realm of the mysterious."[50] Once again we find a scientist speaking like a mystic, and even like a depth psychologist. Jung noticed striking resemblances to ideas of modern science turning up in the dream productions of his analysands. What is an archetype if not a notion of implicate order, of just the type postulated by physicists, biologists, and astronomers? Jung's "abyss of mystery" within the psyche, the illimitable collective unconscious, is an invisible structure giving transient form in the "material" world to various complexes and urges. *There seems to be emerging a unitary, postmodern worldview, in which the mystical traditions, psychology, and the physical sciences all serve to elucidate aspects of the same underlying reality.* That underlying reality reveals the presence of the landscape of the King within the human psyche.

POSTMODERN IDEAS
OF SACRED AND PROFANE

Perhaps we can parallel the two fundamental dimensions of *scientific* reality, the implicate and the explicate, with the sacred and profane dimensions of the sacred king's world. The ancient idea of divine order in mythic time and space seems to agree with ideas of implicate structures, strings, granular space, and invisible operators. This may be an aspect of the divine order we have referred to as Ma'at, Dharma, Tao, and Torah. There is also the shared notion that in the "sacred" time and space of the Planck Era, all things existed in undifferentiated unity. This is strikingly parallel to the pleroma of the Gnostics, the Buddhist nirvana, the Hindu unmanifest Brahman,[51] the Christian paradise,[52] the Jungian collective Self.

Jungian analyst Jolande Jacobi has noted that many prominent scientists, including Planck, Hartmann, Uexhill, Eddington, and Jeans,[53] have come up against an impassable barrier between what empirical knowledge can discover and what metaphysics alone can grasp. We call this Left Brain barrier the "wall of paradise," after the ancient theologian Nicholas of Cusa.[54] On our side of the wall primordial unity manifests in pairs of opposites. On the other side everything exists in complete harmony.

In the Planck Era, the four forces of nature were joined into two, and the two into one. Taoists say that the appearance of "two" signaled the inception of the created world.[55] Before two is the Tao, unknowable in its pure essence. In Babylonian mythology the universe began when Marduk slew Tiamat and divided her into two. The Egyptian universe began when the primordial hill arose from the cosmic ocean, creating two dimensions of reality.

And just as creation myths hold that sacred energy erupted into the profane at a single point, then radiated outward, so the Big Bang theory argues the universe began within an infinitesimally small point. After an unimaginable explosion, radiant energy spread in every direction. Our sphere of space-time is still expanding. We can find a direct parallel to this in the Jewish tradition, which tells us, "The Most Holy One created the world like an embryo. As the embryo grows from the navel, so God began to create the world by the navel and from there it spread out in all directions."[56]

The emerging postmodern worldview is in a way a remythologization of the universe. The teachings of the great spiritual traditions no longer seem so farfetched. From the theory of the archetypes to the "operators" of biological forms, it is once again reasonable to speak of an invisible order trying to incarnate in the lives of individual humans. Of course, physics, astronomy, and biology do not speak the anthropomorphic language of the myths of the King. But they *do* point to a creative ordering which moves the potential into the actual.

Creative ordering through an incarnational process is the central characteristic of the archetypal King. The King is returning in the postmodern world.

WELCOMING THE KING
INTO OUR LIVES

A**N UNSEEN DIMENSION OF REALITY IS BEHIND THE** created world in modern science as in ancient myth. With a burst of heat and light, the Big Bang provided the radiant energy our universe is built upon. The energy dissipated across various cosmic eras, time functioning as a step-down transformer system, slowing the energy until matter was able to take form.[1] Living things on our planet (and possibly on others) depend on the still dissipating energy of the stars. "Entropy" is a law of thermodynamics that order within a closed system will tend to decay, that higher forms of energy will tend to be converted into lower forms. The entropy that characterizes our universe has been recognized as a given in myths of all eras.[2]

Some ancient peoples believed the universe periodically dissolved and then was renewed by a fresh eruption of sacred energy. Most believed as well that a gradual wearing process had begun immediately after creation. Some cosmologists parallel the ancient idea of universal death and rebirth with a theory that the universe will eventually stop expanding, then collapse in upon itself back to another infinitesimal point, which will explode again in another Big Bang, and so on forever.[3] For the Hindus this is the waking and sleeping of Brahman. He falls asleep: The universe collapses. He awakens: The universe expands.[4]

Many ancient peoples believed it was necessary to regenerate the cosmos at intervals much briefer than the cosmic cycles. Regular infusions of divine force from the sacred dimension were required to counteract the effects of universal entropy. For these peoples every act of cultural creation, from raising a new house to crowning a sacred king, was a recapitulation of the creation of the world.[5] Through these acts of renewal the cosmogony was remembered and *present,* much as Catholic doctrine teaches that Christ is present in the Eucharist, renewing all who partake of him.

What is necessary for the cosmos is necessary for us too. Moving from grand speculations about the fundamental importance of cosmic regeneration to a consideration of our own daily needs for renewal need not be thought of as a move from the sublime to the ridiculous. We are simply shifting perspective to a level of being midway between the macrocosm of the galaxies and the microcosm of particles in the quantum field. If we take God to be in part an image of the macrocosm, we can see the sense of the mystic tenet "God is a circle whose center is everywhere and whose circumference is nowhere."[6] Within our holographic universe,[7] inner and outer, above and below, increasingly seem to be subjective perspectives; the whole seems to be entirely present in each of its parts. Depth psychology turns the ancient phrase "as above, so below" into a healing exhortation, "as within, so without." If men can be encouraged to establish order within themselves, the world as a whole will benefit.

We have all experienced the feeling of gradually running out of energy, of needing a "kick start." We all grow weary at times of our life situation, of our friends, of work, home, some nagging problem, even sometimes of our usual favorite entertainments. Think of some of the ways we've tried to relieve ourselves of the feeling that life has become dull, uninteresting, and sterile. Think of a time when buying the new car didn't do the trick. Getting together with the boys at the favorite watering hole wasn't much fun either. Even the vacation to Mexico fell flat. These pursuits may have brought their temporary happiness, but really what we needed was to get back in touch with the "waters of life" running within us. When our profane mini cosmos runs out of Libido, what we need is a transfusion of primordial energy from the sacred realm of the deep psyche.

This same Libido is what we were looking for when we found it impossible to realize our dreams in the everyday world. How many times have we imagined a dream house and then realized we could never afford the payments? How many times has the new job we approached with such great hopes and expectations turned into another dead end? How many of us have been swept away by the ecstasy of love, then discovered only after the marriage ceremony the enormous work it takes to deepen the magic and grow the relationship?[8] Both the imaginal realm and the everyday world are actual and real. They both involve tangible psychological experiences. But it is a difficult process to bring imaginal visions into the material world.

Fantasies, visions, dream figures, and inner voices are the lures the unconscious uses to tempt us toward individuation and toward forming Ego-archetype axes. Our Ego's task is to attend to these messages. We must discover who among these sacred messengers can help us achieve realistic happiness, which of their dream promises we can embody in our profane world, who are the true emissaries of the King within.

PSYCHOTHERAPY:
ATTENDING TO THE UNCONSCIOUS

Modernity has never encouraged men to acquire knowledge of the deeper layers of their masculine psyches. But it is here that the inexhaustible reservoir of masculine identity lies. Self-exploration is prohibited by the rigid rationalistic and materialistic cultural canons of our modern era. Ever since the inscription was carved into the facade of the Temple of Apollo at Delphi—"Know thyself!"—self-exploration has been recognized as the key to authentic human being. With the idea now in disrepute, many (if not most) men are deprived of any real chance to experience themselves as the richly nuanced, Self-empowered male primates they were meant to be.

As we've explored, the Ego that is denied access to the archetypal King will likely be possessed by the King's bipolar Shadow. This poorly accessed King is not solely the result of culturally determined resistance to probing the reaches of inner space. It is also the consequence of inadequate fathering. Many of us have grown up with weakling or tyrant fathers. Often they were absent from us, emotionally or physically, or both, and emotional absence is characteristic of the Shadow King. A man possessed by the Shadow King is not present for us, and so does not see us or celebrate us, and has no desire to do either. Absent fathers do far more damage to masculine identities than many men realize.

Freud drew Western attention to the pervasive mother and father issues of our culture.[9] By a psychological mechanism termed "repetition compulsion,"[10] our unconscious compels us even in adulthood to repeat the childhood traumas we suffered at the hands of our parents. We recapitulate at the same time the negative relational patterns imprinted on us when we were young, before we had any Ego structure to speak of, or any defensible psychological boundaries. While it can be beneficial to consciously reopen the old emotional wounds, too often they possess us unawares.

We retain the dysfunctional patterns of relating learned in childhood. These patterns sabotage our attempts to live lives of realistic greatness, undermining what should be the most generative years of our lives. Our fathers, of course, grew up in a world that damaged them in a similar way. The "father" archetype some analysts speak of we believe to be *one* of the faces of the King. Fathers are always kings to their children, and too often they are tyrants. Once children mature they depose their tyrants—so a father tyrant may feel he has nothing to gain by letting his children grow up. His world taught him, "Kick them first before they kick you," and he can't imagine any other way.

But it is one thing to disavow a father and quite another to do the inner work necessary to reconcile with him. Because painful experiences are so deeply repressed, the average man may have no idea how wounded he is—until he loses his job, or contracts a debilitating illness; or perhaps after his marriage fails, or he faces a major crisis with his children.

Most men do not avail themselves of psychotherapy until such crises arise. Even then the vast majority will not seek help. Cultural mores teach them that it is unmanly to look for any. Men also have been taught not to feel pain, or at least not to show any painful feelings. It can be so painful to break through the repression barrier that shields us from our lifetime store of unlived suffering, it is not too surprising many men would rather self-destruct than try.

Often even when men do engage in a psychotherapeutic process they are completely surprised by the amount of pain that surfaces. In early sessions it is common to hear a man express the belief that he had great parents and a happy home life. Only in later sessions does his devastation, his loneliness, and the desolation of his sense of worthlessness arise. This worthlessness may have been conveyed by both his mother and father.

As these feelings become conscious male counselees frequently develop a resistance to any further self-reflection. Another of our unhelpful cultural lessons is that men should not have feelings of sorrow, vulnerability, helplessness, tenderness, gentleness, or compassion, for themselves or others. Such feelings are supposedly feminine. Most men work so hard, whether consciously or not, to achieve an often-exaggerated culturally defined masculinity that any suggestion they might be less than fully masculine is deeply threatening. Lurking behind the revelation of authentic feeling lies the unconscious fear of once again merging with the mother, of a regression into the passivity of gender-neutral infantilism.

When a man chooses to engage in a psychotherapeutic process he faces inner work that will take his utmost courage and effort. He will have to get to know his inner Child,[11] and come to comfort and confront him. He will have to face his personal Shadow.[12] Initially mortal enemies, he and his Shadow will have to be reconciled. He will have to face his inner feminine by knowing and loving his Anima.[13] Together the two must work out a mutually enhancing relationship, a task requiring as much skill and effort as lifelong intimacies require in the outer world.

This man will become an expert in the delicate art of interpreting his dreams.[14] Dreams will reveal to him the complexual and archetypal inhabitants of his inner world. He will need to reclaim as many split-off parts of himself as he can, in the dangerous but rewarding process of self-integration. He will likely master techniques of imaging and holding dialogues with unconscious aspects of himself. Eventually he will have a series of encounters with the masculine Self at the core of his being.[15] He will come before the cosmic throne at the heart of his total psychic system and at least acquire aspects of Generative Man.

Most psychologies regard the overcoming of the "parental introjects" (internalized images of the parents)[16] as one of the most crucial steps in the development of an autonomous, cohesive Self. Some psychologists speak of "slaying" the parents, others of getting beyond the "imago,"[17] the emotionally imprinted introject carried by the inner Child of both parents, and their positive and negative characteristics. Breaking free of the parents can be an extended undertaking. As infants we are so completely dependent on them, and the time we humans spend in childhood is so substantial, that any negative relational patterns have years in which to be reinforced. We learned as very young children how to repress any anger we may feel toward our parents, so some aspects of our relationships must first be made conscious before we can even begin to cut our ties. But cut them we must, if we wish to be self-empowered.

Many men find it very difficult to free themselves of the internalized father as well as the internalized mother. A major contributing factor to this is the projection dynamic. When a man projects, he unconsciously experiences others as if they were a lost part of himself. He may project aspects of his personal Shadow on another male, and then vilify that person for faults that are really his own unacknowledged issues. He may also project archetypal contents onto others. His parents may continue to have power over him in his adulthood because he projects his King and Queen onto them. It is sensible for a *boy* to see his mother and father as nearly godlike, because they do *in fact* have a lot of power over him, even the power of life and death, as child-abuse statistics so grimly testify.[18]

A boy will *fear* and *idealize* his parents at the same time. He needs to trust in his parents' wisdom and goodness, no matter how harshly they treat him, because his survival and sense of security depend upon them. The projection mechanism at least anchors the boy in the world with some sense of security, however it may be skewed, and introduces him to the archetypal King and Queen through his idealization of his parents. Defense mechanisms can be useful when there is something real to defend against. Eventually during the maturation process they must be discarded, but they may be necessary at certain stages.

At some point the boy will begin to feel a disjunction between his parents and his archetypal projections. At this point he needs to be enabled to withdraw his projections. To the extent that he accomplishes this, he will see that the archetypes are independent of his parents, and that they are within him yet separate from his Ego. If he does not succeed in this, he will never love his parents for the precious, flawed, and mortal people they are.[19] He equally may continue to project the archetypes on his lover or spouse, or authority figures in his later life. If he can free these others of his projections, *he* will be freed in turn of expecting them to be perfectly supportive and loving with him. His adult relationships will then be much more realistic sources of happiness and fulfillment.

We often hear grown men speak of their parents at the idealizing level of a five-year-old. They romanticize the one or two times their fathers took them fishing, for example. And rather than seeing their mothers as the weak or frightened women they often were, these men make of them martyred saints, thereby crippling their own capacity for autonomous, guilt-free functioning. The idealization drops away in stages as a man begins to own his disappointment, sorrow, and rage over his actual treatment. As this happens he can properly return the "perfect parents" to the mythic realm of his imagination.

Once the projections are withdrawn from the parents (or lovers, spouses, sometimes even children), and early traumas have been recovered and processed, a man is on the road to healing. According to our experience, though, traditional psychotherapy is rarely enough to heal him. Objectifying the inner Child, comforting and confronting him, does not *automatically* produce adult structure. While holding dialogues with the personal Shadow, the Anima, and other complexes, the Ego may be overwhelmed by the hostilities of these once-spurned inner entities.[20] Some men are so damaged they have very little adult structure to bring to the dialogic task. Even if made aware of the wounded inner Child, these men may not have the Ego they need to defuse the Child's regressive force.

Many psychologies, social-interactive[21] and Freudian among them, give up at this point. To these systems of thought, we are only what we have been programmed to be. It would seem some programs cannot be undone. Developmental psychologists will often be deeply pessimistic about the prognosis for severely wounded people. They have discovered that we all make our basic decisions about the world, about whether it is fundamentally a supportive or a harmful place, within the first six months to a year of life.[22]

Jungians are a bit more hopeful because the archetypes provide all of us with genetically wired resources for wholeness. The circuits we need for personal well-being are there for us in the unconscious. *For men the masculine archetypes are potentially enormous structured sources of Libido* regardless *of how much damage we have sustained early in life.*

John Weir Perry has demonstrated how these energy sources, especially the King, have the capacity to restructure and reorient the psyches of even profoundly disturbed people. In *Roots of Renewal in Myth and Madness,* Perry cites the case of a man who exhibited the scattered thinking and affect of an acute schizophrenic.[23] At a certain point in his treatment this man drew a square, circle, and cross on the wall in a concentric pattern. He located himself at the center of the drawing. At this central point he saw himself as having the characteristics of

Jesus Christ. He also drew pictures in which he figured himself as the fourth of a divine quaternity also including God the Father, the Virgin Mary, and Jesus.[24]

These archetypal outpourings helped the man to healthfully reorganize his psyche. The visions provided this man with a sense of meaningful structure and purpose in his life. It cannot be said that this man, or the other profoundly disturbed individuals Perry worked with, became "normal" following these visions of wholeness. But their contact with the archetypes, particularly the archetype of the King, helped them achieve a higher level of psychological organization and greater personal integration.

The archetypes offer all of us images of fulfillment, authenticity, and maturity. If a wounded man can get to them, or if they spontaneously come to his rescue through dreams or visions, he can *more or less* transcend his wounding and achieve a significant degree of generativity in his life.[25] The depth psychological process of analysis is, we believe, the most effective way to get to the ground of the psyche. More than any other psychotherapeutic process, depth psychology respects the images of the archetypes the unconscious produces. They are our guides to the achievement of full human being.

If all goes well, they will lead us, too, to a condition of *true humility*. Two admissions bring us true humility: First, we admit that our lives are in some important respect out of control, that we have fallen victim to destructive unconscious compulsions; and second, we admit that we need help. Once we have internalized these admissions, we have gone as far as our boyish heroic consciousness can carry us; from this far edge of legitimate grandiosity we are ready to step with true humility before the King, and receive from him a sense of our *realistic* greatness.

Along the way we will have been gaining an appreciation of how our lives have been possessed by the King's bipolar

In the Service of the King:
The Warrior Receiving His Sword
(from a medieval illuminated manuscript)

Shadow system. We can then objectify both the Shadow system and the King himself. Just as we did with our parents, we need to experience the archetypal system as "out there," and separate from our Ego. For those *tyrants* who have *identified* themselves with the King, this experience is profoundly humbling. These men will feel alarmingly smaller and less powerful than they are used to feeling. Once they understand their real size, they have a profound understanding of the enormity of the power that has

possessed them. For those *weaklings* who have had little awareness of the autonomous forces within them, early attempts to objectify and access the King may seem like exercises in pure
fantasy. But when the King is successfully realized, the Ego is
profoundly moved, even with a sense of divine revelation. The
King may seem to suddenly materialize out of the void, present-
ing himself to the astonished Ego in an awesome aspect. Perhaps
Ezekiel's encounter with the divine chariot[26] and Arjuna's vision
of Krishna[27] were experiences of this sort.

Certainly the man who encounters this numinous King
often suddenly feels that he is in a sacred place, standing on
holy ground. He may feel his flesh creep, or the hairs rising on
the back of his neck. The intuition of holiness is really of the
sacred space at the center of the psyche, from whence the King
energy radiates. The energy concentrated at the center is both
dreadful and wonderful by virtue of its power. It drops us to our
knees with the force of its holiness. We respond as a creature
before his creator.[28]

The wonder of the King is the light and pure healing life-
force he emanates. The anxious Ego relaxes its neurotic grip on
life and lets the King restore it to its proper place in the scheme
of things. The restoration of a proper perspective allows the Ego
to transcend daily difficulties, and experience the reconstitution
of the psyche as a total system. The Ego faces the terror of dying
to a constricting self-image and being reborn through the transcendent function. This revelation of the King evokes for a man
the startling knowledge that his "I" is not the center of things,
as he'd thought. Instead he is freed to become the servant of a
numinous Transpersonal Other.

ACTIVE IMAGINATION AS MEDITATION:
IMAGINING THE UNCONSCIOUS

Since the imagination is the mechanism through which the Ego receives the images and symbols of the unconscious,[29] Jung recommended that patients exercise their imaginations. He called an exercising engagement of the Ego with the unconscious "active imagination."[30] In religious language "active imagination" can be seen as a form of *meditation*. For the world's spiritual traditions meditation consists of a variety of techniques for putting the Ego into an altered state of consciousness, one in which it is focused on inner, spiritual contents (archetypes), and open to their numinous power. The purpose of active imagination techniques is to invite the unconscious to share with the Ego more and more of its contents.

Since at both personal and collective levels the unconscious possesses wisdom and perspective far exceeding the Ego's, and since the split-off aspects of our psyches reside there, the active engagement of the unconscious is essential. Any purposeful reverie is a form of active imagination. Dream analysis, Ego-archetype dialogues, the focused imaging of some meditation techniques, and the free association of spontaneous images, thoughts, and feelings all are means of inviting the unconscious to communicate. We want to explore focused meditation techniques, and use them in relation to the archetypal King.

Some are uncomfortable at first using images in a way that implies their objective reality. With the exception of Catholicism, our Western religions have proscribed the use of images when communing with the divine. Judaism and Islam are particularly adamant about this.[31] Protestant Christians have sometimes been taught that images of the saints, or Christ on the cross, are suspiciously Catholic at best, superstitious and pagan at worst. Even so, Protestant churches often display paintings of Jesus and his followers, since they take the biblical injunction to be specifically against "graven," that is, carved, images.

But Christianity, Judaism, and Islam all supply *verbal* images of God and the spiritual dimension. For the average person the Deity is not merely an intellectual abstraction of goodness, love, wrath, or any other impersonal quality. Most people, after reading texts or hearing them read aloud, have drawn mental images of a more or less anthropomorphic Deity.[32]

Strictly defined, idolatry is the worshiping of something less powerful in the place of an all-powerful God.[33] In this sense, idolatry is making something other than the King carry our transpersonal commitment. It is investing something personal with transpersonal significance. Yet the Gods of all religions manifest both personal and impersonal aspects. The exalted Christian Trinity is also the man Jesus with whom we can "walk in the garden alone." Anthropomorphic images of the Deity point beyond themselves to God.[34] They can serve as aids to worship. Images and symbols, whether verbalized, sculpted, or painted, engage us on an emotional and a cognitive level.

Anthropomorphic images of archetypal realities (of whom the King-God is a culminating one) are helpful to us in reaching the structures of the masculine Self. We would argue that these images are *essential* for psychological health. When God becomes the abstraction he is in our times, the Ego unconsciously depicts *itself* as God-like. If we cannot image the King, we pretend to his throne. Imaging the King helps us objectify and separate the true center of the psyche. After all, it's harder to think you're the King when you're talking to him.

Projection of the King is not always a misguided practice. When we project the inner King onto outer images, we form for ourselves a concrete mental and emotional focus. We provide a screen upon which the archetype can present itself to us. As is true for all archetypal material, the King is ultimately mysteri-

Singing in the Tree of Life:
The King in His Lover Mode
(Ragasthami painting: Krishna in the Tree)

ous and unrepresentable. Nevertheless, we enable ourselves to relate to him by *objectifying* his manifest qualities. He becomes a psychological fact with whom we establish contact.

We have all heard a version of the saying "You are what you think." Following a belief in the power of positive thinking, we are often encouraged to repeat affirmations to ourselves, or image ourselves successfully completing a business task or a tricky athletic move. There is abundant anecdotal and clinical evidence to suggest that dwelling upon certain images helps bring them into our material lives.[35] And all of us know of cases in our own or our friends' lives of self-fulfilling prophecies. Perhaps this works only because repeatedly thinking about a preferred outcome keeps the goal present in our mind's eye, and so helps us work harder over a longer period of time to achieve it. Or perhaps our focus triggers some unconscious mechanism that takes ferocious care to see that we achieve our profound desires. This latter mechanism seems implied in the popular admonition "Be careful what you ask for; you might get it." It would seem likely that just as the unconscious uses the imagination to get through to the Ego, so the Ego can use imagination to activate and influence the unconscious. If this is true, it is best that the Ego make use of the most powerful and appropriate images it knows, the images of the archetypes. By using these with the unconscious, the Ego generates an Ego-masculine Self *axis mundi*, along which mutual imaging can travel unfettered in either direction.

In our view, then, no one needs to be discomfited by a fear of idolatry. The imaging is a creative, suggestive activity, a way of establishing contact with the unconscious, not of mistaking god for God.

A postmodern program of remythologization will be part of our imaging. Most *premodern peoples* accepted myths as being literally true, with little or no reflection upon their deeper significance. *Modernity* has *denied* myth and ritual any significance at all, while at the same time living according to unexamined myths of a scientific and rational nature. A *post-modern reappropriation* of mythic imagination and ritual process acknowledges both their emotional and cognitive significance. We re-create the myths and participate in the rituals, understanding that they are a useful psychological means of getting to otherwise blocked Libido. Myth provides a mind-set within which we can call up the archetypes. Ritual is the process of invitation and dialogue.

It helps the imaging process to collect pictures, photographs, paintings, and other artistic representations of the archetype. These images will become our images of the *deus absconditus*, the "hidden God." The images we select need to convey to us the qualities of the fully expressed King. We need images of his power and vitality, his calm and vigor, his phallic energy and his generativity. They should be decidedly masculine. If effeminate Christs and gentle Buddhas are chosen to represent the King in his Lover aspect, they should be balanced with images suggesting the King's aggressive might. Pictures of a wrathful King should be offset by photographs or other aids illustrating his mercy, his concern for and blessing of his people. Images of the King destroying his mortal enemies in battle need to be viewed as expressions of his struggle against chaos and death. It is best to avoid photographs of actual reigning monarchs. Contemporary men often do not have the power to bring alive for us the archetypal King as well as representations of past rulers do. There is a benefit in choosing unfamiliar, impersonal imagery; the strange will be free of the weight of our preconceptions, which might otherwise influence the content of our reveries.

Useful are images of Egyptian pharaohs, Assyrian kings, and Chinese emperors. Reproductions of associated kingly accoutrements, such as old coins of Greek or Roman Gods or emperors, swords, suits of armor, archaeological drawings of temples, ziggurats, and pyramids can also be helpful. Collecting all these may seem foolish at first, and that is fine; remember, our aim will simply be to use the impersonal power these images hold for the unconscious to evoke feelings, states of mind, and visions of fullness. Our postmodern perspective allows us the freedom not to take ourselves too seriously while we choose to actively engage our images and props during our personal rituals.

Some men find great benefit in setting aside a specific place to hold their personal archetypal reveries. Many wear talismans that remind them of the abiding presence of the archetypal King. Native American medicine bags, rings, chains, and other tokens may serve as portable transformers of King energy. We have found a small crystal pyramid to be a useful portable icon. As we've seen in previous chapters, the pyramid has long been a structure associated with the sacred king. It is at once an image of the quadrated structure of the masculine Self (see Appendix A), and a crystallization of the radiating life-force of the King. A brief meditation or focused-imagination experiment can be a liberating exercise for men who feel beset and besieged. We have recommended the following exercise in active imagination for use with the pyramid icon to many of our counselees and analysands.

> Imagine yourself inside the pyramid, or imagine it inside of you, perhaps in the chest area. It pictures to you your own invincible, unassailable inner structure, that part of you that is eternally durable, that is everlasting and inviolable, whatever may befall you in your day-to-day life. The pyramid's sides are smooth. They are polished and flawless. There are no cracks, holes, or chips in them. When danger threatens, when you feel like you're about to fragment, get inside of the pyramid or imagine it inside of you, protecting your heart, protecting your essence, your

True Self. Picture the danger as the stormy waves of a wind-tossed sea. Visualize the waves crashing against the glass-smooth sides of the pyramid, thundering against them, but harmlessly, unable to shatter them. See the waves breaking against the pyramid, which remains impervious to their battering. Watch the fury of the waves gradually abate until calm is restored. Then imagine yourself wiping the pyramid dry and polishing it to its former brilliance, the danger past. Finally, step back out of the pyramid or set it free of your chest and resume your daily life, your relationship to (and not your detachment from) the vicissitudes of normal human being.

Obviously it will be difficult to read this aloud and meditate on it at the same time. One answer is not to worry about the exact text, but to let your mind follow the gist of the exercise in your own personal terms. If you prefer listening to these words while you meditate, it might be easiest to read this exercise slowly and thoughtfully into a tape recorder, so that you can play it back while you meditate. This leaves your mind free to do the active imagination work.

Some men have never meditated before, and the idea of doing it may seem strange or uncomfortable. If you do meditate, follow your own practice with this work. But if you're new to this, we don't expect you to learn all the breathing techniques of some orthodox practice. All you need to do is find a quiet, private time and place; sit someplace comfortable, in a position you can keep for some time (many like to use a cushion on the floor); then clear your mind of your day-to-day thoughts and concerns, and let your focus turn to the exercise we've given above. Follow whatever spontaneous images occur, and record them so you can return to them later.

Using the pyramid in this way evokes a sense of inner structure, and of defensible psychological boundaries. The adamantine pyramid connects us symbolically to rock and crystal, time-honored images of the enduring masculine Self.[36] A postmodern ritual such as the one above provides us the experience of the archetypal King as a sheltering, indomitable structure and as the tranquil essence at the center of our world.

Through focused imaging we come to realize that Ego and archetype are separate aspects of the psyche. At the same time we can call upon the King to help repair and reconstitute our sense of self. In a sense, meditation confirms Mohammed's saying that the King is "closer than the vein of thy neck."[37]

As we study pictures and artifacts of the King we've collected, we need to *internalize* what they represent. We need to find a quiet, private time to sit before the images, contemplating them, beholding and cherishing them. We need to turn the archetypes around and around in our mind's eye, as if they were fine gems, their facets illuminated by the light of consciousness. We need to let our Left Brain appraise them, and to explore our Right Brain intuitions about them.[38] The symbolic pictures and objects help anchor and objectify our images of the archetype we are seeking inside ourselves.

We might include music to help create a ritual atmosphere. Traditional religious music, for example, the Hebrew "Avinu Malcheinu," serves very well for this. Some find they prefer to choose music with no lyrics, or at least no lyrics in English, because the words can influence and determine the train of thought, rather than letting it run along its individual track. Soundtracks from "sword and sandals" movies like *Spartacus* or *Ben Hur*, or more recently, Peter Gabriel's excellent music from *The Last Temptation of Christ*, all are particularly evocative of King energy.

We can imagine absorbing, as we contemplate, the attributes of the King—his regal calm, his self-assurance, the firm boundaries he maintains for himself, the blessings he bestows on his people, as well as his generosity, his exuberance, creativity, forcefulness, and decisiveness. By absorbing them we allow these qualities to heal the damaged layers of our psyches. According to the most sophisticated of the ancient view of sacred kingship, the king was able to order his kingdom by simply putting his own life in order. He evoked generativity in his subjects by being generative himself. Focused imaging and meditation can work the King's same creative ordering magic for each of us.

The best examples of the power of encounter with the King within come from the experience of those who are experimenting with this kind of important inner work. Large numbers of men from both the United States and abroad have been exploring the changes that occur in their lives when they seek "audiences" with the inner King. We have chosen to let the personal account of a man who recently lost his fight with cancer illustrate for us the generative and ennobling power of actually forming a relationship with the Great Lord Within. Before his recent death Bill generously gave us permission to share his experience with others in the hope that others might benefit from his explorations in the inner world. In his public life he was the editor of a major magazine and was widely respected as a public leader. In his early sixties, however, he became aware that he had lost a sense of meaning in his life and work and began to experience a great deal of despair. He had prided himself on being a tough-minded intellectual with little interest in either depth psychology or human spirituality. Not long after he entered his "dark night of the soul," he had to face the additional shock of hearing his doctor tell him that he had cancer. He sought out analysis to help him face his life situation. Reluctantly and with many doubts he began to experiment with active imagination and inner dialogues. Much to his surprise he found that helpful, caring companions awaited him in his inner world, companions who at Bill's eleventh hour opened up depths of meaning he had never dreamed of. Ultimately, the Pharaoh (the King) eased

Bill's transition from the profane dimension of time and space into the sacred dimension beyond the grave. The following account in his own words tells us of the ritual he developed in cooperation with a great Pharaoh in the King's Chamber within.

VISITS WITH THE PHARAOH

Morning Ritual

We have a large, old-fashioned bathtub. Every morning I get into the tub before I turn on the water. I visualize myself at the power center of a pyramid. I am in a large circular room with a large bathtub in the center. There is a golden light above. This room with the tub is the only room inside this pyramid. It is the Pharaoh's exclusive bathing pyramid. He is allowing me to use it.

I turn on the water to flow slowly, and lie down. A long line of Egyptian women in long dresses enters the room single file. Each carries a ceramic pitcher of water. This is special healing water from the king's secret well. As each woman moves by me she empties her pitcher over my body into the tub. Each woman then moves on to form a circle around me. Then they begin singing and swaying or dancing with the music. The music is Wagner's Venusburg music from Tannhäuser (not Egyptian, obviously).

After all of them have emptied their pitchers (I turn off the water faucet), they dance around me and sing for a short while longer, then file out. As they leave the young magician/teacher, Imhotep, and his mentor/teacher, enter with a magic, healing potion. Imhotep pours the elixir into the tub (as I pour some bath oil or other aromatic liquid into the tub). Then I often put on my headphones and listen to a tape called *Journey of the Drums*.

Soon, as Imhotep remains at the end of the tub, a group of men enter. They are Native Americans with shields, spears, feathers, loincloths and some wear feathered headdresses. They dance around and sing with the drums. Then the king, the Pharaoh, enters and sits in a large throne at the foot of my tub, and oversees the whole ceremony. He is dressed in a long robe. He has long hair, is tall with a deep resonant masculine voice like Paul Robeson. He does not always participate in a noticeable way. But sometimes he simply holds his arms up in some kind of all-encompassing spiritual gesture. Usually I lie quietly during this period and meditate. Sometimes I try to sense the power of the pyramid, the golden light, the power of the water and the potion, the masculine energy of the men and the power of the king. The men and I sometimes chant "OM" or "RAM" during this time. Sometimes the Pharaoh chants mysterious words in a language I don't understand. Later the men leave. Then sometimes the king and I talk briefly. He may bless me, I may ask for something, or I may thank him for the good things I now have. He leaves and the ritual is over.

Afternoon Ritual

I light some incense and make myself comfortable in my recliner. Then I begin to visualize. I am outside on the north side of the Great Cheops Pyramid. I enter the tunnel leading to the king's chamber. I follow it down and then upward as shown in the schematic drawings of this pyramid. Toward the top of the ascending tunnel, I pass through a space that is beautifully tiled. A mysterious light fills the chamber. I get to the top and enter the antechamber. There, a knight (more like a medieval knight) with a spear and shield greets me. He guards the king's chamber. He allows me to enter the chamber and aids me in opening the heavy granite door. I try to notice the odor of the incense. There is a golden light above the king. Inside I find the Pharaoh, facing east, sitting in his throne or standing nearby. He is expecting me and speaks to me. We converse. I ask for his blessing, thank him for his blessings. I ask him questions. Sometimes we talk about me and he offers suggestions and advice. Sometimes we talk about my disease and I ask him for help in conquering it. Sometimes we just sit quietly meditating together. At other times I move or he moves and our bodies meld into one. I try to feel the essence and presence of his body and spirit— sometimes specifically, going from my head to my toes visualizing our bodies melding and me sensing the power and energy of the king. After a few minutes we separate. We may converse some more. He blesses me and sometimes says the universal Judeo/Christian benediction ("The Lord bless you and keep you . . ."). And I leave. I leave by the same tunnels (this is the only way in and out of the king's chamber). I salute the warrior/knight and begin my walk down the descending tunnel. If I feel especially exuberant, I may slide as if on skis on my feet all the way down. Then I hike up the ascending tunnel and come out into the bright sun. I turn east toward the sun and hold my arms high and wide in a gesture of joy and appreciation. End of visualization.

Notes

I try to do both of these rituals every day. But this is sometimes not possible. If I have an early appointment, on that day I simply take a shower and skip the ritual. Once in a while I will postpone the ritual and do it later in the day.

I try to do the afternoon ritual every afternoon at about 3:00 P.M. This is more difficult to do every day than the morning ritual. If someone else is in the house I sometimes find it difficult to do. At other times I find myself wrapped up in getting a job done and forget to stop for it. Other times I feel like I don't have time to do it. Sometimes when I have not done the afternoon ritual I try to do it at bedtime.

In conjunction with the morning ritual I usually do these things: Before the ritual, I do some self-affirmations in front of the bathroom mirror. Then I shave and brush my teeth. After the ritual I usually do some other healing rituals. I may visualize my brain ordering my glands to send out good chemicals throughout my body to heal my disease. Often I drum for a few minutes and try to meditate during the drumming after the bath ritual.

What the Pharaoh Does for Me

It is very difficult to put into words just how visualization with the Pharaoh affects me. I know that I feel better about myself when I do the rituals. When I am discouraged or depressed because of my therapy or disease, I neglect to do the rituals. When I do them I feel better. I am not sure which comes first. I do know that when I do the rituals I feel better. I have self-esteem and somehow a reason for living—for continuing to fight my disease. Sometimes there is no specific thing I feel after meditating with the king. By this I mean, I don't always feel like "Wow, I really feel great!" immediately after meditating. More often it is just that I feel better, in general, over a period of time. I guess I'm trying to say it doesn't often happen instantly. By "feeling better" I mean having a sense of well-being, fullness, a zest for life, self-esteem—those kinds of things.

Yet there are times during the meditation when I definitely feel something spiritual. During a meditation, I may have a warm feeling about myself, and about other people. I love others in a way I have not loved before—myself too, I suppose. If I talk to the Pharaoh about my family and children, for example, I experience a new feeling—a sense of love and appreciation for my children I have never felt before—I guess it is love. I know this feeling I have for my wife and children is new. It not only happens during the meditation, but outside of it. I haven't felt this before. I'm sure some of the credit goes to the conversations and meditations with the Pharaoh. I have noticed that much of the time I have dry eyes—the tear glands don't seem to excrete enough tears. But when I am with the king in either of the rituals, my eyes are always moist. Sometimes they are even wet—as I sometimes am moved to tears.

Sometimes when I am with the king, I feel a sense of fullness or belongingness or spirituality that I can't really describe. I suppose it is the sense of unity of all things that the mystics talk and write about. It doesn't happen often. I wish it would happen more often.

Obviously, this man felt that he had benefited from his encounters with the inner King. He found strength to face his illness with courage and grace, and energy to seek to improve his relationships with his family. This in itself would have made his efforts at active imagination and inner dialogue with the King worthwhile. However, in his case as in many others we find that an encounter with the King had an impact that reached beyond his private life. He began to express a new and deeper concern for others and for his public responsibilities. He organized the first cancer group for men in our city, making it possible for men to support each other in fighting their illness and giving attention to the particular problems of men facing serious, life-threatening illness. He had hopes of providing leadership for others in forming and maintaining groups for seriously ill men. He was not, however, interested simply in illness-related topics. He became excited about the possibilities for leadership that exist for men and women in their sixties and older if they will accept the challenge of providing mature leadership for the building of a viable planetary human community. At the time of his death he was working on an article for *Modern Maturity* magazine in which he hoped to challenge older men and women to assume once again their roles as *human elders*—mediating generativity for the human community. Those of us who had the privilege of knowing him were amazed at the power of the generative and nurturing life-force that surrounded him in the last months and days of his life. Part of this radiance he brought to his family, friends, and city was no doubt the result of his *face-to-face relationship* with the loving King whom he met in the King's Chamber of his soul. Perhaps some of you who are reading this can carry forward Bill's vision.

ACTIVE IMAGINATION AS "PRAYER": INVOKING THE UNCONSCIOUS

Another active imagination technique, what religions call "prayer," provides a number of techniques for establishing the *axis mundi* between the Ego and the King. There are five techniques presented here, each of which generates the axis in a slightly different way.

A *prayer of petition* is the kind most commonly used. It is the prayer the Ego uses to ask the archetypes for help. At best the prayer is spoken with the twofold dynamic of true humility: the recognition that our lives are dependent on a greater

Invoking the King:
Revelation of the Vision Serpent
(vision rite from Yaxchilán)

power than the Ego, and the decision to get the help we need from that power.

The Ego asks the King for any qualities of courage, insight, endurance, patience, wisdom, clarity, or vision that it might need. The Ego may also ask for a change of outer circumstances, the answer to an apparently insoluble problem, a sense of well-being through deliverance from a real outer-world oppression, or any of a host of other things that could make for a greater fullness of being.

A prayer of intercession is a kind of petition prayer the Ego makes before the archetypes on behalf of an outer issue—other human beings, the natural world, or an important cause, for example.

In the prayer of petition the Ego assumes its realistic size by approaching the archetype as its creature and servant, ready to receive whatever answer it is given, ready also to implement any answer it receives. The Ego sincerely acknowledges the ultimate futility of its own devices and seeks the creative power only the archetype can supply. The Ego's efforts and will are not enough. It needs a powerful ally. True humility invites an incarnational process by allowing the creative power of the King to manifest in the profane world through a man's own life.

Once the petition is made, it is best if the Ego closes the prayer with an attitude of faith that the archetype will respond in some way. The Ego needs to put itself in the frame of mind to listen and watch for an answer. It has performed the focused imaging of a particular good it desires and conveyed that image to the unconscious. Via the imagination the unconscious will respond. Since archetypes usually speak in images and symbols, it is important that the Ego be prepared to interpret its answer in these terms.

Many of these symbolic responses will be conveyed to the Ego in dreams. Learning to interpret dreams in a manner the Ego can comprehend becomes vitally important to the man seeking to access the archetypal King. A very readable introduction to Jungian dream interpretation is one written by analyst John Sanford, *Dreams: God's Forgotten Language*.[39] There is a wealth of other literature in the field well worth looking into.

The unconscious may speak to us also through waking visions, daydreams, spontaneous thoughts, or insights that pop into our heads. Also, the unconscious may communicate through what Jung called "synchronistic events." By this he meant events that seem to have no causal connection with each other, but which cluster together at certain times of crisis or searching in our lives, and which often point to a particular theme or issue we need to address.

A man who had sought counseling (which act is in itself a kind of prayer of petition) after separating from his wife asked his counselor whether he should "bury" the relationship or try to revive it. After mirroring the man's concern, his counselor suggested he continue to weigh the decision, holding the opposite possibilities in tension until the unconscious had an opportunity to respond. Several mornings later his car was stopped at an intersection by a funeral procession. He drove on, not thinking much about it. A few blocks farther on he had to stop for another funeral procession. This time he thought, "Two in one day. That's weird!" On his way home that evening, he was held up by a third procession! As he sat waiting for it to pass, like a bolt from the blue the thought came to the man that his relationship with his wife was really "dead." Then he realized the three funeral processions, acausally connected with his particular dilemma, might have been steering him to his problem's solution.

The prayer of petition, followed by eyes, ears, and mind open to the answer, allows the higher will of the true psychological center to guide us through our troubles. In serving the King a man creates a little more order within himself. Each time he realizes a little more inner structure in his struggle to solve the dilemmas of daily life, he moves the whole of the created world forward.

A *prayer of confession* is the Ego's spontaneous response to the immediate and overwhelming power of the archetype. In the presence of the fully realized King, the Ego feels profoundly unworthy, not guilty or ashamed, but *realistically lacking*. With no sense of humiliation the Ego confesses its mistakes, and submits to the power upon whose wisdom, strength, courage, and life-force it depends. The prayer of confession is the prayer through which the Ego can experience its necessary deflation. This prayer prepares the Ego for a more authentic embracing of the life tasks the masculine Self demands it should accept. In this sense the prayer of confession constellates more than any other the Ego-archetypal axis, opening the Ego to a sense of gratitude and *realistic* greatness.

The *prayer of thanksgiving* expresses the Ego's gratitude for the good it already has. An attitude of deeply felt, exuberant appreciation is the opposite of grandiosity. When we are grandiose we feel we owe nothing to anyone, that everything we have achieved has been owed to us. We do not celebrate the act of grace real goodness is. We pass over it as something of no great importance, something almost worthless. Far more interesting to us are the things we do *not* have, but feel we deserve. These are our obsessive focus.

The prayer of thanksgiving puts us in a proper relationship with the King. If we are caught in his Shadow system, we feel that nothing we have is good enough for us. The weakling is a chronic complainer, always feeling he has been shortchanged. The tyrant believes he has had to do everything on his own. Neither of these Shadow kings realizes goodness is never owned, and can never be assumed.

The King has a superabundance of Libido and goodness.

And the unconscious showers us with blessings when we prepare our minds to receive them. Gratitude and thanksgiving prepare our state of mind.

By its prayer of praise and worship, the Ego puts itself in a position subordinate to the archetype. It praises the King, realizing he is the source of all life and all blessing. In the prayer of praise and worship the Ego spontaneously expresses its joy, and unrestricted admiration for the King. The capacity to admire and praise others is the hallmark of mature psychological structures. A consolidated sense of self is full enough that it can overflow and touch others with its radiance.

In the *prayer of dialogue* the Ego-King axis is constellated by verbal interaction between the differentiated, accessing Ego and the archetype. Although the unconscious uses largely the language of symbols, there are times when the archetypal energy is so charged and the conscious attitude so receptive that the Ego can hear the voice of the King. The words that reach the Ego are often oracular, cryptic, and mysterious. Yet this fifth form of prayer can be an important means of actively interacting with the archetype.

The best way to begin such a dialogue is with pen and paper.[40] A man seeking this kind of communication needs to find a quiet time and place, to clear his mind and to await patiently whatever the unconscious has to say. It can help him to write a sort of letter to the archetype, asking questions, inviting responses. After writing a page or two, often quite suddenly the man may hear an inner voice responding to him. Frequently he finds himself writing so quickly he feels as if he were taking dictation. It is of the utmost importance that he not censor anything that is communicated. He should write it down exactly as it comes.

Some voices that come to us may seem hostile or persecuting.[41] Then the question religions speak of as the "discernment of spirits" arises.[42] Hindu and Buddhist traditions warn of illusory demons which suddenly appear when the person seeking enlightenment steps over his inner threshold.[43] Common sense should lead us to ask ourselves whether the voices have any legitimate criticisms to offer us, or if instead they seem bent on destroying our sense of well-being. Some of the "entities" encountered in dialogue prayers may simply be parental or sibling introjects, or the internalized voice of our therapist or even what Freud called our superego.[44]

The dangers inherent in turning inward are manageable with common sense and discretion. If a voice turns hostile, end the session. If inner persecutors are encountered on a regular basis, it is probably wise to consult a counselor, psychotherapist, analyst, or some other professional familiar with such phenomena. But the man who can discern the voice of the King—and you will know it when you hear it—will earn plentiful rewards. You will be guided by the King's wisdom, supported by his blessing, strengthened by his protective might, and enlivened by his procreative force. You will enact for yourself a royal audience, in which the King and your Ego are made real to each other. You should write as long as the energy is flowing; when it begins to ebb, you simply end the session, but afterward take careful steps to remember what it was you did to gain access to your King. That way you will know how to call on the King again in the future.

AS IF: GETTING INTO
THE CONSCIOUSNESS OF THE KING

There is another active imagination exercise we can try when other means of access fail us. We can act "as if" some situation were true, and proceed from there. This is a method actors use as a technique for getting into character. When the imagination fails and the character just will not come, an actor behaves "as if" he were the character. He comes at the role from the outside rather than the inside. The "as if" technique is an effective ruse to employ to invoke the unconscious, which often supplies the actor with material he would never have come across consciously. Often an actor's trouble with a role stems from the inaccessibility of repressed but pertinent personal experience, and behaving "as if" gives the unconscious the opportunity to supply the information.

Among the ways an actor begins to behave "as if" he is another person is by adopting a certain walk, a vocal habit, or a verbal pattern characteristic of the role. He tries it out on his own body and experiments with how the new habits make him feel. It is a very conscious and questioning technique, but his goal is to get himself past a stuck place to where he can genuinely inhabit his role. He evokes (literally, "calls out") the character from his unconscious.

If we are having trouble imagining the King within us, we may need to involve him by behaving "as if" we were already vested with our own kingship. The approach may seem shallow at first. Indeed, acting against our feelings can reinforce a false persona[45] when that way of acting becomes a substitute for authentic feelings. If we continue a false persona over time, we may elicit a variety of personality disorders.[46] But there is no danger in using the technique almost like a game, or an experiment, to see how behaving like a king might feel.

If we are becoming unglued and we hear our voices rising with anxiety and tension, we can remind ourselves to take a deep breath, slow down, and consciously lower our voices. By speaking calmly and carefully, we soon recover control. We may feel the Ego-King axis materialize within us. We can imagine the *axis mundi* rising through our spines, or picture ourselves as the World Tree, our roots deep in the earth, our topmost branches reaching to the clouds.

When we feel rage begin to take us over, we can catch

ourselves clenching our fists and cramping the muscles in our necks. We can then imagine ourselves growing steady and quiet, taking our king's place at the center of the situation. A strange thing may happen. As we take control of ourselves, the external situation will become calmer as well. If you are calm in a crisis, others will take their cue from you. By acting "as if" you are the King you can manage to do a little world building too.

A young man was once sitting at the bar in one of his favorite restaurants. It was happy hour and a lot of people were getting loaded. An obviously drunk man behind him suddenly dropped his glass on the floor. The drunk challenged the young man, saying, "Hey, you son of a bitch! You knocked that drink out of my hand!" The young man felt a rush of fear and anger. The frightened bartender looked around helplessly, and some of the bystanders began to form an eager circle to watch the coming fight.

The young man resisted getting hooked by his aggressor's need to prove himself, found his center, and assessed his options. He gave his attacker a blank stare. Acting "as if" he were in control of the situation, he got up from his stool, calmly paid for his drink, and walked deliberately out the door. The non-plussed drunk did not follow. Because he had centered himself, the young man was able to coolly take charge, control his fear and anger, and deescalate the drunk's hostility. He had evoked "divine order" in potentially destructive circumstances. The King was embodied in him, and creative order held chaos in check.

Finally, getting into the "mind of the king" and seeking to think and feel "as if" one is the True King is a technique that can have many far-reaching implications in addition to the more personal and private ones noted above. One of the exercises we have used in many workshops for men on kingship issues is that of imagining oneself the king who has just returned from a "far country" to his city and who now walks the streets in disguise to take stock of the condition of his people during his absence. In this exercise one seeks to look with the king's eyes, hear with his ears, and feel with his heart. In a workshop setting one can take an imaginal walk through one's city or other places in one's "realm." *An even more powerful experience can be had in actually observing conditions in our cities, our forests, or our rivers while practicing putting on the consciousness of the king.* Men who have done these exercises report that they find themselves not only able to stop denying the enormous public social needs that challenge us, but that instead of being overwhelmed, they feel an influx of the power and determination to respond to them in a proactive way.

EMULATION: ADMIRING MEN

It is of vital importance that a man access the mature masculine archetypes *through other men.* While historical figures provide an inner sense of what maturity is like, these men cannot be intimately known. They cannot be held. They cannot be smelled. We will never be able to look into their eyes. Biographies and histories make for useful reading, and do give us imaginal examples to emulate. *But there is no adequate substitute for bonding with living men.*

Male bonding is a familiar idea in our culture. It is a nearly universal behavioral pattern, found in the vast majority of cultures in all historical epochs. Primate instinct may account for male clustering, for chimpanzees bond in much the same way as men.[47] Anthropologists theorize that male bonding occurs in order to further societal goals of communal protection and provisioning.[48] Psychologists speculate that men also need the company of other men to reinforce their male identity against the regressive infantile impulse.[49]

Manhood is *in part* an artificial societal construct.[50] While arising in the structures of the masculine brain as a natural genetic and hormonal endowment, the cultural expressions of manhood must be reinforced in order to keep men from a regression into sexless infantilism. It takes work to become a man. Achieving adult male status requires personal courage and the support and nurturing of older men. In many traditional societies the older man's function was to initiate young men into the mysteries of life, work, responsibility, marriage, and masculinity.[51] Lacking these culturally sanctioned and ritualized avenues of contact, modern men often fall back on less serious forms of male bonding. Not that there is anything wrong in getting loaded with the boys. But ultimately something more is needed. Men need to bond with other men they can genuinely admire.

A man does not have to be perfect to merit our admiration. No man *is* perfect, but many are admirable. We especially need to be able to admire men who show qualities of character we feel we lack. Artists need to admire warriors and love them for the ways they express their masculinity. Warriors need to love and admire artists for the same reason. CEOs need to bond with the warehouse and assembly-line workers who earn their livings by the sweat of their brows. And these workers need to bond with the magicians and kings the CEOs are trying to become.

We need to admire our friends for their strengths, strengths we may not possess. And we need to love them in their weaknesses, for we know weakness too. We need to seek out men who consciously or not are in touch with the mature masculine archetypes. Even the pure emotional act of admiring other men supports our own maturity, our sense of security and worth. If we can all absorb archetypal and personal aspects of manhood from each other we will help each other become generative men. We will help each other embody the archetypal structures of authentic masculinity.

*   *   *

Once we are proficient with our active imagination skills, and we have some familiarity with our inner terrain, once we have sought out and bonded with other men, we will be able to call upon archetypal energies at any time, and at any place. If things break down at the construction site, if communication goes awry at an important meeting, if the hotel accommodations for the overnight business trip are a bust, if the wife is suffering an emotional crisis and the kids are into something they shouldn't be, we will be able to find our center, constellate the *axis mundi*, call out the inner King, and even against enormous odds, make a world where before only chaos and destruction had reigned.

DANCING THE FOUR QUARTERS: THE CHALLENGE OF MASCULINE WHOLENESS

BY ACCIDENT OR DESIGN, THE DIRECTOR OF THE FILM *David, the King* represents the title character engaged in one of the fundamental acts of sacred kingship: dancing the four quarters. Beyond the simple pleasure to be had watching actor Richard Gere's sincere if unsuccessful effort to dance, the film offers a valuable visual reference for a rarely noted aspect of King energy. King David is shown dancing into Jerusalem after his predecessor dies. Taking the crown is for him a joyous, anticipated event—he shows no hesitancy at all about assuming his royal responsibilities.

Of necessity we have focused in many of our chapters on

what can go wrong with King energy. We have also provided the profile of an ideal generative man in order to make sure the man who needs one has a specific image of what maturity can be. But what happens after the King energy is there in the psyche, and the three other foundational archetypes are generatively embodied as well? If the King is the center of the world, and he is responsible for a kingdom stretching impossibly far away from him in every direction, what is he to do to fulfill his responsibilities? The answer is that he begins to dance the four quarters.

This is why the image of King David dancing is so important. His playful dance has a serious intent. By dancing he keeps the world created. Some scholars believe King David underlies the Hebrew image of God. The Christian teaching at least is that he is Christ's ancestor. Jesus is called in some traditions "Lord of the Dance," and in this circumstance he is parallel to the Indian God Shiva. The dance here is a metaphor for the chaotic, actively shifting universe along with the emergence of creative order, which the archetypal King engenders. Shiva does his dance right on the verge between chaos and creation. His dance makes the world, and unmakes parts of it as well. Anyone who has seen a traditional Indian image of Shiva, one leg and four arms raised and variously moving, will attest to the striking serenity of Shiva's countenance at the center of the image, still in the midst of the swirling motion. [1]

By dancing the four quarters, one after the other, the King keeps them created and infused with sacred energy. This demands a certain ceaseless activity. The King must not stop in his progress through the world because if he stops the world stops with him. How can a man seeking to access the archetype manage this uninterrupted movement? One answer some men accept is to scurry around, expending a tremendous amount of frenetic energy in a tense, frightened attempt to keep things from grinding to a halt. The assumption behind this answer is that disaster is looming, and everything needs to be done quickly to stave it off. But because the disaster is expected, it comes, and it comes as often as not like an unwelcome relative, whenever it wants.

The better answer is to dance the four quarters. This answer assumes change is the engine of life, and the best thing you can do for yourself is to hitch yourself up to that engine and go for a ride. You can have the serenity of Shiva if you're changing exactly as fast as the rest of the world—for then it takes no effort to move at all. With a light, careful step you can visit every district of your world. Gracefully moving from quarter to quarter, you regenerate the world even as you move through it with elegance and pleasure. There is no wasted, nervous effort to this dance.

There was a time in our country when these dances were performed as a matter of course. *Black Elk Speaks* is the life story of a Sioux holy man, as told to a white poet he met. Here he describes the preparations his tribe made for a dance done in honor of one of his pivotal visions. A sacred tepee was built and decorated at the center of a circular camp.

> On the west side they painted a bow and a cup of water; on the north, white geese and the herb; on the east, the daybreak star and the pipe; on the south, the flowering stick and the nation's hoop. Also, they painted horses, elk, and bison. Then over the door of the sacred tepee, they painted the flaming rainbow. It took them all day to do this, and it was beautiful.[2]

The dance took place around the tent, with specific events taking place in particular quadrants marked out in the circular space. Afterward, here is what had happened inside the tepee they had danced around:

> Then . . . we began going into the tepee to see what might have happened there while we were dancing. The Grand-

fathers had sprinkled fresh soil on the nation's hoop that they had made in there with the red and black roads across it, and all around this little circle of the nation's hoop we saw the prints of tiny pony hoofs as though the spirit horses had been dancing while we danced.[3]

It's hard to read such a passage without experiencing a sense of loss. Like Vietnam, the massacres of the Native American nations are an unmourned national tragedy. This is perhaps one reason why so many men have been moved and encouraged by the film *Dances with Wolves*.

We have lost much of the Indian lore. But many of the records we do have (like *Black Elk Speaks*) are truly remarkable. Joseph Campbell said a perceptive thing to Bill Moyers during his popular series of television interviews. He said that once we saw the first image of the earth taken from a camera on a spaceship, we were given the chance to start a world mythology. There is no plainer image to be had of the one world we all have to share. The Gaia movement has taken some steps to found this new planetary myth. But we can go further.

We have the opportunity, for the first time in human history, to offer a truly global initiation to our younger generations. Tribe by tribe, people have always felt they have done this, but always they have been limited by tribal concerns. But the opportunity has presented itself to us, with all the knowledge we possess about comparative mythology and the human need for initiation, to begin initiating new generations into a nurturing myth that makes a real effort to care for the world. If we do not take advantage of this opportunity, it will be because of our pathological denial of the problems facing our world today.

We should all aim to dance the four quarters. The King who *is* Lord of the Four Quarters is the leader too of the four foundational structures of the psyche. When he is dancing, he is accessing himself and the Warrior, Magician, and Lover in a balanced and generative way. He is balancing the four into one generative unity. And he accomplishes the balance *playfully*— the psyche that has reached this stage of maturity can't help but take pleasure in itself, and all the things of creation.

Inner work is fundamentally important to an individual's capacity for pleasure. If our feelings are deadened by unresolved issues, there may be very few things in the world for us to take pleasure in. But we shouldn't lose sight of the pleasure available to us once we have worked through the Shadow material that frustrates our progress. Erikson's Generative Man has a deep capacity for play. Another word for adult play is *recreation*—something we have associated with the King all along. When a child plays he may be trying out a sense of an integrated Ego, or rehearsing for personal mastery (succeeding in the limited world of the game, an important compensation for a life in the outside world in which he is *not* a master). Erikson felt there was no great difference between the play of adults and children, though, as Browning notes, "the adult's play is recreation, whereas the child's is preparation." Here are Browning's reflections on some of the phenomena of adult play:

All through Erikson's work is the implication that the creative adult (the generative adult) is precisely the person who can infuse his life with play; . . . the great cultural synthesizers—the religious, political and cultural geniuses such as Luther, Freud and Gandhi—were supreme in their playfulness, especially in their work. Their great works of synthesis were personal attempts to restore the active mastery of their egos in the context of the tensions and dichotomies of their personal and public historical situations. All great historical syntheses are as much play as they are work. They are work because they are indeed attentive to the real contradictions and tensions that most people of a given historical period both sense and suffer. They are a result of play because the creative genius does not simply conform to, adjust to, and accommodate to these tensions. Instead, he bends and reshapes these tensions until they submit to a new synthesis which not only enlivens and activates him but which also enlivens and activates a whole people and an entire era.[4]

The kind of synthesis Browning is talking about is a healing structure. Luther offered a corrective to the corrupt Catholicism of his era, and it was popular because so many people hungered for one. Freud looked into forbidden topics, and Europeans responded because they had secretly been longing to explore the same oppressive taboos themselves. Gandhi synthesized the antipathies of his countrymen into a useful and creative means of protest, and won India away from the British Empire as a result.

Both *synthesize* and *heal* are words that mean "to make something whole." The synthesis we would like to communicate to men today is how to make the quadrated psyche whole. It is not enough to develop only one or two of the archetypes. We need all four of them in our lives, because once they are activated in our souls, we can make a real difference in our society at large.

We cannot solve our national problems with men who have no Warrior or men who have nothing *but* the Warrior to guide them. We need that aggressive energy to attack, and sustain us in our battles against, our social ills, but we need it stewarded and integrated into functioning along with our other energies. As this book has made plain, we need the energies of the King to put our world in order, and to fuel our caring, nurturing efforts, and our efforts to bestow constituitive blessings upon people. When we develop our Magician we give ourselves the gift of seeing through the fundamentalisms that fragment our best organizations, leaving them incoherent and purposeless.

And with the Lover beside us, we'll give our emotions free rein to guide us—emotions are often wiser than our Egos would like to think. They stem from a deeper level of consciousness, and they have much to tell us. The Lover also ensures our joyful embodiment, so that we can enjoy ourselves and gather the necessary rewards for what we do.

It is not enough, though, to make peace with your Shadow material, and explore your Anima, and *start* down the path to being a generative man. If you do this you are doing a lot already, much more than so many men have done in our society. But we cannot stop at this. Depth psychology has been a thread in this country's social fabric for more than a generation now, and a significant number of the "best and the brightest" have been through a course of one kind of therapy or another—and what do we have to show for it? There is more Shadow material abroad in our country than ever. What are we to do about it?

Men who have made it through drug and alcohol recovery programs have done courageous work, and we are all indebted to them for it. For we are all aspects of one another, and when a man brings order back to his life, he increases the stock of order at large in the world for all of us to draw on. But we cannot settle for this. Recovery for *what?*, we finally have to ask ourselves; maturation *to what end?*

There is a tradition within at least two of the major religions in this country, American Protestantism and Roman Catholicism, of emphasis only on salvation of the individual. Once that happens, then what? Often very little. Frequently churches are not set up with the vision to provide anything more. The same problem faces therapists, once an analysand has completed a course of treatment. What can they be encouraged to *do* afterward?

We need to recognize that therapy, recovery, or conversion isn't enough. As a man gets personally stronger, he must find things that will relate him back to the world. He needs to take responsibility for making changes in the world, and not only in himself. Because once you consider the state our society is in, you must recognize that we have no choice. Know thyself, by all means—try to get that far. And know that once you are on the way with this work, there is even more satisfying work to come.

KINGSHIP AS STEWARDSHIP
AND SERVANT LEADERSHIP

A friend of ours told of an incident reported in the local Washington papers. Apparently a wild stag walked up to the front gate of the White House. There he hooked his horns in the iron of the gate and twisted his head until he broke off his rack. He left it hanging there on the White House gate and walked around the streets of Washington for several hours afterward in a catatonic daze. Finally some National Park Service employees caught the stag and took him away to the woods.

This is another example of a Jungian synchronistic event. One of the most searching of tasks facing the men of our culture involves conserving and stewarding the ecological resources of our planet. The stag couldn't consciously have picked a better place to make his unconscious protest. It might have meant something too, if only our president had been listening.

Generativity means primarily a concern for the future. There are degrees to generativity—you can be generative in providing for your own children without going much farther afield than that. Or you can be a generative civic leader, concerned for your community; or a generative prophet who makes the world at large his concern. There is a tradition in our country of emphasis on the individual. No doubt this has made for some of the more spectacular events in our history. But it is time we started to move away from being concerned *only* for the individual and to move toward a more encompassing concern.

The world is currently crying out for our help. There are dozens of things a man can do to help, from organizing his family's recycling habits to joining with a group in the community to clean and care for the parks to working on a national or international scale with groups like Greenpeace. The kind of male bonding that is occurring spontaneously in various places across the country strikes us as being the ideal ground for building new environmental and social-justice-concerns groups where none existed previously to do the work that a community notices needs doing.

This is why we see this kind of male bonding as a very positive thing. Some people seem to think that when men get together in emotionally connected groups, Nazism isn't far away. We think that it is the Shadow side of male bonding these people are afraid of and it comes from men who are not in touch with their King. So the obvious solution to the problem is to help *get* them in touch with their King. That doesn't mean the best approach is to discourage male aggressive behaviors. Male Warrior energy is an *excellent* incitement to getting things done, particularly when it is in the service of the King.

There's a marvelous sense of magnificence to some of the servant Warriors of the past. The Knights Templars shouted to each other "Be glorious!" on their way into battle. And around the world in America, the Lakota had a cry in a similar spirit—"Black Elk, this is the kind of day in which to do something great!"[5] If we can hold on to that kind of inspiration for settling the conflicts of our lives, without losing our King's perspective of purposeful caring, we will make a difference in our world.

It can be more important to make a difference than to make a mark. Cooperative groups will accomplish more than a group with a chaos of leaders. We have no wish to *shame* men into world-building work; the impetus has to come from within. We do believe shame shouldn't be the universally despised mechanism it has become today. Most often a man is taught to feel ashamed of his gifts, and this is an unhealthy, dysfunctional shaming. But if you were to meet a true saint, you would feel what John Bradshaw calls *healthy shame*. Call it humility in this situation, if you prefer. Humility is instructive. It is what our Ego feels when it recognizes how much more it could be doing.

If it doesn't make sense for you in your life to join an environmentalist group, or found your own, consider what you can do in the human groups around you. There are hundreds of groups already in place to help men help others. Think of the Boy Scouts, Big Brothers, Junior Achievement, the 4-H Clubs—all these groups are available to the man who wishes to sponsor the younger generation. The efforts of these organizations are largely unsung, and we are indebted to them. Or think of the similarly unsung groups engaged in urban renewal, the NAACP, or the men's clubs that do such a variety of good works—the Rotary Club, the Masons, Kiwanis, Lions, the Knights of Columbus, the Elks. If we have missed naming any groups it is only because our list is informal, designed to spur men on into seeing what kinds of organizations are already in place and waiting for them to get involved in civic regeneration.

You don't necessarily have to look any farther than your job. What can you do for the young men you work with? Are there any men you find yourself drawn to, that you might be able to encourage and mentor in their work? Or are there older men with gifts they are waiting to pass on, that no man has seen fit to ask for? Of course, if you are an executive, this should be a part of your job description already. If you are an executive and you are not making the people who work for you feel magical, you are not doing your job. This is a context in which shame has no place. The days in which the view "If I really ride them they'll work harder" could be sanctioned are no longer with us. You must empower your workers to do their work, and that means *you* must be drawing empowerment from your King energy yourself.

This is one arena in which men have a lesson to learn from the women's movement. Because of the empowering spirit of the movement, women have been getting together and forming spontaneous groups to fight the social problems they identify. Many of these groups don't even consider themselves "feminists," though they've drawn support and encouragement from the feminist example. We're thinking of the anti–drug-traffic groups women are forming in inner-city neighborhoods, groups, too, on a national scale like Mothers Against Drunk Driving. The first group in years in Ireland to have an impact on the violence in that society was a group of ordinary housewives who found their common cause.

If individuation is as Jung sees it, it is a moral struggle that brings some cosmic healing into the world. It occurs to us that the ultimate purpose of this healing may be to bring the King and Queen back together in a common cause. It's as if Zeus and Hera need some marriage counseling, and that is the task before our culture now. Not many of us can imagine men and women living together peacefully, and that isn't only because of tyrant or weakling kings. There are plenty of queens out there who are not looking to cooperate. They are looking for *consorts*, yes—but it is time for both sexes to find their common ground.

A brief history of humanity can be seen to support the notion that the two sexes need to come together now in a mutually balanced dynamic. If women powered the prehistoric shift from a nomadic to an agricultural way of life (and from the fertility objects and mother-goddess religions of these agrarian communities, this is what may have happened), and men have largely powered the shift of the last several thousand years into city life and technological mastery (which has been taken to such an extreme that many now feel the need to redress the balance), then it would stand to reason that what we are facing now is the necessity of bringing these two separate energies into harmonious cooperation for a new shift into the future. We have developed each energy to a high level in our human history. Our time could witness the exciting spectacle of what the two energies can accomplish together.

Robert Greenleaf was a highly principled Quaker, and a management theorist who spent the last twenty years of his life changing the way leaders worked with people. A mentoring college professor wished aloud in class one day for a man who would work from inside the institutions that serve us to change them around until they really *would* serve us, and Greenleaf decided to do exactly that. He worked for thirty-eight years with AT&T, rising from the ranks of the telephone linemen to an executive position. For the last twenty of those years he planned the work he was to do after retirement, and he found this second "career" to be the most rewarding period of his life. He consulted for companies, churches, and foundations, making sure they reoriented themselves to the people they served.

He helped many colleges through the turbulence they faced in the sixties, and it was in this context that he worked out the metaphors of the theories he has passed along to us. He noticed the shelves of the college bookstores were filled at the time with the works of Hermann Hesse. Always open to new ideas, he picked up some of these works to see what attractions they held for the students. One story in particular, *Journey to the East*,[6] resonated with ideas he had held since childhood.

In the story a group of men undertake a pilgrimage. They take with them a servant, Leo, who performs for them all their menial tasks but somehow also eases the journey along by his entertaining spirit and his songs. One day Leo is missing, and not long after, the pilgrims grow fractious and the pilgrimage itself loses focus and is abandoned. Years later the narrator, one of the original pilgrims, runs into Leo, who invites him to a meeting of the Order that had originally sponsored the journey; once at the meeting he discovers Leo is in fact the titular head of the Order. He met a noble leader he'd taken at first to be a servant.

The theme of the story was simple for Greenleaf—that the leader led simply and naturally because he first appeared to the pilgrims as their servant. He wrote his first essay, "The Servant as Leader,"[7] around this theme. For example, rather than blame the students for their irresponsible rebelliousness, he took a long hard look at why their collegiate institutions were doing little to serve them. His conclusion was that most colleges had lost sight of what it was they were set up to do. They no longer attempted to serve the student body.

Perhaps because of the sense of limitlessness the first European settlers felt when they began their lives here, we have a problem with scale in America; if an organization is successful, our immediate instinct is to make it bigger before we give it a vision. And as Proverbs 29:18 reminds us, "Where there is no vision, the people perish." Greenleaf believed that big institutions had the capacity to be creative and nurturing; he had seen in his experience some that were. But he found the movement into caring began always with a single person, who served as a servant leader. Often this leader's legacy included a division of the larger institution into smaller "communities," because people seem to work better in these smaller groups.

The idea of the leader as servant is in accord with most of our practical experience in dealing with people, although it is at odds with some things we are often *told*. We are *told* that to get respect we have to demand it. But the demanding tyrant is respected by no one; the easiest way to gain someone's respect is first to respect him. We are perceptive beings, and our co-workers know our faults as intimately as we know theirs. The tyrant may feel he has to intimidate people so that they will have no opportunity to notice his flaws. Here is one manager's experience with the opposite approach, after having taken over a tyrant's directorship position.

> I felt I couldn't help the staff if I didn't know what their problems were, but they were not about to share with one who "never makes a mistake." I began the practice of starting the weekly staff meeting by disclosing my two dumbest mistakes of the previous week. At first there was shock, but then the people began to share, and I was able to resolve a lot of things that would have been swept under the rug. When I've told this story at management development conferences, I've had some weak-egoed managers confront me with the question of whether this practice didn't lessen the staff's respect for me. On the contrary, they respected my humanness, open communication, and willingness to work with them to solve problems.[8]

In order to lead others, a man must be willing to lead himself into unfamiliar territory as well. Change is based on influence, and influence is a mutual process. If you are helping someone, make sure to find a way to help that teaches you something as well. That way, as you develop his best potentials, you develop your own, and both parties are mutually empowered.

The first skill the servant leader must learn is to listen. Once he can listen, he must be able to accept what he hears. This means he cannot scold, chide, or kill the messenger. The servant leader must articulate a vision that his people can support. If he doesn't credit his people for letting him know their feelings, and if he doesn't let those feelings influence the vision, they will never support his vision. They will feel alienated from the visionary process, and to their minds the vision will remain *his*.

Once a mutually inspired vision is articulated and implemented, Robert Greenleaf believed, the servant leader had then to ask some pretty tough questions. "Do those being served grow as persons: do they, while being served, become healthier, wiser, freer, more autonomous, more likely themselves to become servants? *And* what is the effect on the least privileged in society; will she or he benefit, or, at least, not be further deprived?" To this he added one further stipulation: "No one will be knowingly hurt by the action, *directly or indirectly*."[9]

This injunction is perhaps the most difficult to uphold, and also the most important. Greenleaf believes in persuasion over coercion. Although it takes more time to *persuade* a man of something, he generally will *stay* persuaded. If he believes his leader's path is true, he will follow to the ends of the earth. On the other hand, if he has been coerced he will abandon the fold at the first opportunity. It is the leader's duty to maintain the truth and scope of his vision.

Return to the image of the dance. If the leader does not set a cooperative rhythm—whether he is dancing with a group or a single partner—the dance will be one nobody enjoys, or profits from.

Our most familiar model for the servant King is probably Jesus of Nazareth, the Good Shepherd. Though he chose twelve very plain men for his followers, he made sure to spend his time and energies among them, sharing meals, traveling and planning with them. In return, after a growing comprehension and commitment to his vision, they internalized it as their own, and spread it after his death across the known world.[10] In Matthew 20:26–28 Jesus is absolutely clear about the purposes behind his practice, telling his apostles, "Whoever wants to be great among you must be your servant, and whoever wants to be first must be your slave—just as the Son of Man did not come to be served, but to serve, and to give his life as a ransom for many." As servant kings to our communities, we *may* not be called upon to give our lives, but surely we are challenged to dedicate them in service.

THE RETURN OF THE TRUE KING

CONSCIOUSLY OR NOT, MEN HAVE ALWAYS BEEN IN touch with the archetypal King. Whether as the push of the instinctual primate—the protecting, providing, procreating Alpha Male, enforcing law and order in a society of chaotic emotion, or as the sacred king in the pyramid's summit temple, communing in trance with his ancestral Gods, the King has always driven us from the unconscious depths of our animality and lured us from the high heavens of the imagination with visions of transcendent wholeness.

Perhaps more often than not we feel ourselves swinging like a pendulum between the poles of his Shadow form. We may lack the Ego structure or the maturity we need to accommodate him. Perhaps, like a giant oblivious to his own strength, he crushes us as he gathers us in his arms. Perhaps because he is himself so charged with energy, he finds it impossible to see our undeveloped images. Once we acquire authentic selves, perhaps he will be better able to behold us.

When we consolidate our personality, the King can enter into a healthy incarnational relationship with us. Together we can constellate the *axis mundi*, and along it we can pass his sacred energy into the created world. The King may need *us* to become fully *himself*.

In concert with an open Ego the King can materialize the Center, in which the eternal dialectics of Tyrant and Weakling, of light and darkness, life and death, masculine and feminine, inner and outer, can reconcile and resolve into a transcendent third. The King can make of a willing Ego a Transformer, filled to the brim with concentrated divine energy, rendering this energy useful to everyone. Through an imaginative, playful Ego, the King drives the Procreator in a man, infusing the world with creative Libido. To a humble Ego, the King manifests as the Structurer, bringing human affairs into harmony with the mythic music of the universe.

As often as it seems that high civilization is out of step with the cosmic "right order," it must be remembered that any civilization arises from the natural order and cannot be totally estranged from it. If the Tao appears to have been violated, it is because we misunderstand the Tao—nothing that occurs in nature is unnatural. Still, things work out better for us as individuals when we embrace a *conscious* attitude of cooperation with the universe. When we try to bring repressed material back into consciousness, we are bringing our individual consciousness back in tune with the world's Dharma, we are accepting the world-building challenge brought by the archetypal King, and proving our worth as individuals.

Our present world situation is in desperate need of men

willing to call up the sacred King in themselves. We are dangerously divided against each other. This may always have been true of human societies, but the possible consequences of our divisions are today more serious than ever. We are in need of a visionary, realizable Center. We need a Structurer to bring an order to human affairs preferable to today's law of the jungle. Confronted by infantile displays of mismanaged Libido, we need the example of a Transformer to teach us the way to contain and focus our energies. With a mature Procreator, we might finally address the crises rooted in the brutalized childhoods so many of us share. We could "break the chain" of brutality that is otherwise passed on to each new generation, to international politics, and to our disregarded ecosystem.

Now as never before we need to access the dynamic masculine and feminine archetypal structures to fight the powers of infantilism and evil that threaten our world. We need to build worlds as far into the future as our imaginations can carry us. The Creator's word of truth comes to us along the *axis mundi*, from the deep unconscious. The silent word of truth has found expression in every sacred king who ever worked to raise his people's consciousness, to expand the boundaries of civilization and to make order out of chaos. Not only can individual men not *be* men without vital connection with the King encoded within them. But also, if the men of earth do not form a living bond with their archetypal roots *all* the world-making adventures through which the life-force stretches us toward a richer and more authentic way of being human will elude us. But from his centered position between the planes of reality—sacred and profane—the mortal man who grasps the scepter offered to him by his own deep psyche can dream dreams and *act* to make them come true. The King is on his throne within *you* at that central point in *you* where worlds explode in contained thunder and flash and flower into being from out of *your* mind, *your* soul, *your* words, and *your* deeds.

The man who built the second pyramid at Giza, Cephron,

had himself sculpted in stone, seated on the throne of Egypt. His head, site of the mind of God in human form, is protected by the enfolding hawk wings of Horus. Cephron's eyes are calm, direct, unafraid to behold whatever is before him, in this world and the next. His lips hold the same mysterious smile seen on the enlightened Zeuses and Buddhas from Spain to Java, the smile of the deep joy of gnosis. His body is upright, alert, but not tense; he is relaxed and concentrated, ready for any necessary action. His feet are grounded on the Primordial Hill. In his right hand, resting on his thigh, he holds the phallic scepter—his left hand is left open on his knee, palm downward, in an attitude of benediction. This sculpture is an image of benevolence and might, of an offering of life, of a declaration of authority.

We began this book by calling attention to the ancient and widespread longing of our species for the return of the liberating and life-enhancing King—a longing that is echoed throughout the mythology of many cultures. We have argued in this book that this longing is not just an infantile fantasy in response to our feelings of hopelessness and helplessness in a chaotic world. Rather, we are convinced that this ancient imago within us is an image of the biologically encoded potentials for generativity and inclusive nurture which are a part of the evolutionary potential within everyman. *Masculinity is not in its essence abusive. We have within us the innate potential to use our masculine power for blessing, stewardship, and servant leadership. Our ancient longings may yet be fulfilled—not through one messianic person, but through an inner revolution in the maturation of masculine consciousness in which millions of men may participate.* You can be a part in this revolution in masculine consciousness—in the return of the True King. He is within you waiting for you to welcome him into your life and to bring his vision to your family, your community, and planet Earth. If we each do our part, perhaps we will soon join men and women from other races, cultures, and creeds at an *inner* Round Table—and begin to plan the great public struggle which could lead to the *real* Camelot, a world community of Shalom—of peace with justice.

APPENDICES

APPENDIX A

DECODING
THE DIAMOND BODY:
BEYOND JUNG

IN THE FOLLOWING BRIEF DISCUSSION WE WILL SHOW how we have furthered Jung's work on the deep structure of the Self. Our work builds upon his fundamental metapsychological assumptions.

Many Jungians have forgotten the nature and depth of Jung's commitment to the *quaternio* and *double quaternio* structures of the human self. Jung believed that the human preoccupation with quadration reflected a structural reality in the collective unconscious. His best-known work on quadration is his typology—particularly in his explication of the four functions of intuition, thinking, feeling, and sensation. Less well known is his idea that the totality of the archetypal Self has been imaged clearly in the octahedron.

He presented his most extensive exposition of this double quaternio of the deep self in his essay "The Structure and Dynamics of the Self" in *Aion*. Jung's intent was to articulate the various ways in which an octahedral shape of the Self may be shown to contain psychological insight (Figure 1). While he struggles mightily to make his case, many have found his exposition hopelessly opaque.

A few prominent Jungians have continued to search for the key to Jung's fascination with this particular octahedron. Others have adopted a similar octahedral shape to explain the deep Self, but have reinterpreted the meanings of the diamond's various facets and planes. Notable among these is John Layard's exegesis in *A Celtic Quest* (Figure 2). Layard suggests that an analysis of Celtic mythology leads to an octahedron that locates the archetypal Self in the lower pyramid and the human individuating Ego in the upper. The archetypal feminine joins the Self below. While somewhat more intelligible than Jung's study, Layard's ingenious interpretation of the diamond body has not become widely known for any clinical usefulness.

One more useful schema has been offered by Toni Wolff. In her essay *Structural Forms of the Feminine Psyche*, Wolff demonstrated how a feminine quadration could be seen to be expressed by more than typological distinctions (Figure 3). She delineates the four major feminine structures as the Mother, the Amazon, the Medial woman, and the Hetaira. Her work comes closest to anticipating our structural decoding, though her model has certain limitations. For a more thorough study of these, see Appendix C. Suffice it to say here that while she correctly sees these four forms to be important feminine structures, she nearly misses their underlying archetypal dimension. In our terminology these dimensions are described as the Queen, Warrior, Lover, and Magician. Wolff discerns aspects of the archetypes

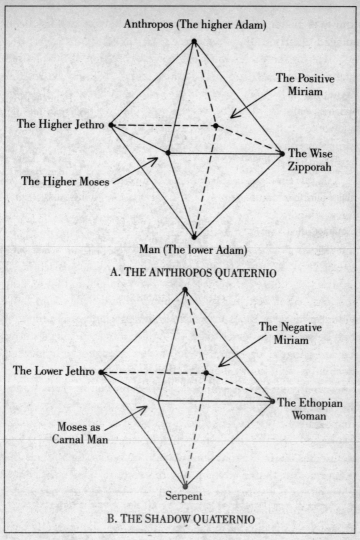

Figure 1: From Carl Jung, "The Structure and Dynamics of the Self" in *Aion*, Volume 9, Part 2, of the *Collected Works*, p. 231.

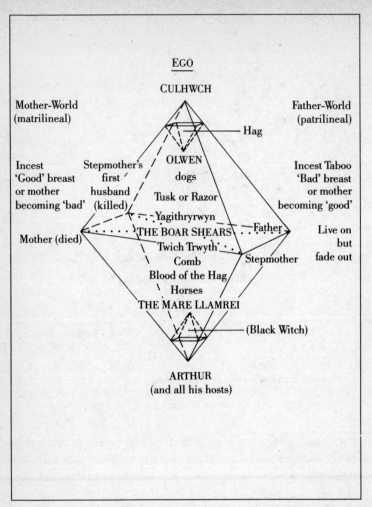

Figure 2: From John Layard, *A Celtic Quest* (Dallas: Spring, 1975), p. 202.

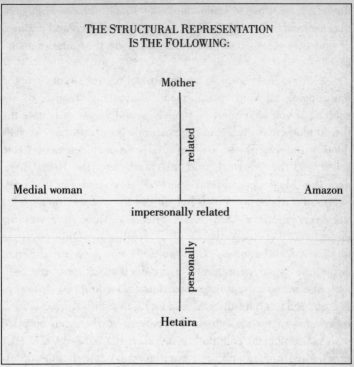

THE STRUCTURAL REPRESENTATION
IS THE FOLLOWING:

Figure 3: From Toni Wolff, "Structural Forms of the Feminine Psyche," privately printed for the Students Association, C. G. Jung Institute, Zurich, July 1956, p. 4.

but describes for the most part traits of the feminine bipolar Shadows. Her model omits a necessary emphasis on balancing these four aspects in the movement toward individuation. Also she seems unable to interpret the dialectics that she correctly observes to exist between the Mother and the Medial woman, the Amazon and the Hetaira.

Ironically, we investigated these other models only after constructing our own. We did not approach this topic deductively, fitting psychological data into an a priori octahedral structure. Rather, we came to the double-pyramid model inductively, seeking to understand the shape our research findings seemed to be urging. Later we were astounded and gratified to find that others had struggled to decode the same diamond body.

Our model (Figure 4) has grown out of over twenty years of anthropological field research and clinical psychoanalytic research. If you examine this model carefully, you will note the two fundamental dialectical oppositions built into the psyche's deep structure. These are between eros and aggression (the Lover and the Warrior), and ruler and sage (the King/Queen and the Magician). Freud focused of course on the eros/ aggression dialectic, and Adler on the ruler/sage (compare his work on superiority and social interest). Thus Jung was not entirely correct to ascribe Freud and Adler's conflict purely to typological differences. The two were focusing on different structural dynamics inherent in the deep structure of the Self.

We believe the human predilection for fourfold structures is grounded in an intuition of an inner quaternio. Each quadrant represents in a way a distinct "program" or biogram encoded with psychological potentials necessary to a cohesive and fully functioning human self. The King program contains the ordering and nurturing potentials. The Warrior program holds potentials for boundary foundation and maintenance, effective organization, action, vocation, and fidelity. Within the Magician program lie potentials for cognitive functioning, understanding, death, and rebirth. Receptiveness, affiliation, healthy dependency, embodied sexuality, empathy, and intimacy are all potentials characteristic of the Lover program.

All of these programs must be adequately accessed, then balanced one against another in a healthy dynamic tension, analogous to the tension of a well-functioning human musculature. Individuation and wholeness are not just esoteric concepts. The psyche has clear and discernible components available to it, which require deliberate sustained efforts to be

DECODING THE DIAMOND BODY:
THE DEEP STRUCTURES OF THE HUMAN SELF

1. Models of the engendered self in quadrated form (the quaternios)

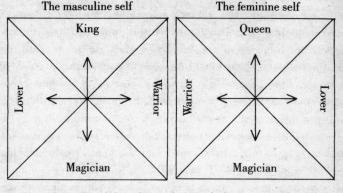

The masculine self   The feminine self

Arrows above indicate dialectical tension built into the deep structure of the psyche

2. Models of the complete bisexual Archetypal Self
in octahedral form (the double-quaternio)

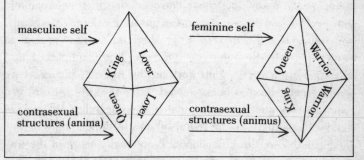

Figure 4: Adapted with permission from Robert L. Moore, *The Magician and the Analyst: Ritual, Sacred Space, and Psychotherapy* (Chicago: Center for the Scientific Study of Religion, 1991).

attained, consolidated, and maintained. On the basis of our model, individuation requires development along four axes. This development counteracts the dialectical tensions built into psychic structure.

We chose the pyramid for our model because it most graphically illustrates the struggle involved in individuation. Individuation in this sense is the Ego's struggle to reunite the archetypal polar opposites at the base of each of the faces of the pyramid. (See pages 41 to 42 in Chapter 2.) *Wholeness is imaged in the capstone of the pyramid.* From the eye of illumination printed on our one-dollar bill to the temple on top of the Maya pyramids, we have noticed the support mythological traditions give to our intuited model of the goal of psychological and spiritual quest. *We believe we have been privileged to stumble, in the course of our researches, across the actual encoded psychological structure underlying these mythic images.*

While the relation of the four foundational archetypes to Jung's theory of typology has yet to be researched, there does not seem to be any one-to-one correspondence. It seems likely that we will find sensation and feeling in the Lover's quadrant, and intuition and thinking in the Magician's—but typological theory neglects the other two quarters. Jung's insistence that Shadow work precede deep work on the Anima/Animus is, we think, clearly imaged in our model. Here the contrasexual is a realm as rich and diverse as that of the engendered Ego—yet deeper in the psyche and more difficult to understand.

Finally, we think our model helps make sense of the way in which male and female developmental challenges are similar—in the four powers there are to be accessed and integrated—and different—in their structural organization. This structural asymmetry will, we conjecture, help us understand gender differences in developmental trajectories, psychopathology distributions, and perceptual and communication styles. In short, it seems that Jung did in fact intuit the biomorphic form of the psyche's deep structures. We believe our model is a decoding of that structure, enabling us to relate together research data from many different sources, and confirming Jung's assumption that the psyche is structured as an octahedral double quaternio.

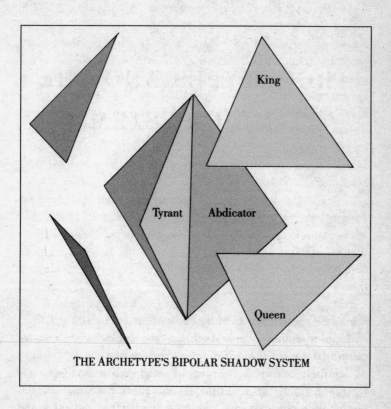

THE ARCHETYPE'S BIPOLAR SHADOW SYSTEM

APPENDIX B

ARCHETYPES AND THE
LIMBIC SYSTEM

ACCORDING TO A NUMBER OF BRAIN RESEARCHERS, most notably Paul MacLean, the limbic system (augmenting the more basic instincts of the underlying R-complex, or reptilian brain) is the seat of mammalian and species-typical instincts for all primates, including humans. Located in the paleocortical area, the limbic system consists of the fornix, hippocampus, cingulate cortex, anterior thalamic nucleus, amygdala, septum, the mammillary bodies, and associated hypothalamic areas. The paleocortex (as the term's Greek roots suggest) is the older brain, a region we share with other mammals. Ours is genetically configured particularly like the paleocortices of other primates.

Because the mechanism of evolution serves to develop new structures gradually, based upon older ones, there remain in our bodies any number of archaic structures that continue to fulfill their more primitive functions. One familiar vestigial organ, the appendix, no longer serves any apparent function (it is believed to have once aided the digestion of grasses) and because of this is now a frequent site of infection. The limbic system, however, continues in its inherited functions, and suggestively seems to be the locus for archetypal structures—suggestively because this would appear to link human archetypes with the instinctive patterns of other species.

Paul Broca, in 1878, was the first to identify a large convolution common to the brains of all mammals as the "great limbic lobe."[1] In 1937 James Papez realized that this limbic system was the seat of the experience and expression of emotion.[2] Paul MacLean later developed the full concept of the limbic system.[3] MacLean came to believe the system was not only the center for emotion but also the integration center for correlating "every form of internal and external perception." It has, he claims, "many strong connections with the hypothalamus for discharging its impression."[4] While some researchers do not accept this notion, there appears to be no other neurological system available to play such an integrative role.

Within the limbic system are three primary subsystems:

1. the affiliative/attachment subsystem[5]
2. the autonomy/aggression subsystem[6]
3. the integrative/inhibition subsystem[7]

The affiliation/attachment subsystem, as the name implies, is almost certainly responsible for general mammalian tendencies to form social units characterized by nurturing, affection, and play. In humans and other primates these affiliative impulses may result in such complex psychological and social phenomena as reliance, dependence, and collaboration. The affiliative impulse seems to arise (along with each species's particular structures of affiliation) primarily in the cingulate gyrus.[8] MacLean has proposed that the concept of "family," for example, may be structured into the limbic system.[9]

Exploration, fear, defensive strategies, fighting, the acquisition of territory, the need for control (over the inner and outer worlds), and other self-definitive, self-preservative behaviors are a result of the autonomy/aggression instinct. This impulse enables humans to form cohesive selves through adversity. It may also give rise to the instinct to order society hierarchically.[10] The autonomy/aggression subsystem appears to be located in the amygdaloid complex.[11] There is evidence that in primates the amygdala plays a hierarchically ordering role for our societies.[12]

The third major limbic subsystem mediates the integration/inhibition instinct and is apparently located in the hippocampus and the septum.[13] MacLean believes this subsystem to be the integrative center for the entire nervous system.[14] The hippocampus can be thought of as the gatekeeper of the limbic system, which system is the capital of the nervous system as a whole. Teamed with the neocortex (which brings cognitive functions into play), the hippocampus "gate mechanism" seems to be responsible for regulating, arranging, prioritizing, and modulating data from nearly every aspect of the nervous system. The hippocampus regulates alternating affiliative/attachment and autonomous/aggressive behaviors. When properly operating, this system regulates these competing drives to appropriately interact with any set of environmental stimuli, both inner and outer.

We believe the archetypes arise in the limbic system, and are then elaborated and refined as they pass upward through the neocortex. This elaboration may be primarily achieved either by the Left Brain's rational, logical functions, or by the Right Brain's intuitive, holistic mode. They may be given "humane" form especially in the frontal lobes, which seem to be responsible for largely empathetic and altruistic emotions as well as for refined cognitive processes. In order for the Ego to know and access any of the four major archetypes, it must experience a particular archetype as an asymmetrical composite of each of the others. In light of the brain research we've cited, a provocative correspondence suggests itself between the archetypal and the limbic systems.

It seems clear that what we call the Lover arises originally in the affiliative/attachment subsystem, and our Warrior arises in the autonomy/aggression subsystem. The Magician (which some other psychologies mistake as the Ego) arises in the integration/inhibition subsystem at its interface with the neocortical structures. We'd locate the Ego within the neocortex proper. This maintains the Ego's status as the apparent center of waking consciousness. Here it is separate from the Magician, but initially more closely related to this archetype than it is to the Lover or the Warrior.

The King manifests as the integrated, mature functioning of all the neocortical and limbic subsystems. Though it seems to arise in the septal-hippocampal subsystem, it transcends this subsystem's gatekeeping functions. More than a regulator, the King embraces the Warrior, Magician, and Lover in an integrated, constituitive manner.

On page 272 we have provided an elaboration of George Everly's diagram of the limbic system, including with it our four archetypes of mature masculinity.

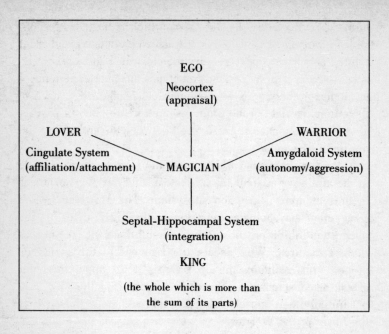

APPENDIX C

ARCHETYPES AND
THE ANIMA

I N THIS APPENDIX WE WILL SKETCH OUT SOME OF THE structures and dynamics of the feminine psyche. Our particular interest will be in the Anima, the inner feminine element of the masculine psyche. We follow Jung in emphasizing that Shadow integration must precede serious work with the contrasexual Anima or Animus. Implicit in Jung's approach is his understanding that integration of the personal Shadow solidifies the integrity of the Ego, and its achievement of a healthy psychosexual identity. Without a cohesive nuclear self, work with inner contrasexual structures can be confusing at best, and dangerous at worst.

We add to Jung's insights a description of the actual structural configurations of the contrasexual Anima. The structure is similar for the feminine Animus (the inner masculine subpersonality in a woman), as we will make plain. As we've argued, the Shadow system involves both a personal Shadow and the bipolar Shadow of each of the four archetypes. After attending to the initiatory and integrative processes involved in mastering this Shadow system, a man can safely turn his attention to his Anima.

The aim of a relationship with the contrasexual should not be to develop androgyny. Androgynous personalities entertain grandiose fantasies of "completeness within the Self." While there may be some biologically based androgynous personalities, as some brain research seems to suggest, for most men and women, androgyny is a masturbatory narcissistic stance, a kind of psychological hermaphroditism. For most people, any attempt to join the contrasexual to the Ego results in a regressive merger, rather than a mature complementary relationship. A merger with the Anima renders a man incapable of forming a mature relationship with his inner feminine energies, as surely as it skews his outer-world relationships with women. Jung believed that as a man's Ego grows stronger, his awareness of the contrasexual as truly "other" will increase, until finally he can initiate what should become a lifelong relationship with his personified Anima through dreamwork, active imagination, and any other techniques he finds useful.

Contrary to what some contemporary Jungians claim, we believe the Anima is not an amorphous, ethereal "mood." The Anima has a dynamic structure that mirrors that of the masculine archetypes. As our diagram on page 276 (explicated in Appendix A) illustrates, the Anima is the feminine inverse of the four-faceted masculine archetypal pyramid. Turned upside down, the model becomes that of a feminine psyche. A woman's pyramid is composed of Queen, Lover, Warrior, and Magician archetypal facets, and her inverse pyramid is the masculine structure we've delineated. This masculine structure is her Animus.

Just as the masculine psyche demonstrates genetically determined archetypal patternings, the feminine psyche has its own distinct coloring. These masculine and feminine psychic systems each retain their distinct characteristics when operating as contrasexual subsystems. Because of this we will quickly examine the deep structures of the feminine psyche, as they are the same as those in place in the male Anima.

Years ago Toni Wolff, a Zurich-trained Jungian analyst, described in *Structural Forms of the Feminine Psyche* four foundational personality types in women. These "forms" she called the Mother, the Amazon, the Medial woman, and the Hetaira. These forms parallel rather closely our concept of the four feminine archetypes, and by extension, the Anima. (See Appendix A.)

Wolff seems to us to have been very close to decoding the feminine psyche. However, her work includes a number of missteps which kept her from finally succeeding. Her first error was in focusing on the form of the Mother instead of the Queen. While the Mother (like the Father) can be argued to be an archetype, the maternal and paternal forms are less inclusive than the King and Queen, and are more properly aspects of the royal archetypes than archetypes themselves.

The Queen is a numinous, mature structure, including and exceeding the Mother. The Great Goddess imagery of the ancient religions issues from the Queen's impact on the psyche. The Mother's focus is on a single family, where she is especially concerned with the needs of the infant human. The Mother is therefore less fertile than the Queen, from whom the earth itself derives fertility, and less nurturing, because the Queen nurtures the planet she engenders, and not only her own children. And like the fully expressed King, the Queen encompasses

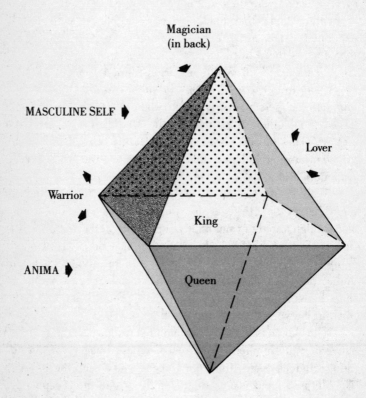

Magician
(in back)

MASCULINE SELF

Lover

Warrior

King

ANIMA

Queen

each of the other three archetypes. Wolff excludes her other three forms from the Mother's influence.

Others might argue that the Mother does, in fact, integrate the feminine Warrior, Magician, and Lover. But to the extent she does so she is approaching identity with the Queen. Though the Mother archetype provides a strong image of nurturing and blessing, she offers to a somewhat lesser degree an image of teaching and discipline (the Magician and Warrior) and no image at all of erotic love (the Lover). The Queen, however, provides images of all of these traits.

Wolff's second mistake is to weight the feminine Warrior with the culturally compromised image of the Amazon. Our Warrior is clearly related to her Amazon, but the legendary Greek form she's chosen often misdirects the aggressive energy that is this archetype's domain. Instead of being a Warrior using this energy in the service of the royal couple, supporting and extending the created cosmos, the Amazon of the myths all too frequently uses her aggression against males, even to the point of exiling her sons.

The fully expressed feminine Warrior helps a woman consolidate an independent Self by defining and defending legitimate psychological boundaries. The Warrior enables a woman to achieve other difficult tasks through strategic thinking, self-discipline, and hard work. But the feminine Warrior is not in any sense antimale, as the Amazon often tends to be. The Warrior does not misinterpret the battles she must fight as narrow tribal disputes, except in the legitimate defense of a woman's offspring. Where her children are threatened, a woman accessing her Warrior is programmed to react with swift and relentless ruthlessness. Otherwise, the woman in an axis with her Warrior correctly sees her battles as primarily personal efforts to establish a Self, and transpersonal efforts to defend creation.

But by using the largely negative image of the Amazon,

Wolff ends up really examining primarily the Shadow Warrior, in her sadistic expression. Possessed by the Sadist, a woman's fury is directed not only against men in general but against other women as well, and even against her own children.[1] A woman who allows the Amazonian Sadist to act for her in her life misses all the potential benefits of the full expression of the feminine Warrior.

We hope the resources of the feminine Warrior will be accepted more fully into our culture. We would then see women engaged in a more active psychological and physical defense of themselves and their mates, as well as a fuller participation in the struggle against communal and global forces of destruction. There is evidence that our culture is increasingly learning to steward this energy—especially in the arenas of social and environmental reform.

The Hetaira is, like the Amazon, a culture-bound term. In ancient Greece the hetaira functioned much as the more familiar geisha did in Japanese culture—as a well-educated female companion and prostitute. Any prostitute is a manifestation of the Shadow Lover, no matter how well-educated. In Wolff's system the Hetaira displays both aspects of the Lover's bipolar Shadow, the Addict and the Impotent Lover. The Addict is operative in Wolff's claim that women under the influence of the Hetaira have a tendency to go from one man to another. The Impotent Lover is disclosed by the knowledge that psychologically a prostitute is often engaged in a fruitless repetition of her unsuccessful childhood attempt to gain her father's admiration and love.

The Hetaira seems to be a second-generation archetype, composed of fragments of more basic ones. She includes both poles of the Magician's Shadow—as a Manipulator she causes a woman to use men for their money and her own narrow interests, and as the Innocent One she lures a woman into displaying her naïveté about relationships. The Sadist manifests in a woman's underlying anger toward men. The Warrior's other Shadow pole, the Masochist, appears in her willingness to place herself in harm's way.

To the extent Wolff's final type, the Medial, approaches the concept of the shaman, it is an appropriate and full expression of the archetype of the Magician. It is Wolff's least limiting term.

Despite any other shortcomings, it is striking that Wolff's conceptualization of the archetypal dynamics of the *feminine* psyche agrees so closely with our own system of thought concerning the *male* psyche. We interpret this as a verification of our instinct to extend the concept of the quadrated psyche from the masculine to the feminine Self, and to the Anima or Animus.

To our thinking then, a woman's quadrated psyche functions just as does a man's. She balances the energies of four foundational archetypes—the Queen, Warrior, Magician, and Lover. The Queen guides a woman toward a centered calm, a sense of inner order she can extend into the outer world. She becomes gifted with the capacity to bless and join in fructifying union with the other members of her "realm." The Warrior guides a woman in self-discipline and self-defense, and the defense of others. Her achievements are encouraged by the Warrior, and her sense of service to a Transpersonal Other reinforced. The Magician affords a desire to introject, to raise and contain power, to heal and to act as a mediator between the human and the divine spheres. Drawing on the Magician's powers, a woman may serve as a spiritual guide to others, especially in the task of initiating younger women into the mysteries of adult responsibilities and joys. And the Lover empowers a woman to be passionately and creatively engaged with all things, to be uninhibited sexually (playing and displaying) and profoundly spiritual.

Of course, the relationship between the masculine and

feminine aspects of the Self are often problematic. For the Anima is a whole structure, and no man experiences it simply piece by piece, pair by pair. Just as he balances the energies of *his* four foundational archetypes, he must balance the four different signals that reach him from his Anima. It can be useful to separate out the different sources of these signals in order to distinguish their characteristics, so long as we remember that they operate as a whole.

The feminine energies beside each of the male archetypes give them depth and definition. But when a man is caught in one or more of the bipolar Shadow systems of the masculine archetype, he encounters all of the Anima's complementary Shadow energies too. At the Warrior's *active* Sadist pole, for example, he will meet with the *passive* poles of the Shadow Anima, the Abdicator, the Innocent One, the Impotent Lover, and especially with the Masochist. If he is Ego-identified instead with the Masochist, he will be confronted by the feminine Tyrant, the Manipulator, the Addict, and especially with the woman Warrior at her Sadist pole.

Relations between the masculine and feminine Warriors can be particularly strained. The only really successful mode for a relationship between them is as comrades-in-arms.[2] Otherwise the aggressive/aversive energies they each channel can be directed against the other, causing empathic breaks in man-woman relationships that are difficult to repair. A Warrior needs an enemy, and too often the masculine and feminine Warriors make enemies of each other.

A man who does not access the fully expressed Warrior (whose feminine counterpart is his comrade-in-arms) will tend to experience his Anima, and all the women in his life, in a split and shadowy way. He will see one aspect of the feminine as the Tyrant Queen—his sophomorically idealized and "virginal" mother. Women who are not like her he sees as whores, and we've seen what a complex mixture of Shadow elements a prostitute carries. The Tyrant Queen sends this man to his death to defend her. He "fucks" a whore (rather than "making love" with her) in an act of revenge against his mother, overcoming "her" resistance with brutality. Here is the power issue the rapist fails to manage. He wants power over what he sees as an inordinately powerful, abusive woman. Perhaps his mother was physically or verbally abusive of him, or perhaps she was neglectful and uninterested. Such a man is of course not accessing his Warrior appropriately. Instead, he is a psychotic boy without any experience of his legitimate power.

Until a man becomes secure in his masculine identity, he will remain a sadomasochist in his relationships with women. If he is not secure he feels that he is risking invasion by his Anima. He has yet to learn to respect the legitimate territories of the feminine psyche, both within and without. The maturing male learns there is a space within him he can never invade, and that will never be "his." He must approach his Anima with respect. Once he learns to deal with this "other" with discipline and respect, he has the prerequisite knowledge necessary to deal respectfully with any "other," including the women he loves, and other men, other species, and finally the Transpersonal Other we all need to serve.

The octahedral Self we diagrammed above gives a good visual model for imagining these Anima dynamics. While it does not portray the vital interpenetration of the masculine and feminine structures, it does show how the contrasexual system is contained *within* the total structure, and is in no way external to it. The two structures together form the "diamond body" of the great Self. Though it is in some sense merely a pictorial construct, it is an appropriately suggestive and allusive one. Like the implicit structure of a crystal, we each have a perfect diamond Self within, waiting the chance to form. We are gifted then with an inner vision of the possible human which has the clarity, radiance, and perfection of a jewel.

NOTES

Complete bibliographical information on works cited in these notes will be found in the Bibliography that follows.

PREFACE

1. Tolkien.
2. Herbert
3. Forsyth.
4. Blake.

CHAPTER 1: GENDER IDENTITY,
GENDER ASYMMETRY, AND
THE SEXUAL IMBALANCE OF POWER

1. By "radical androgyny" we refer to the claims made by some feminists, whether male or female, that there are no differences between the sexes (except what they regard as incidental biological divergences). When it comes to assigning blame, however, particularly for aggressive behavior and fear of intimacy, some feminists draw very clear distinctions between the sexes, always at the expense of the male. One would think from their claims that women have no Shadow. A woman's only weakness seems to be that she "loves men too much." It is impossible to love someone too much. What *is* possible is to become so addicted to another that personal responsibilities are relinquished. However, shadowy business of this kind is common to both sexes. The idealization of androgyny is against nature and scientific evidence; it is also hypocritical. For related discussion, see Ardrey, in toto but especially pp. 143 ff.; Ashbrook, pp. 57–59, 96–97, 105, 322 ff, 324–327, 339; Keen, pp. 195 ff.; Moir and Jessel; Stevens, *Archetypes*, pp. 23 ff., 48 ff., 81–84, 174 ff.; E. Wilson, in toto but especially pp. 16, 18–21, 121 ff.

2. An example of this phenomenon is Riane Eisler's *The Chalice and the Blade: Our History, Our Future*. Although Ms. Eisler purports to demonstrate a "partnership" model of male/female relationships, she provides a stereotypic negative metaphor of the "Blade" to designate male qualities. Her central image of partnership is of a mother Goddess nurturing her child, by implication her son—hardly a relationship between equals. Also see Daley, *Beyond God the Father* and *Gyn/Ecology*; Ruether, pp. 104 ff.

3. Miller, *The Drama of the Gifted Child, For Your Own Good*, and *Thou Shalt Not Be Aware*.

4. Research in this area clearly links the development of high civilization (beyond the "high culture" of the late Neolithic) with the advent of sacral kingships and the attendant assemblage of larger nation-states. For an extensive record of sources, see the Bibliography's Kingship listing. See especially Basham; Emery; Kwanten; Frankfort, *The Birth of Civilization in the Near East*; Jaynes; Perry, *Lord of the Four Quarters*; Schele and Freidel; Wales; E. Wilson, pp. 89–90.

5. Jung's *Aion* in *The Portable Jung*, pp. 148 ff; Jacobi, *The Psychology of C. G. Jung*, pp. 5, 114 ff; 120–121; Jung, *Man and His*

Symbols, pp. 186 ff., and *Mysterium Coniunctionis;* Pedersen; Sanford, *The Invisible Partners;* Stevens, *Archetypes*, pp. 174 ff., 193–194.

6. Ibid., pp. 79–80; E. Wilson, pp. 132–137.

7. See Bibliography under Brain Research.

8. Gilmore: See Index under Work.

9. Browning, pp. 145 ff.

10. Niebuhr isn't always as frank about his distrust of power as Lord Acton was when he said, "Power corrupts, absolute power corrupts absolutely." He does frequently, however, cast the desire for power, and its achievement and uses, in an exaggeratedly negative light. He assumes (as liberal Christians have for centuries, and some feminists do today) that the quest for power is inherently mistaken, and that its achievement is invariably destructive for principal and subordinate alike. Writers such as Keen, Ruether, Eisler, and Daley betray an unconscious utopianism in their works—and as Stevens notes in *Archetypes* (p. 139), utopianism will always fail.

11. Lauzun, pp. 64–65; Niebuhr, pp. 44, 192.

12. Stevens, *The Roots of War*, pp. 36–38; Storr, in toto and especially pp. 11, 21, 23, 34, 42. Even Gilmore (op. cit.) affirms the almost universal necessity for aggressive male behaviors, as channeled into the culturally defined roles of protector, provider, and procreator. Keen finds himself (op. cit., pp. 112 ff.) endorsing "fierce gentlemen" as if they were vital to the survival of the species. This comes after his emphatic rejection of sociobiological claims and the notion of an aggressive instinct, and despite his embrasure of the romantic socialization model of gender definition.

13. Cultures have seldom celebrated initiation ceremonies for their girls. By and large girls have been considered naturally initiated by their first menstruation. Boys have been, in contrast, forcibly taken through initiation rituals designed to awaken in them an awareness of their risk-taking and self-sacrificial responsibilities. This may also reflect a widespread human awareness that innate masculine aggressive potentials require extremely careful containment and channeling if they are not to become dangerous to the human community in the behavior of irresponsible, immature, "monster boy" males. See the Bibliography under Initiation; see also Eliade, *Rites and Symbols of Initiation;* Gilmore; Henderson; Keen, pp. 27–33; Turner; Webster.

CHAPTER 2: DECODING THE MALE PSYCHE

1. See Bibliography under Jungian Thought.

2. Jung, "The Relations of the Ego and the Unconscious," in *The Portable Jung*, p. 75; Jacobi, *The Psychology of C. G. Jung*, p. 1; Jaffé, pp. 40–42; Jung, *Psychology and Alchemy*, p. 215; Stevens, *Archetypes*, pp. 43–47.

3. Jacobi, *The Psychology of C. G. Jung*, p. 1; Stevens, *Archetypes*, pp. 43–47.

4. Campbell, *The Hero with a Thousand Faces*, pp. 3 ff.; Jacobi, *The Psychology of C. G. Jung:* See Index under Mythology/Myths.

5. Campbell, *The Hero with a Thousand Faces*, p. 258.

6. Eliade, *Cosmos and History*, p. 3; Jacobi, *The Psychology of C. G. Jung*, pp. 5–10; Jaynes: See the first two chapters on the nature of consciousness; Frankfort, *Kingship and the Gods*, pp. 27–29.

7. Jung, "Aion," in *Psyche and Symbol*, pp. 1–6.

8. Beahrs, especially Chapters 1 and 4.

9. Nearly every school of psychology acknowledges this, in one way or another. The Jungian approach to the Shadow, the work of developmental psychologists with the inner Child (see especially Alice Miller), and the work of hypnotherapists like Dr. John Beahrs with multiple-personality disorders all are particularly relevant.

10. Jung, "The Structure and Dynamics of the Psyche," in *The Portable Jung*, especially p. 52; Stevens, *Archetypes*, especially pp. 26, 40, 51 ff.

11. Jung, "The Concept of the Collective Unconscious," in *The Portable Jung*, pp. 59–69.

12. Bettleheim, pp. 53–64; Lauzun: See Index under Id.

13. Browning, p. 158.

14. Ibid., p. 158.

15. Ibid., p. 159.

16. Ibid., pp. 145–147, 158, 159; Jacobi, op. cit.: See Index under Libido; Lauzun: See Index under Libido.

17. See Bibliography. Although Jean Bolen does not do this, she tends to identify the Gods and Goddesses with human personality types. Bolen's Gods and Goddesses do parallel cognition, feeling, and behavioral styles observable in men and women. *But no human being is an archetype, and neither is any God or Goddess*. Bolen's work describes complex configurations of archetypes (our foundational four from the

psyches of men and women, as well as countless others which determine our modes of perception) as expressed through different Ego identities, personal complexes, cultural and Superego conditioning, etc. Her Gods and Goddesses are simpler than human personalities, and so on this level they approach the archetypes more nearly than all but the most dysfunctional human personalities. But we believe the Libido takes form at the most basic levels of drive as either a King (or Queen), Warrior, Magician, or Lover, and then after progressive explication and diversification, presents itself in complex manifestations. These foundational four are the node around which collect the culture-specific ideals, parental introjects, and other family myths that provide so many layers of archetypal functioning.

18. Jacobi, *The Psychology of C. G. Jung*, pp. 1–9 ff.; de Laszlo, pp. 6–9.

19. von Franz: See Index under Shadow, Projection of.

20. Individuation is a matter, for Jungians, of bringing into Ego consciousness (1) what has been otherwise split off and repressed, as well as (2) awakening insights that have never been conscious. For the distinction between complexes and archetypes, and their relation to the two categories above, see Jolande Jacobi's *Complex, Archetype, Symbol*.

21. See Theodore Millon's excellent work with the concept of bipolarity in *Modern Psychopathology*.

22. Millon, *Disorders of Personality*, in toto but especially p. 58.

23. Hillman, et al., especially Hillman's chapter "Senex and Puer: An Aspect of the Historical and Psychological Present."

24. Tillich, *Systematic Theology: III*, especially Chapter 1 and "The Kingdom of God as the End of History."

25. Ibid.: See Index under Hegel; also see Sean Kelly's forthcoming *Individuation and the Absolute: Hegel, Jung, and the Path Toward Wholeness*.

26. See Bibliography under Theology and Philosophy; see also Whitehead, *Process and Reality*.

27. Jung, *Psychology and Alchemy:* See Index under Coniunctio.

28. In Greek mythology and legend, the Symplegades were two great rocks in the middle of the ocean. When a ship tried to pass between them, they would rush together and destroy the ship.

29. Stevens, *Archetypes*, pp. 259–275.

30. Ibid., pp. 260, 264. For the relevance of the limbic system to the four foundational archetypes, see Appendix B.

31. Otto, in toto but especially pp. 12 ff., 25.

32. Eliade, *Cosmos and History*, pp. 12 ff., and *Patterns in Comparative Religion:* See Index under Temple; Tree, Cosmic; Palace; Mountain, Cosmic.

33. Ibid.: See Index under Kings, Rulers. The literature on sacral kingship, and the king's mediation of the sacred and profane worlds, is vast. See also the Bibliography under Kingship.

34. See Bibliography under Kingship. Also see Frazer: See index under King; Queen; Perry, *Lord of the Four Quarters*, p. 32.

35. Goodall, *In the Shadow of Man*, p. 284.

36. Goodall, *Through a Window*, p. 13.

37. See Bibliography under Primate Ethology. Also see de Waal; Goodall, *Through a Window* and *In the Shadow of Man*; MacKinnon.

38. Bourne, pp. 321 ff.

39. de Waal: See Index under Alpha Male; Goodall, *In the Shadow of Man*, pp. 112 ff.

40. de Waal, pp. 109–110, 200, 204–205.

41. Goodall, *Through a Window*, p. 57.

42. Goodall, *In the Shadow of Man*, pp. 73–74; MacKinnon, p. 85.

43. Bourne, p. 407.

CHAPTER 3: HISTORIC IMAGES OF THE SACRED KING

1. Gilmore, in toto. See especially the Index under Gregor, Thomas.

2. There is some debate in Jungian circles as to whether or not archetypes evolve over time. If they are carried in the genes, then they must be very conservative structures. Genes rarely mutate, and occasional mutations are seldom passed on to the next generation because more often than not they are disadvantageous. If, as we believe, the archetypes arise in the most conservative area of the brain, the limbic system if not the R-complex, this would lend additional support to the idea that archetypes are very conservative elements of the psyche. The limbic system has remained virtually unchanged since the advent of the primates. It would follow that culture has no power to change the essential characteristics of the archetypes, even if it augments or minimizes particular archetypal intents.

3. Perry, *Lord of the Four Quarters.*

4. The Hebrew kings were seen as merely mortal men, at least by the authors of the Bible. These kings were not only clearly distinct from God, they quite often were his enemies. See Karl Ruttan's doctoral dissertation, *The Evolution of the Kingship Archetypes in the Old Testament.*

5. We have derived this term from Edward Edinger's "Ego-Self axis." A man's Ego can form an axis with any of the four archetypes, or any combination of them. Because the masculine Self is composed of the four foundational archetypes, to the extent that a fully effective axis is formed with an archetype, it also provides an axial relationship with the masculine Self and with the contrasexual archetype in the Anima. An integrated and balanced accessing of all of the eight archetypes of the Diamond Body constitutes Edinger's Ego-Self axis.

6. Evidence for this can be found in Kabbalistic and other Medieval occult literature. In the popular imagination, David was the ancestor of the Messiah. There is evidence that during his reign he performed sacral kingship ceremonies, reminiscent of earlier Canaanite kingship practices. (See Aubrey Johnson's *Sacral Kingship in Ancient Israel.*) Solomon was believed to have been specially chosen by God to receive divine wisdom and extraordinary magical powers. See Jobes, pp. 1472–1473; Scholem, *Major Trends in Jewish Mysticism* and *Origins of the Jewish Kabbalah.* Numerous apocryphal books were assigned to Solomon. See Barnstone, ed.; Hadas.

7. In theory the pharaoh was the King-God incarnate.

8. This was especially the case with Akhenaten. See Bibliography for works on Egyptian history.

9. See Bibliography.

10. Jung, *Mysterium Coniunctionis:* See Index under King.

11. Perry, *Roots of Renewal in Myth and Madness:* See, for example, pp. 68–73.

12. Following and extending Frazer, Eliade is without doubt the most significant figure in the field. For a representative sample of his writing, see Bibliography under Mythology and Religion.

13. Eliade, *The Sacred and the Profane:* See especially the Introduction and Chapter 1.

14. Eliade, *The Sacred and the Profane,* pp. 80–113; *Patterns in Comparative Religion* (see Index under Time), and *Rites and Symbols of Initiation* (see Introduction).

15. Eliade, *Cosmos and History*, pp. 16–18, and *The Sacred and the Profane*, pp. 45–47.

16. Eliade, *The Sacred and the Profane*, pp. 39–47, *Cosmos and History*, pp. 6–11, 77–78, and *Patterns in Comparative Religion*, Chapter 10.

17. Schele and Freidel, pp. 70 ff., 313.

18. Eliade, *Cosmos and History*, pp. 12–13, and *The Sacred and the Profane* (see Index under Axis Mundi; Center).

19. Eliade, *The Sacred and the Profane*, p. 48, and *Cosmos and History* (see Index under Kings); Perry, *Lord of the Four Quarters:* See Introduction.

20. Eliade, *The Sacred and the Profane*, pp. 53–54, and *Patterns in Comparative Religion*, p. 405; Perry, *Lord of the Four Quarters:* See Introduction; Schele and Freidel, pp. 66–73.

21. Eliade, *The Sacred and the Profane*, pp. 29, 47–50; Perry, *Lord of the Four Quarters:* See Index under Kings and Kingship; Baal; Marduk, for examples.

22. See Bibliography under Kingship. See especially Hadfield; Martin and O'Meara, pp. 185–187.

23. Freud, *Totem and Taboo*, Chapter 2, especially pp. 41–42; Perry, *Lord of the Four Quarters*, pp. 33–34.

24. Hadfield, pp. 10, 13; Seligman, pp. 22–24, 61.

25. Frazer: See Index under King; Meyerowitz, pp. 106–107; Seligman, p. 24.

26. Frazer: See Index under King; Hadfield, p. 116; Martin and O'Meara, pp. 185–186; Perry, *Lord of the Four Quarters:* See Introduction.

27. Frankfort, *Kingship and the Gods*, p. 16; J. Wilson, pp. 19 ff.

28. Emery, pp. 42 ff.; J. Wilson, pp. 15–23.

29. Ibid., pp. 47–49.

30. Frankfort, *Kingship and the Gods*, pp. 207 ff., and *The Birth of Civilization in the Near East* (see Appendix, pp. 121 ff.).

31. Emery, pp. 38 ff.; Frankfort, *Kingship and the Gods*, p. 15; J. Wilson, pp. 36 ff.

32. Breasted, *The Dawn of Conscience*, pp. 109, 111, 113; Frankfort, *Kingship and the Gods*, pp. 176, 186; Kirk and Raven: See Index under Egypt; Mythology; J. Wilson, pp. 124, 310 ff.

33. Breasted, *The Dawn of Conscience*, pp. xiv ff.; Frankfort, *Ancient Egyptian Religion*, p. 88; Jung, *Mysterium Coniunctionis* (see In-

dex under Trinity, Quaternio; Egypt) and *Psychology and Religion*, Part II, "A Psychological Approach to the Dogma of the Trinity," especially pp. 115–117, 131.

34. Breasted, *The Dawn of Conscience*, pp. 10, 19; Hooke, *Middle Eastern Mythology*, p. 66; J. Wilson, pp. 43, 47.

35. The pharaoh's incarnational nature has been extensively documented. For specific reference to his incarnating Ra, see, for example, Breasted, *The Dawn of Conscience*, pp. 27, 74; Frankfort, *Kingship and the Gods*, pp. 42, 57, 77, 101, 106, 148.

36. Engnell, p. 6; Frankfort, *Ancient Egyptian Religion* (see Index under Re, Parallelism between Pharaoh and; also see Chapter 1 and pp. 52, 88) and *Kingship and the Gods*, p. 211.

37. Ibid., pp. 61 ff., especially 66 and 77.

38. Ibid., pp. 25, 66.

39. Ibid., p. 152.

40. Breasted, *The Dawn of Conscience*, pp. 202–203; Frankfort, *Kingship and the Gods*, p. 173.

41. Breasted, *The Dawn of Conscience*, pp. 202–205; Frankfort, *Kingship and the Gods*, pp. 51–52.

42. Frankfort, *Ancient Egyptian Religion*, pp. 84–87, and *Kingship and the Gods*, pp. 150, 183; Hooke, *Middle Eastern Mythology*, pp. 74, 75; J. Wilson, pp. 160, 161.

43. Steindorff and Seele, p. 60.

44. Breasted, *A History of Egypt*, p. 461; J. Wilson, pp. 252–253.

45. Frankfort, *Kingship and the Gods:* See Index under Sed Festival.

46. Breasted, *The Dawn of Conscience*, pp. 107–109, and the whole of Chapters 7 and 8; Frankfort, *Ancient Egyptian Religion*, Chapter 4, especially pp. 103 ff., and *Kingship and the Gods* (see Index under Osiris).

47. Ibid., pp. 112 ff.

48. Basham, p. 486; Dodds, pp. 72, 98 ff., 128; *Encyclopaedia Britannica*, Vol. 18, under Plotinus, pp. 58–60; Jung, *Psychology and Religion*, p. 441; J. Kelly, pp. 20 ff., 127, 270, 274–275.

49. Gonda, Vol. III, pp. 44–45, 60.

50. Ibid., Vol. III, pp. 50–55; Perry, *Lord of the Four Quarters*, p. 14.

51. Gonda, Vol. III, and Vol. IV, pp. 36 ff.; Perry, *Lord of the Four Quarters*, pp. 124–125.

52. Gonda, Vol. III, pp. 45, 66 and Vol. IV, pp. 41, 57.

53. Richards, p. 152.

54. Gaer, pp. 134 ff.; Malandra; Perry, *Lord of the Four Quarters*, pp. 134–139; Richards, p. 150, 157.

55. Richards, p. 146.

56. Campbell, *The Masks of God: Occidental Mythology*, pp. 189 ff., Chapter 5; Cumont, pp. 142–143, and "The Doctrines of the Mithraic Mysteries" in toto; Gaer, pp. 134 ff.; Malandra, pp. 47 ff.; Perry, *Lord of the Four Quarters*, pp. 135–139.

57. Campbell, *The Masks of God: Occidental Mythology* See Index under Aryan Culture.

58. Chaney, pp. 7–19.

59. Ibid., p. 19.

60. Tucci, p. 197.

61. Ibid., pp. 197–205, especially p. 200.

62. Jung borrowed the term "mandala" from Tibetan Buddhism. He used it to describe images of the psychological center that occur throughout the art and architecture of every culture. He found that many of his analysands spontaneously drew or painted mandalas during the course of their analysis. They also reported powerful healing dreams in which images of a sacred center would appear. These various mandalas appeared in either a circular or square form, and were often quadrated. John Weir Perry and other Jungians have done further original work in this area. See, for example, Jung, *Psychology and Religion:* See Index under Mandala; Perry, *Roots of Renewal*, pp. 38–39, 91.

63. Perry, *Lord of the Four Quarters*, pp. 204–210.

64. Ibid., pp. 214–216.

65. Ibid., p. 214.

66. Ibid., p. 215.

67. Ibid., pp. 215–218. For further reading, see Gernet: See Index under Taoism; Wei, especially Part II.

68. See Bibliography under Jungian Thought. For a popular description of inner/outer correspondence, with a construct of the Imago, see also Hendrix.

69. Waida, "Symbolism of 'Descent' in Tibetan Sacred Kingship," pp. 60–78, especially pp. 68 ff.

70. Turnbull.

71. Waida, "Sacred Kingship in Early Japan," pp. 319–342.

72. Ibid., p. 319.

73. For an excellent discussion of Maya kingship, see Schele and Freidel.

74. Morley, et al., especially Chapters 2 and 3; Thompson, especially Chapter 2.

75. Schele and Freidel: See Index under Wars of Conquest.

76. Peterson: See Index under Sacrifices, Human; Wars of the Flowers.

77. Ibid., p. 113.

78. Ibid., p. 114.

79. Ibid., p. 114. See also Leonard and the Editors of Time-Life Books, *Ancient America*, p. 101.

80. Carrasco; Perry, *Lord of the Four Quarters*, pp. 194, 195–199, 201; Peterson: See Index under Quetzalcoatl; Wheatley.

81. Ibid., pg. 85.

82. Zuidema; pp. 39–95; *Encyclopaedia Britannica*, Vol. I, under Andean Civilization.

83. See Bibliography under Kingship for a sampling of the literature on this subject. Also see Frankfort, *Kingship and the Gods*, pp. 215–248; Wales, pp. 21–28.

84. Frankfort, *Kingship and the Gods*, pp. 224 ff., 295 ff.

85. Ibid., pp. 215–248; Grottanelli, pp. 317–322; Hocart, pp. 7–8.

86. Frankfort, *Kingship and the Gods*, pp. 217–218; J. Wilson, op. cit., pp. 8–17.

87. Cohn-Haft, p. 12; Perry, *Lord of the Four Quarters*, pp. 59–61.

88. Frankfort, *Ancient Egyptian Religion*, p. 60, and *Kingship and the Gods*, pp. 277–279; Perry, *Lord of the Four Quarters*, p. 59.

89. Eliade, *Cosmos and History*, pp. 59-60, and *Patterns in Comparative Religion* (see Index under Marduk); Frankfort, *Kingship and the Gods:* See Index under Marduk; New Year; New Year's Festival.

90. Ibid., pp. 215, 218.

91. Emery, pp. 30 ff.; Frankfort, *The Birth of Civilzation*, especially "The Prehistory of the Ancient Near East" and the Appendix; J. Wilson, pp. 37–42.

92. Frankfort, *Kingship and the Gods*, pp. 218–221.

93. Frankfort, *The Birth of Civilization*, pp. 82–89.

94. Frankfort, *Kingship and the Gods*, pp. 228.

95. Albright, *Yahweh and the Gods of Canaan*, p. 69.

96. Frankfort, *Kingship and the Gods,*, pp. 224.

97. Ibid., pp. 251 ff.

98. Ibid., p. 238.

99. Ibid., pp. 238–240, 299–301.

100. Eliade, *Cosmos and History* (see Index under Palaces) and *Patterns in Comparative Religion*, pp. 374 ff.; Perry, *Lord of the Four Quarters*, p. 19.

101. Frankfort, *Kingship and the Gods*, p. 320.

102. Eliade, *Cosmos and History*, pp. 54–58.

103. Frankfort, *Kingship and the Gods*, pp. 295 ff.

104. Albright, *Yahweh and the Gods of Canaan*, pp. 101–109.

105. Barnett and Forman.

106. Eliade, *The Sacred and the Profane*, pp. 47–50; Perry, *Lord of the Four Quarters*, pp. 15, 16.

107. The literature on the Mesopotamian influence is extensive. See Bibliography under Kingship. Also see Perry, *Lord of the Four Quarters*, pp. 8–111; Albright, *Yahweh and the Gods of Canaan;* Frankfort, *Kingship and the Gods:* See Index under Syria; Palestine; Anatolia; Gurney: See Index under Assyria(n); Babylon(ia); Sumeria(n).

108. Hocart, p. 8; Perry, *Lord of the Four Quarters*, pp. 145–156.

109. Engnell, p. 67; Frankfort, *Kingship and the Gods*, p. 338.

110. Albright, *The Archeology of Palestine*, especially Chapters 5 and 6; Engnell, p. 74; The Editors of Time, *The Epic of Man*, Chapter 7; Grottanelli, p. 320.

111. Engnell, Chapters 4 and 6.

112. Albright, *Yahweh and the Gods of Canaan*, Chapter 2, especially pp. 67–68, 76–77, 84–85.

113. Ibid., pp. 57, 153 ff.

114. Ibid., p. 65.

115. Frankfort, *Kingship and the Gods*, p. 339.

116. Ibid., pp. 339 ff.; Ruttan.

117. Ibid., pp. 31–35.

118. Ibid.

119. Albright, *Yahweh and the Gods of Canaan*, pp. 120, 171. El-olam and El-elyon, "God of the earth" and "God of the highest" respectively, were the Canaanite names for the supreme Creator. His northern Hebrew name was Elohim, which means "the totality of the Gods and Goddesses." Elohim is therefore a distinct conception, though related to El-elyon—since the latter was for the Canaanites the father of the Gods, he could be conceived of also as their totality.

120. Kenik, pp. 391–403. Ruttan (op. cit.) makes the case that in

the Hebrew king's enthronement rituals, he is to some extent identified with the enthronement of Yahweh, and the king's role in other high events of the cultus extends this identification. The king therefore recapitulates the original cosmogony, and as with other sacred kings he is seen to bring blessing or blight upon his kingdom, depending in his case upon his adherence to the Torah. See, for example, I Kings 16:25–17:1.

121. Jobes, pp. 1472–1473.

122. Frankfort, *Kingship and the Gods*, pp. 339 ff.; I Samuel 8.

123. The literature on this is comprehensive. See Bibliography, and also Basham: See Index under Indra; Eliade, *Patterns in Comparative Religion:* See Index under Amon; Amon-Ra; Ahura-Mazda; Indra; Yahweh; Malandra; Perry, *Lord of the Four Quarters:* See Index under Ahura-Mazda; Indra; Zeus; Seltman, pp. 37–53.

124. Campbell, *The Masks of God: Occidental Mythology*, pp. 125–126; Eliade, *Patterns in Comparative Religion*, pp. 94–95; Freud, *Moses and Monotheism*. The complex of ideas behind the God, Yahweh, resists a simple ascription to a Kenite or Midian God of volcanoes, as Albright points out in *Yahweh and the Gods of Canaan*. But his volcanic origins seem to explain his sharp divergence from such weather Gods as Thor and Zeus. Yahweh's use of thunder, lightning, fire, smoke, cloud, and earthquake point to a volcanic model. Exodus 19:16–22 can be read as a divine hierophany in the context of a volcanic eruption.

125. Campbell, *The Masks of God:* See Index under Monotheism; Eliade, *Patterns in Comparative Religion*, pp. 94–95, and Index under Monotheism; Frankfort, *Kingship and the Gods*, p. 343.

126. Albright, *Yahweh and the Gods of Canaan*, pp. 120, 171.

127. Frankfort, *Kingship and the Gods:* See Index under Ptah, as Creator; Genesis 1: Compare this creation story with the Egyptian myth of creation in which Ptah makes the world through divine utterance.

128. Ruttan, especially Chapter 2.

129. Exodus 3:6; 33:17–23.

130. Campbell, *The Masks of God: Occidental Mythology*, p. 105; Genesis 6–8 (the Flood), 11 (the Tower of Babel), 18, 19 (Sodom and Gomorrah).

131. Jung, *Psychology and Religion*, pp. 152–157.

132. Not only had the Persian religions influenced their Jewish and Greco-Roman counterparts by the first century A.D., they also had taken a prominent place alongside the Empire's state religion. This was especially true of Mithraism, practiced by many Roman soldiers. Vast num-

bers of Egyptian, Greek, and Roman converts to Christianity brought their own spiritual assumptions with them into their new faith, assumptions molded by centuries of sacred king beliefs and practices. The apostle Paul borrowed ideas for his budding theology and recommended praxis from the mystery religions of Greece and Asia Minor. By so doing he made Christianity a world religion. Gnostic Christian writings display an intimate familiarity with the Hermetic tradition of the Hellenistic world. See Bibliography, and also Campbell, *The Masks of God: Occidental Mythology*, pp. 95–110, and Index under Christ; Orpheus; Tammuz; Cumont; Jung, *Psychology and Religion*, "A Psychological Approach to the Dogma of the Trinity," and also Index under Hermes Trismegistus; Hermetic Philosophy; Mylonas, in toto but see especially p. 274.

133. For example, Herakles, Dionysus, Tammuz, Ba'al, Osiris, and Orpheus.

134. Norris, pp. 2–3; Philippians 2:5–11. For a magnificent depiction of Christus Pantocrator, see Thompson, gen. ed., *The World's Great Religions*, pp. 180–181.

135. Campbell, *The Hero with a Thousand Faces*, p. 41; John 1:1–14; Perry, *Lord of the Four Quarters*, p. 14; Ruttan. Once we relate the concepts of Ma'at, Dharma, Tao, the Torah, and the Greco-Roman Logos, their close parallels become apparent. They are each instances of the divine creative ordering of the cosmos, including human, natural, and spiritual planes. The Torah has, strictly speaking, more to do with human society and its relationship in cultus and praxis to the divine, but the notion of Wisdom in Proverbs picks up the cosmic dimension.

136. This is equally true of John's Christ-as-Logos creation myth, and Christ's reordering of the world through his crucifixion. Christ hangs crucified upon the World Tree, the *axis mundi*, and by means of his sacrificial death and atonement (at-one-ment) with his Father he reconstitutes this axis so that the superabundance of God's healing, redeeming, restorative love can flood again into the earthly dimension.

137. See the Gospels for the multiplication of loaves and fishes, the withering of a fig tree, the calming of a storm, and numerous accounts of exorcisms and healings. See also Smith, *Jesus the Magician*.

138. John 5:19. The Son's "obedience" (a receptivity to the power and will of the Father) constitutes Jesus' "right ordering" of his own inner world.

139. John 1:4, 5, and 8:12; Philippians 2:5–8; Waida, "Symbolism of 'Descent.' "

140. Hebrews, in toto but note especially 3:1; 4:14–15; 9.

141. Kelly: See Index under Christology; Norris, in toto.

142. Myers; Peters, in toto but especially pp. 30 ff.

143. Ibid., p. 56.

144. Frazer, pp. 103–105; Peters, pp. 82, 102, 182 ff.

145. Frazer, pp. 103–104.

146. Kantorowicz.

147. Hocart, Chapter 10.

148. Eliade, *Patterns in Comparative Religion:* See Index under Tree, of Immortality; Tree, of Life.

149. Hocart. Also see Bibliography under Kingship.

150. Gilmore.

151. Sullivan, ed.

CHAPTER 4: THE KING IN HIS FULLNESS

1. Incarnation is really a process, wherein an individual modulates childhood grandiosity gradually until the world as experienced as *other*, something *outside* the self. Not only is the objective reality of the world perceived more and more, it is also fully entered into and engaged by the Ego. Thus the process of incarnation parallels Heinz Kohut's theory of "transmuting internalization."

2. Campbell, *The Hero with a Thousand Faces*, pp. 193, 217 ff., 238–243, 347 ff.; Engnell, p. 63; Frankfort, *Kingship and the Gods*, pp. 51–52, 252 ff., and Index under Hammurabi; Gonda: Note discussion of Dharma and the king's authority throughout; Perry, *Lord of the Four Quarters*, pp. 14–15; Schele and Freidel pp. 70–73; Tucci, especially pp. 197, 199–200; Waida, "Notes on Sacred Kingship in Central Asia," especially p. 186, and "Symbolism of 'Descent.' "

3. Stevens, *Archetypes*, pp. 174 ff.

4. See Appendix C on the Anima.

5. Hadfield, pp. 10–11, 14–15; Kantorowicz; Murray, pp. 17–23; Tucci, pp. 198–199.

6. This is the initiatory experience so richly elaborated by depth psychologists. See Bibliography under Jungian Thought.

7. I Corinthians 15:54–55.

8. Yahweh brings life and blessing to those who obey his laws, and chastisement and death to those who don't (the wicked, the Egyptians, and the foes of Israel).

9. Campbell, *The Hero with a Thousand Faces*, pp. 115, 126–171; Nikhilananda: See the General Introduction; Prabhupada: The central revelation of the Bhagavad-Gita is one of divine unity in which the terrible and the sublime are experienced as one.

10. The personal Shadow does not contain only negative and destructive qualities. Often it serves as the conservator of unlived "golden" positive qualities and resources. See Bibliography under Jung. For an example, see Jacobi, *The Psychology of C. G. Jung*, pp. 5–23. For a non-Jungian view of the same phenomenon, see Beahrs, pp. 147–150.

11. Castañeda, pp. 39–47, 84–85; Edinger, *Ego and Archetype*, p. 15; Eliade, *Rites and Symbols of Initiation:* See Index under Death; Godwin, pp. 11–15; Moody; Underhill; Whitehead, *Adventures of Ideas*, pp. 259 ff., especially 284–296.

12. Frankfort, *Kingship and the Gods*, p. 21.

13. Ibid., p. 21.

14. Eliade, *The Sacred and the Profane*, pp. 17–22; Frankfort, *Kingship and the Gods*, pp. 295–297; Grottanelli, p. 316; Hocart, Chapter 8; Perry, *Lord of the Four Quarters*, p. 32; Wales, p. 130.

15. Frazer, pp. 164–167; Hocart, pp. 106–110; Jung, *Mysterium Coniunctionis;* See Index under King; Rex; Regina.

16. The Arthur legends are available in a number of imaginative sources. Among them are Lacy, ed.; Malory; Tennyson; Weston: See Index under Fisher King, and especially p. 48; White.

17. Neumann.

18. Eliade, *The Sacred and the Profane*, pp. 49, 370–373. For a related Talmudic idea, see Goldin, pp. 43–46. Here the concept and practice of "building a hedge around the Torah" is explained. After the Romans destroyed the Jewish temple, the Scriptures (and especially the Torah) became the sacred space of the Jewish people. In Exodus 19:21–24, Yahweh sets a boundary at Sinai separating the sacred from the profane. The boundary here is maintained for several reasons, not merely to protect the people from the raw power of Yahweh. Just prior to this, in Exodus 19:10–15, Yahweh seems to set the boundary so that the sacred mountain, and presumably his own sacred essence as well, will not be defiled.

19. Exodus 33:17–23.

20. Graves, p. 56.

21. Prabhupada, pp. 177–188.

22. II Samuel 6:1–11.

23. Freud, *Totem and Taboo*, pp. 46, 47.

24. Frazer, pp. 686–689.

25. Hadfield, p. 116. Also see Note 1 to this chapter.

26. Covering the face or raising the arms reverentially (palms up-turned in blessing) are examples of this, as are bowing, kneeling, and "kowtowing."

27. There is a considerable literature covering this. See, for example, Eliade, *Patterns in Comparative Religion*, pp. 231, 381; Frank-fort, *Kingship and the Gods*, pp. 271–274, 318 ff.; Turner, especially Chapter 3.

28. Possession, too, is well documented. See, for example, Jacobi, *Complex, Archetype, Symbol*, pp. 12–19, 66–68; Jung, *Psyche and Symbol*, pp. 9 ff., especially 13–14; Stevens, *Archetypes*, pp. 121 ff., 212–214, 221.

29. Ibid., pp. 122–124.

30. Genesis 1:22, 28.

31. Watts and Elisofan.

32. Eliade, *Patterns in Comparative Religion:* See Index under Tree, Cosmic; Tree, of Life; Engnell, pp. 12, 23, 25, 61, 67; Perry, *Lord of the Four Quarters*, pp. 16–17; Schele and Freidel, pp. 90–91; Wales: See Index under Tree, Sacred.

33. Eliade, *Patterns in Comparative Religion*, pp. 257.

34. John 15:1–7.

35. Frankfort, *Kingship and the Gods*, Chapter 5; Perry, *Lord of the Four Quarters*, p. 35.

36. Miller, *The Drama of the Gifted Child*, pp. 16, 32, 35.

37. See Bibliography.

38. Whether the king served as the high priest and performed sacrifices—vegetable, animal, or human—*or* was himself offered as the supreme sacrifice, the aim was to appease or provision the Gods so that they would provision the kingdom. In the Book of Hebrews, Christ serves as both high priest and sacrifice. His purpose is to provision the world with new life, restructure the cosmos according to the divine order, and appease the Father. The literature in this area is sizable. See, for example, Engnell, p. 35; Hadfield, p. 31; Hocart: See Index under Sacrifice; Murray; Schele and Freidel: See Index under Bloodletting Rituals;

Frazer: See Index under King, Sacrifice(s); Sacrificial King at Rome; Valeri.

39. Again, the literature in this field is remarkably extensive. A few examples must suffice: Frankfort, *The Birth of Civilization:* see Appendix; Perry, *Lord of the Four Quarters,* p. 212; Schele and Freidel, pp. 45–55; The Editors of Time-Life Books, *The Age of the God-Kings,* pp. 37 ff.

40. Cohn-Haft, pp. 77 ff.; Frankfort, *Kingship and the Gods,* pp. 51–52, 149, 251, 252, 277–278; Gonda, pp. 36–37, 52–54; Hocart: See Index under Law; Commandments; Perry, *Lord of the Four Quarters,* p. 14–16; Richards, p. 153; Tucci, p. 197; Waida, "Symbolism of 'Descent,' " pp. 64, 69, 78; Wheatley, pp. 65–71, 86–87, 91, 102–103.

41. Breasted, *The Dawn of Conscience,* pp. 99–101; Frankfort, *Ancient Egyptian Religion,* p. 130, *Kingship and the Gods,* pp. 207, 212, and *The Birth of Civilization* (see Appendix); Keightley, pp. 211–225; Richards, pp. 146–147; Waida, "Sacred Kingship in Early Japan," p. 334; Wheatley, p. 66.

42. Ibid., p. 85.

43. Hooke, *Myth, Ritual, and Kingship,* pp. 159 ff.

44. Engnell, p. 12, 37, 68; Hooke, *Myth, Ritual and Kingship,* p. 205; Myers, pp. 258–262.

45. Engnell, pp. 68; Frankfort, *Kingship and the Gods:* See Index under Apophis, as Enemy of Re; Marduk, as Hero of Creation Story; Hooke, *Myth, Ritual and Kingship,* p. 205; Myers, pp. 12, 15, 37, 68; Perry, *Lord of the Four Quarters,* pp. 206–207; Thomas, ed., pp. 128 ff.

46. This is the concept known as sympathetic magic. What is done on earth through ritual process is accomplished in the divine realm as well. See Edwards, p. 291; Eliade, *Patterns in Comparative Religion:* See Index under Magic; Frazer, pp. 12 ff.

47. Breasted, *The Dawn of Conscience,* p. 201.

48. Ibid., pp. 202–203.

49. Engnell, pp. 33 ff.; Frankfort, *Kingship and the Gods,* p. 295; Wales, p. 28.

50. Eliade, *Cosmos and History.*

51. Jonson, p. 352.

52. In parallel to the ancient idea "as above, so below" (an idea grounded in sympathetic magic), Jungians cite the psychological corollary "as within, so without."

53. See, for example, Perry, *Lord of the Four Quarters*, pp. 216–217.

54. An Ego must objectify its inner psychic contents and the outer world, and experience the two as separate, in order to achieve a consolidated sense of its own reality.

55. This unwanted material is primarily Shadow territory. But it may equally be a man's Anima, or any number of other complexes, which are trying to communicate lost elements of the Self to the Ego.

56. Hamilton, p. 328.

57. I Kings 3:16–27.

58. Frankfort, *Kingship and the Gods:* See Index under Ptah, as Creator; Language.

59. John Kelly: See Index under Logos.

60. Campbell, *The Masks of God: Occidental Mythology*, p. 83.

61. Eliade, *Patterns in Comparative Religion:* See Index under Mountain; Mountain, Cosmic; Wales.

62. Schele and Freidel, p. 239.

63. Edwards, pp. 287–293.

64. Following are only a few references from the vast literature on this cross-cultural belief: Breasted, *The Dawn of Conscience*, Chapters 2–6; Eliade, *Patterns in Comparative Religion*, Chapter 3; Hadfield, p. 12; Malandra; Peterson: See Index under Sun Worship; Quetzalcoatl; Sacrifice, Human; Reichel-Dolmatoff, Part Two; Waida, "Sacred Kingship in Early Japan," pp. 321, 327–330, 335–336; Wales, pp. 23–24.

65. Breasted, *The Dawn of Conscience*, Chapters 2–6; Cohn-Haft, pp. 77 ff. (Hammurabi is portrayed here as the sun. By his association with the sun he has the task of "enlightening" the land and furthering the welfare of the people); Campbell, *The Masks of God: Occidental Mythology*, p. 75 ff.; Edwards, pp. 291–292; Gonda, Part I, pp. 49, 60; Parrinder, pp. 111–121; Malandra; Waida, "Sacred Kingship in Early Japan"; J. Wilson, Chapters 2–4: He links the emergence of Egyptian civilization with the theology of the pharaoh as the son of the Sun. Also, in China, the emergence of advanced civilization is associated with the shift from chthonic to sky-oriented religion.

66. Perry, *Lord of the Four Quarters*, pp. 23 ff.

67. Miller, *The Drama of the Gifted Child*; Rubin, Chapters 3 and 6.

68. Ibid., pp. 54–59.

69. Gilmore, for example, pp. 93–98; Gillette, "Men and Intimacy."

CHAPTER 5: GENERATIVE MAN

1. See Bibliography.

2. Gilmore makes two exceptions to the general pattern. He finds the protector and provider functions absent in the cultures of Tahiti and the Semai. To us it seems these two cultures are possessed by or "mainlining" the Lover. Gilmore uses the old socialization model to account for gender differences, but we prefer a depth psychological biosocial orientation. See Gillette's review of *Manhood in the Making* in *Wingspan*.

3. See Browning, Chapters 6 and 7, and Epilogue.

4. Ibid., pp. 158–159.

5. Ibid., p. 183.

6. Ibid., p. 154.

7. Ibid., p. 145.

8. John 8:19.

9. Proverbs 29:18.

10. Heinz Kohut and others talk about mirroring as being the method by which we affirm each other's sense of self. We can mirror others only by truly beholding them. By paying full and appreciative attention to them we confirm their sense of reality, including the reality and validity of their feelings, whether or not these feelings seem appropriate to a given situation.

11. This touches on the psychological issue of merger. Merger is in evidence when we experience others as mere extensions of ourselves, or ourselves as extensions of others. We feel the other should act and feel the same as we do. If we find it difficult to imagine acting autonomously from others, we can be sure we are merged with them. In the dysfunctional system of merger (referred to now as "codependency") neither person is free to value either self or other. There is no "confirming face." Mergers may also be viewed as archaic self-object relationships.

12. Firmness is a kind of aversive/aggressive response to abuse and invasion at the hands of another. It is a declaration of legitimate autonomy. Every individual has a right to repel the verbally and physicall abusive behaviors of others. Firm, controlled aggression is very different from repressed rage. No one is gratuitously or unnecessarily hurt by firmness.

Used judiciously, it is an expression of territorial integrity. Ernest Wolf offers a helpful discussion of adversarial self-object needs and self functions in his outstanding recent book *Treating the Self*.

13. Those who have paranoiac tendencies may imagine unreal dangers. Yet naïveté about life's dangers can be equally destructive. Dangers to our psychological and physical well-being do indeed exist. A generative man is Self-confirmed enough to distinguish between real and imagined dangers, and to respond according to the destructive potentials of real dangers. Firmness without hostility will under most circumstances defuse the danger. In other circumstances, however, the emotional force anger provides may be needed as an ally. Violence may be the only appropriate response in still other circumstances. It is never wise to ignore a danger, or minimize the genuine threats it carries. Clear and present dangers must be confronted and dealt with by some combination of firmness, anger, and force. Inability to understand this we believe to be a manifestation of massive denial and clear evidence of the absence of an adequate Warrior initiation.

14. Ulanov provides a thorough explanation of the dynamics of envy.

15. Children see through exaggerated praise. Furthermore, such praise can encourage them to develop a false Self, often histrionic or coquettish. False praise also may undermine a parent's credibility—consequently depriving the child of the sense of security and parent-mediated confirmation of reality.

16. Grandiosity is one part of an inflated sense of talent and ability. It stems from an infantile sense of primacy. Realistic greatness, on the other hand, involves a grounded sense of actual capabilities (both strengths and weaknesses). When experienced as a negative inflation, grandiosity can make a person feel worthless. A sense of realistic greatness affirms that the truth lies somewhere in between. It allows a person to be fully and realistically engaged with the world. See the important works of Heinz Kohut and Ernest Wolf for the most outstanding psychoanalytic discussions of these topics.

17. Often we are unaware of our inner worlds, our unconscious defects and resources. A generative man attempts to hold another's true Self (his realistic greatness) up for him and show it to him, so that he can eventually take it back and live out of it.

18. This technique, a major part of a depth psychological process, is also used in hypnotherapy. See Beahrs; Hannah.

19. The rule of a sacred king was based on a just ordering of

society—one that favored the weak over the strong. Since the generative man is concerned with "mutuality" (Browning, p. 153), it follows that by accessing the King he will be affirming the rights of the oppressed, including the oppressed of the feminine gender, of other races, cultures, creeds, and species.

20. See Browning's discussion of Erikson's thinking with respect to industrial society and ecology (pp. 191–192).

21. This applies to his own internal dialogues, as well as his relationships with others. He seldom takes things at face value, but always has an eye out for what is behind the surface personality. He listens for the subtle valences that betray inner unconscious agendas.

22. According to Jung, maturation involves growing toward greater consciousness. This means integrating split-off, repressed, and rejected parts of our Selves. Erikson also sees a growth in maturity as the hallmark of Generative Man. See Browning, Chapters 6 and 7.

23. Moral seriousness endows a man with the capacity and the willingness to take responsibility to reconcile with the positive aspects of his Shadow. At the same time a morally serious man confronts Shadow aspects which, after a thorough process of sifting and examining, can be seen to be negative or evil. This man takes seriously all of the repressed or underdeveloped aspects of his once whole Self. He confronts and comforts everything that he is.

24. The Transpersonal Other we are referring to here is the Jungian image of the Self, the Diamond Body within, and the religious image of God. Where a man's purposes become scattered, his causes fanatical, and his personality shallow, he has no genuine experience of and commitment to his deep Self.

25. Neumann.

26. Browning, pp. 193–197; Gillette, "Men and Intimacy."

CHAPTER 6: THE SHADOW KING AS THE TYRANT USURPER

1. Jungians have a saying that the rhinoceros can gore you only if you have a hole the size and shape of his horn.

2. For a similar, Jungian view of this situation, see Stein, ed., *Jungian Analysis*, especially Chapter 16: "Psychopathology and Analysis" by Sandner and Beebe; Jung, "Dream Symbolism in Relation to Alchemy," in *The Portable Jung*, especially pp. 416–420.

3. Jacobi, *Complex, Archetype, Symbol*, pp. 22–25, and the chapter titled "Archetype."

4. Edinger, *Ego and Archetype*, p. 15, provides a discussion of negative inflation; Jacobi, *Complex, Archetype, Symbol:* See Index under Inflation; Stein, ed.: See Index under Inflation.

5. This is what psychologists call the "objective Ego" or the "observing Ego." See Beahrs: See Index under Ego; Stein, ed., p. 178.

6. See Note 4 to this chapter. Also see Jung, *Psychology and Religion:* See Index under Possession.

7. See Note 6 to this chapter.

8. Edinger, *Ego and Archetype*, pp. 31 ff.; Nilsson, pp. 52–59, "Hybris and Nemesis."

9. Walker: See headings under Vain; Vainglory.

10. See Notes 5 to 8 to this chapter. Pretensions to godhood are the result of the Self's inflation of the Ego. The Ego remains in the original merged condition with the Self, having failed to distinguish itself and establish what Edinger calls an Ego-Self axis.

11. Euripedes, *The Bacchae.*

12. Aeschylus, *Agamemnon*, in Oates and Murphey, pp. 163 ff.

13. Hamilton, pp. 278–279.

14. Sophocles, *Antigone*, in Oates and Murphey, pp. 273 ff.

15. Sophocles, *Antigone*, in Grene and Lattimore, eds., *Sophocles I*, p. 204.

16. See, for example, such stories as the punishment of the pharaoh (Exodus 1–15), the Tower of Babel (Genesis 11:1–9), the punishment of David for his arrogance in the Bathsheba and Uriah incident (II Samuel 12:1–23) and the wicked kings of Israel (throughout the Books of Kings and Chronicles).

17. Barnstone, ed., pp. 29–30, "The Fall of Satan" (from the Jewish Haggadah). This myth may be based on the much earlier Canaanite story of Ashtar the Tyrant, found in the Ba'al cycle of myths which were unearthed at Ugarit; Pritchard, ed., p. 111–112.

18. See Notes 3 and 5 to this chapter. Also see Jung, *Psyche and Symbol*, pp. 125–127.

19. Campbell, *The Power of Myth*, pp. 117–118.

20. Campbell, *The Hero with a Thousand Faces:* See Index under Holdfast.

21. Inflation frequently induces paranoia, because unconsciously the inflated person knows his condition to be false. He needs to maintain

it, though, as a defense against his feelings of inadequacy, shame, and worthlessness. Paranoia is an uncontrolled state of heightened vigilance. The vigilance must be sustained for the inflated person to recognize any potential threats to his exaggerated sense of importance. Because he believes he is the center of the world, the paranoid believes that others have nothing better to do than persecute *him*.

22. Edinger, *Ego and Archetype*, Chapter 1; Marcuse, Chapter 2, pp. 168–169; Miller, *The Drama of the Gifted Child;* Stevens, *Archetypes*, pp. 140 ff.

23. Moore and Gillette.

24. Like any of the full conceptions of the sacred king, or of the Self, the Transpersonal Other reflects the basic biological and psychological truth that most men and women are asymmetric mixtures of masculine and feminine qualities.

25. Millon, *Disorders of Personality*.

26. Ibid.

CHAPTER 7: THE SHADOW KING AS THE WEAKLING ABDICATOR

1. Aldred.
2. See Bibliography under Literature; King Arthur.
3. Peters, especially Chapters 1–4.
4. Myers, pp. 247–278; Peters, pp. 37–59, 197–198.
5. Ibid., p. 4.
6. Jacobi, *Complex, Archetype, Symbol*, p. 48 and note 48.

CHAPTER 8: HISTORICAL PATTERNS OF ACCESSING THE KING

1. Breasted, *A History of Egypt:* See Index under Imhotep. (Imhotep has been called the first individual in history); Campbell, *The Power of Myth*, p. 58; Frankfort, *The Birth of Civilization*, p. 107; Neumann: See Index under Individual(s); J. Wilson, p. 33.

2. Breasted, *A History of Egypt*, Chapter 5, especially p. 105; J. Wilson: See Index under Art; Intellect.

3. Eliade, *Cosmos and History:* See Index under History.

4. Pritchard, ed., pp. 36–37.

5. Jung, *Man and His Symbols*, pp. 73–75.

6. Jung, *Psyche and Symbol*, pp. xxvii–xxxi. In depth psychology individuals are encouraged to become progressively more conscious of the split-off aspects of themselves, for this is the path to maturity. Jungians call this process individuation. See Bibliography under Jungian Thought and also Edinger, *The Creation of Consciousness*; Jacobi, *The Psychology of C. G. Jung*, pp. 21 ff. For a similar, non-Jungian approach, see Browning, especially his discussion of Erikson's work.

7. Gilmore, pp. 30 ff.; Webster, pp. 59 ff.

8. Ibid.

9. Breasted, *A History of Egypt*, pp. 98 ff.; J. Wilson, p. 263.

10. Barr, pp. 77–79, 230–232, also Index under Democracy.

11. Kirk and Raven: See Index under God(s). Xenophanes is of special interest in connection with this. See pp. 167–172.

12. Ibid.

13. Plato: See "Apology," "Phaedo," pp. 86, 115, "Republic": Book VIII, p. 415, Book IX, p. 476, and Book X.

14. Dodds, in toto but especially p. 81; Pagels, Chapter 6.

15. Dodds, p. 82.

16. Plato, pp. 52, 56.

17. Pagels, Chapter 6. Note p. 161; Robinson, ed., *The Nag Hammadi Library*, pp. 141, 205, 231, 233, 235.

18. Jesus says he has come to fulfill the Torah (Matthew 5:17 ff). Then he proceeds to explain what he means—he proposes that to fulfill it he has internalized the Torah.

19. John 8:19.

20. John 6:38.

21. His human Ego is displayed when Jesus pleads to be saved from death (Matthew 26:26–46). At the same time the Christ in him calls himself the "Son of Man," and proclaims himself at the trial before Caiaphas (Matthew 26:64).

22. Luke 17:2–21.

23. John 14:20.

24. Pagels: See Index under Light Within; Robinson: See Index under Light.

25. Pagels, Chapter 5. Note p. 128.

26. Pagels, p. 179.

27. Tillich, *Systematic Theology*, pp. 13, 180, 208.

28. These two formative documents of the young United States were written by men steeped in the classical cultures of Greece and Rome, as well as the prophetic tradition of the Hebraic Old Testament. See Huston Smith, p. 254.

29. See Peter Berger's work on modernity, *Facing Up to Modernity*, in toto; Jung, *Mysterium Coniunctionis*, pp. 124, 362, and *Psychology and Alchemy*, pp. 16, 480.

30. The demythologization of the Judeo-Christian tradition was led by the great biblical scholar Rudolf Bultmann. He examined Christian myths and legends, and the miraculous events they depicted, in order to reveal their oral and literary development, and to hypothesize about the natural causes and events that might lie behind them. For a discussion of demythologization, refer to Tillich, *Systematic Theology*, and see Index under Demythologization.

31. Through his rational thinking Kant restored the central mystery of the soul. He demonstrated that we can know nothing of a supposedly objective reality beyond what comes to us through the subjective modes of perception and cognition. Einstein proved mathematically that Newtonian theory is valid only for a kind of shorthand understanding of the "real" world. Time and space, Einstein found, are not what we perceive them to be. Heisenberg discovered that there is no way to observe subatomic phenomena without interfering with them. He was among the subatomic physicists to disclose the mysterious nature of the subatomic dimension.

32. Jung, *Man and His Symbols*, pp. 75 ff., and *Psyche and Symbol*, pp. xxxi ff., 30–31, 38.

33. Ibid.

34. Jung, *Man and His Symbols*, pp. 72–75, 84 ff, 91, and *Psyche and Symbol*, pp. 23–24, 126.

35. Jung, *Man and His Symbols*, pp. 92.

36. Jung, *Man and His Symbols*, pp. 93–94, and *Modern Man in Search of a Soul*, p. 215.

37. Capra: Note especially the impact subatomic physics has had on the culture, as examined in Chapter 1.

38. Ibid., Chapter 12, especially p. 184.

39. Ibid., pp. 153 ff.

40. Ibid., Chapter 14.

41. Ibid., p. 215.

42. Ibid.

43. The Editors of Time-Life Books, *Voyage Through the Universe*, pp. 104 ff.

44. Ibid., p. 105.

45. Ibid., pp. 105 ff.

46. Ibid.

47. Ibid., pp. 108 ff.

48. Jaffé, pp. 29 ff.

49. Ibid., p. 30.

50. Ibid., p. 35.

51. Nikhilananda, "Discussion of Brahman in the Upanishads," pp. 25 ff.

52. Nicholas of Cusa.

53. Jaffé, Chapter 4.

54. Nicholas of Cusa.

55. Wei, pp. 181–183.

56. Eliade, *The Sacred and the Profane*, p. 45.

CHAPTER 9: WELCOMING THE KING INTO OUR LIVES

1. The Editors of Time-Life Books, *Voyage Through the Universe*, pp. 119 ff.

2. Eliade, *Cosmos and History*, Chapter 2.

3. The Editors of Time-Life Books, *Voyage Through the Universe*, p. 118; Eliade, *Cosmos and History*, pp. 114–115; Ferris, Chapter 9; Morris: See Index under Universe.

4. Basham, pp. 320–322.

5. Eliade, *Cosmos and History*, Chapter 2, *Patterns in Comparative Religion* (see Index under Creation, Reenactment), and *The Sacred and the Profane*, Chapter 1; Frankfort, *Kingship and the Gods*: See Index under New Year's Festival; Sed Festival. See also Parts III and V, Chapter 17.

6. Jung, *Psychology and Religion*, p. 155, note 6.

7. Jung, *Psyche and Symbol*, especially p. 253; Loye: See Index under Holography.

8. The plethora of books marketed on love and relationships is ample testimony to this. Among the most useful are Hendrix; R. Johnson; Rubin.

9. Freud believed the Oedipus complex was the central feature of

neurosis, which he saw as primarily a relational problem between child and father. Much of Freud's work is about father issues. This is really the thrust of his *Totem and Taboo*—he frankly admits that he doesn't know what to make of the "mother-goddess" (read "Mother") in his reconstruction of the psychological basis of childhood/tribal relational issues.

10. Miller, *The Drama of the Gifted Child:* See Index under Compulsion to Repeat.

11. Miller, *The Drama of the Gifted Child.* See Bibliography for Miller's other books. Hendrix is also instructive. Also see, for comparison, Jung, *Psyche and Symbol*, pp. 113–147.

12. The Jungian literature on the Shadow is extensive. See, for example, Jacobi, *The Psychology of C. G. Jung:* See Index under Shadow; Jung, *Man and His Symbols*, "Approaching the Unconscious," and *Psyche and Symbol*, pp. 6–9.

13. The literature on the Anima is also comprehensive. See, for example, Jacobi, *The Psychology of C. G. Jung:* See Index under Anima/ Animus; Jung, *Psyche and Symbol*, pp. 9–22; Pedersen: See Index under Anima; Sanford, *The Invisible Partners.*

14. A few examples from the vast number of works on dreams and Jungian dream interpretation: Jung, *Man and His Symbols*, pp. 27–45, *Psychology and Alchemy*, Part II, "Individual Dream Symbolism in Relation to Alchemy," and *Psychology and Religion* (see Index under Dream(s)); Sanford, *Dreams.*

15. Our theory of the masculine Self is a gender-specific extension of Jung's concept of the androgynous Self. For comparison, see Bibliography under Jungian Thought. Refer to Indexes under Self. In addition, see Campbell, *The Hero with a Thousand Faces*, pp. 126–149.

16. Miller, *The Drama of the Gifted Child:* See Index under Introject and Introjection.

17. See Hendrix. He developed a theory of the Imago (emotionally formed images of parents and other significant persons from the first few years of life), which the inner Child carries. This bears comparison with the concept of parental introjects.

18. Miller, *The Drama of the Gifted Child*, for example, p. 86.

19. Robert Johnson, especially Chapters 14 and 19; Miller, *The Drama of the Gifted Child*, pp. 112–113.

20. Beahrs, Chapter 6.

21. Millon, *Disorders of the Personality.*

22. Miller, *The Drama of the Gifted Child*, for example, p. 101.

23. Millon, *Disorders of the Personality*, Chapter 14; Perry, *Roots of Renewal*, pp. 61 ff.

24. Ibid., pp. 206–208.

25. Neumann, especially Chapter 4.

26. Scholem, *Major Trends in Jewish Mysticism*, pp. 43 ff.

27. Prabhupada, pp. 180 ff.

28. See Bibliography. See also the story of Moses and the burning bush (Exodus 3:1–6) and the various encounters between Jacob and the god El (Genesis 28–35, especially 28:16–17). See also James, Lecture III, "The Reality of the Unseen"; Otto.

29. The archetypes can never be known directly. Like the DNA-encoded potentials of an organism, archetypes are primordial structures. They can be known only indirectly, through the images and symbols that present themselves to the Ego. For further discussion, see Jacobi, *Complex, Archetype, Symbol,* "Symbol," especially pp. 77 ff.

30. There is an ample literature on active imagination. See Bibliography under Jungian Thought; see also, for example, Jung, *Man and His Symbols*, pp. 206, 207; Hannah, in toto.

31. The injunction against representations of the Deity is here carried to the extreme. See Exodus 20:3–6.

32. For a Freudian analysis of the formation of an individual's God-image, see Rizzuto.

33. Tillich, *Systematic Theology*, pp. 200, 206, 355.

34. Jaffé, pp. 44–49; Scholem, *Major Trends in Jewish Mysticism* (see Index under En Sof) and *Origins of the Kaballah* (see Index under En Sof); Tillich, *The Courage to Be*, pp. 182–190.

35. This is certainly true insofar as what we expect from life is usually what we will experience. Complexes work along these lines. They filter out data that would contradict their assumptions and threaten their existence (their continued "life"). They will allow the Ego to experience only those aspects of reality that confirm their natures. Thus many of us live lives of self-fulfilling prophecies. Not only do complexes color experience; they also affect the outside world so that it changes to fit the expectations held by the complex. See Millon, *Disorders of Personality*, pp. 212–213, 396. Presumably, more positive expectations will also be met.

36. See Chapter 1.

37. Huston Smith, p. 232.

38. See Ashbrook.

39. See Bibliography under Jungian Thought.

40. If you carry out the dialogue with pen and paper, the content of the dialogue will become more conscious. In addition, the dialogue is available then for review later, and you can perhaps discover feelings and ideas which were not apparent initially.

41. Beahrs: See Index under Persecutor Alter-personalities.

42. See, for example, I Corinthians 12:10 and I John 4:1.

43. Evans-Wente, ed., pp. xxxv–lxxxiv.

44. Bettelheim, Chapter 8, especially pp. 58 ff.; Lauzun: See Index under Superego.

45. Jacobi, *The Psychology of C. G. Jung:* See Index under Persona.

46. Millon, *Disorders of Personality*, Chapters 4 and 5.

47. de Waal: Note especially pp. 120–123; Goodall, *In the Shadow of Man*, pp. 186–187.

48. Gilmore, especially Chapter 10; MacKinnon: See Index under Man, Reproductive Behavior; Social Organization, In Apes; Social Organization, In Man.

49. Gilmore, pp. 26–29.

50. Ibid., Chapters 1 and 10.

51. See Bibliography under Mythology and Religion, and Indexes under Initiation.

CHAPTER 10: DANCING THE FOUR QUARTERS

1. Campbell, *The Mythic Image*, p. 359.
2. Neihardt, p. 162.
3. Ibid., pp. 174–175.
4. Browning, p. 189.
5. Neihardt, p. 265.
6. Hesse.
7. Greenleaf, *Servant Leadership*.
8. Bothwell, p. 146.
9. Greenleaf, *Servant*, p. 24.
10. Muvosvi, pp. 8–11.

APPENDIX B: ARCHETYPES AND THE LIMBIC SYSTEM

The argument of this appendix owes a great debt to George S. Everly, Jr.'s synthesis of the most recent work of a number of brain researchers, in his paper *The Biological Bases of Personality: The Contribution of Paleocortical Anatomy and Physiology to Personality and Personality Disorders*. He presented this paper at the First International Congress on Disorders of Personality, in Copenhagen, Denmark, in August 1988.

1. MacLean, p. 257.
2. Ibid., p. 264.
3. Ibid., in toto.
4. George S. Everly, Jr., p. 5.
5. Ibid., p. 5.
6. Ibid., p. 5.
7. Ibid., p. 5.
8. Ibid., p. 6.
9. MacLean, Chapter 21.
10. Everly, p. 7.
11. Everly, p. 8; MacLean, Chapter 19.
12. MacLean, pp. 322 ff.
13. Everly, p. 9; MacLean, Chapters 18–27.
14. MacLean, pp. 497, 498, Chapter 27.

APPENDIX C: ARCHETYPES AND THE ANIMA

1. See Alice Miller's discussion of "poisonous pedagogy" and the role of the mother in destroying her children's sense of Self (references in Bibliography under Miller).

2. An example of this can be found in the Canaanite Baʻal cycle of myths. In them Baʻal, king of the created world, has two enemies to defeat—chaos (Yamm) and death (Mot). He succeeds against Yamm, but is slain by Mot. His sister and his queen, Anath, kills Baʻal and resurrects Baʻal. Anath further proves herself to be Baʻal's comrade-in-arms when she summons his enemies to a banquet, locks the doors, and kills them all.

BIBLIOGRAPHY

1. Brain Research

Ashbrook, James B. *The Human Mind and the Mind of God: Theological Promise in Brain Research*. Lanham, Md.: University Press of America, 1984.

Everly, George S., Jr. "The Biological Bases of Personality: The Contribution of Paleocortical Anatomy and Physiology to Personality and Personality Disorders" (a paper presented to the First International Congress on Disorders of Personality, Copenhagen, Denmark, August 1988).

Harth, Erich. *Windows on the Mind: Reflections on the Physical Basis of Consciousness*. New York: Quill, 1983.

Jaynes, Julian. *The Origin of Consciousness in the Breakdown of the Bicameral Mind*. Boston: Houghton Mifflin, 1976.

MacLean, Paul D. *The Triune Brain in Evolution: Role in Paleocerebral Functions*. New York: Plenum Press, 1990.

Moir, Anne, and David Jessel. *Brain Sex: The Real Difference Between Men and Women*. New York: Carol Publishing Group, 1991.

Restak, Richard M. *The Brain*. New York: Bantam Books, 1984.

2. Jungian Thought

de Castillejo, Irene Claremont Day. *Knowing Woman: A Feminine Psychology*. New York: Harper and Row, 1974. Originally published, New York: G. P. Putnam's Sons, 1973.

Edinger, Edward. *The Creation of Consciousness: Jung's Myth for Modern Man*. Inner City Books, 1984.

―――. *Ego and Archetype*. New York: Penguin Books, 1974. First published, New York: G. P. Putnam's Sons, 1972.

Evans, Richard I. *Jung on Elementary Psychology: A Discussion Between C. G. Jung and Richard I. Evans*. New York: E. P. Dutton, 1976.

Hannah, Barbara. *Encounters with the Soul: Active Imagination as Developed by C. G. Jung*. Boston: Sigo Press, 1981.

Hillman, James, et al. *Puer Papers*. Dallas: Spring Publications, 1979. Especially the chapter by Hillman, "Senex and Puer: An Aspect of the Historical and Psychological Present."

Jacobi, Jolande. *Complex, Archetype, Symbol in the Psychology of C. G. Jung*. Princeton: Princeton University Press, 1959. Originally published as *Komplex/Archetypus/Symbol in der Psychologie C. G. Jungs*. Zurich and Stuttgart: Rascher Verlag, 1957.

―――. *The Psychology of C. G. Jung*. New Haven: Yale University Press, 1973. First published, London: Routledge and Kegan Paul, 1942.

Jaffé, Aniela. *The Myth of Meaning: Jung and the Expansion of Consciousness*. New York: Penguin Books, 1975.

Johnson, Robert. *We: Understanding the Psychology of Romantic Love*. San Francisco: Harper and Row, 1983.

Jung, Carl. *Aion: Researches into the Phenomenology of the Self*, Vol. IX of *The Collected Works of C. G. Jung*. Princeton: Princeton University Press, 1959.

―――. *Man and His Symbols*. New York: Dell, 1964; London: Aldus Books, 1964.

————. *Modern Man in Search of a Soul*. New York: Harcourt Brace Jovanovich, 1933.

————. *Mysterium Coniunctionis: An Inquiry into the Separation and Synthesis of Psychic Opposites in Alchemy*, 2nd ed. Princeton: Princeton University Press, 1970.

————. *The Portable Jung*. Joseph Campbell, ed. New York: Penguin Books, 1971. Reprint of Jung's work in *Aion*, pp. 148 ff.

————. *Psyche and Symbol: A Selection from the Writings of C. G. Jung*. Violet deLaszlo, ed. New York: Doubleday, 1958.

————. *Psychology and Alchemy*, 2nd ed. Princeton, Princeton University Press, 1980, New York: Bollingen Foundation, 1953.

————. *Psychology and Religion: West and East*, 2nd ed. Volume XI of *The Collected Works of C. G. Jung*. Princeton: Princeton University Press, 1958.

Layard, John. *A Celtic Quest*. Dallas: Spring, 1975.

Moore, Robert, and Doug Gillette. *King, Warrior, Magician, Lover: Rediscovering the Archetypes of Mature Masculinity*. San Francisco: Harper, 1990.

Neumann, Erich. *Art and the Creative Unconscious*. Princeton: Princeton University Press, 1959.

Pedersen, Loren E. *Dark Hearts: The Unconscious Forces that Shape Men's Life*. Boston: Shambhala, 1991.

Perry, John Weir. *Roots of Renewal in Myth and Madness: The Meaning of Psychotic Episodes*. San Francisco: Jossey-Bass, 1976.

Sanford, John A. *Dreams: God's Forgotten Language*. New York: J. B. Lippincott, 1968.

————. *The Invisible Partners: How the Male and Female in Each of Us Affects Our Relationships*. New York: Paulist Press, 1980.

Stein, Murray, ed. *Jungian Analysis*. Boston: Shambhala, 1984.

Stevens, Anthony. *Archetypes: A Natural History of the Self*. New York: Quill, 1983. Originally published as *Archetype: A Natural History of the Self*. London: Routledge and Kegan, 1982.

————. *The Roots of War: A Jungian Perspective*. New York: Paragon House, 1989.

Von Franz, Marie Louise. *Projection and Recollection in Jungian Psychology*. Peru, Ill.: Open Court, 1980. Originally published as *Spiegelungen der Seele: Projektion und innere Sammlung*. Stuttgart: Kreuz Verlag, 1978.

Wolff, Toni. "Structural Forms of the Feminine Psyche." Privately printed for the Students Association, C. G. Jung Institute, Zurich, July 1956.

3. Kingship

Basham, A. L. *The Wonder That Was India*. New York: Grove Press, 1959. Originally published 1954.

Bricker, Victoria Reifler. *The Indian Christ, the Indian King: The Historical Substrate of Maya Myth and Ritual*. Austin: University of Texas Press, 1981.

Chaney, William A. *The Cult of Kingship in Anglo-Saxon England*. Berkeley: University of California Press, 1970.

Emery, W. B. *Archaic Egypt*. Harmondsworth, Middlesex, England: Penguin Books, 1961.

Engnell, Ivan. *Studies in Divine Kingship in the Ancient Near East*. Oxford: Basil Blackwell, 1967. First published, Uppsala: Almquist and Wiksells, 1943.

Evans-Pritchard, Edward E. *The Divine Kingship of the Shilluk of the Nilotic Sudan*. Cambridge, Eng.: Cambridge University Press, 1948.

Frankfort Henri. *The Birth of Civilization in the Near East*. New York: Doubleday, 1956.

————. *Kingship and the Gods: A Study of Ancient Near Eastern Religion as the Integration of Society and Nature*. Chicago: University of Chicago Press, 1948.

Gadd, C. J. *Ideas of Divine Rule in the Ancient East*. Schweich Lectures on Biblical Archeology. London: British Academy, 1948.

Gonda, Jan. "Ancient Indian Kingship from the Religious Point of View." *Numen*, Vol. III (1955), pp. 36–71, 122–155; Vol. IV (1956), pp. 4, 24–58, 127–164.

Grottanelli, Christiano. "Kingship in the Ancient Mediterranean World." *Encyclopedia of Religions*, Mircea Eliade, editor in chief. 1987. Vol. VIII, pp. 317–322.

Hadfield, Percival. *Traits of Divine Kingship in Africa*. Westport, Conn.: Greenwood Press, 1979.

Hocart, Arthur Maurice. *Kingship*. London: Oxford University Press, 1927.

Hooke, S. H. *Myth, Ritual, and Kingship: Essays on the Theory and Practice of Kingship in the Ancient Near East and in Israel*. Oxford: Clarendon Press, 1958.

Johnson, Aubrey R. *Sacral Kingship in Ancient Israel.* Cardiff: University of Wales Press, 1955.

Kantorowicz, Ernest H. *The King's Two Bodies: A Study in Medieval Political Theology.* Princeton: Princeton University Press, 1957.

Keightley, David N. "The Religious Commitment: Shang Theology and the Genesis of Chinese Political Culture." *History of Religions,* Vol. XVII, No. 2 (November 1977 or February-May 1978), pp. 211–225.

Kenik, Helen A. "Code of Conduct for a King: Psalm 101." *Journal of Biblical Literature,* Vol. XCV, No. 3 (1976), pp. 391–403.

Kwanten. *Imperial Nomads: A History of Central Asia, 500–1500.* Pittsburgh: University of Pennsylvania Press, 1979.

Malandra, William W. *An Introduction to Ancient Iranian Religion: Readings from the "Avesta" and "Achaemenid" Inscriptions.* Minneapolis: University of Minnesota Press, 1983.

Meyerowitz, Eva L. R. *The Divine Kingship in Ghana and Ancient Egypt.* London: Faber and Faber, 1940.

Mumford, Lewis. *The City in History: Its Origins, Transformations, and Prospects.* New York: Harcourt, Brace and World, 1968.

Murray, M. A. "Evidence for the Custom of Killing the King in Ancient Egypt." *Man,* Vol. XIV (1914), pp. 17–23; London: Royal Anthropological Institute, 1914.

Myers, Henry Allen. *Medieval Kingship.* Chicago: Nelson-Hall, 1982.

Parrinder, Edward G. "Divine Kingship in West Africa." *Numen,* Vol. III (1956), pp. 111–121.

Peters, Edward. *The Shadow King: Rex Inutilis in Medieval Law and Literature, 751–1327.* New Haven: Yale University Press, 1970.

Richards, J. W. "Sacral Kings of Iran." *Mankind Quarterly,* Vol. XX, Nos. 1–2 (1979), pp. 143–160.

Ruttan, Karl. "The Evolution of the Kingship Archetype in the Old Testament." Thesis, Chicago Theological Seminary, 1975.

Schele, Linda, and David A. Freidel. *A Forest of Kings: The Untold Story of the Ancient Maya.* New York: William Morrow, 1990.

Seligman, C. G. *Egypt and Negro Africa: A Study in Divine Kingship.* London: G. Routledge and Sons, 1934.

Tucci, Giuseppe. "The Secret Characters of the Kings of Ancient Tibet." *East and West,* Year VI, No. 3 (October 1955), pp. 197–205.

Valeri, Valerio. *Kingship and Sacrifice: Ritual and Society in Ancient Hawaii,* trans. from Hawaiian by Paula Wissing. Chicago: University of Chicago Press, 1985.

Waida, Manabu. "Notes on Sacred Kingship in Central Asia." *Numen*, Vol. XXIII (December 1976), pp. 179–190.

———. "Sacred Kingship in Early Japan." Ph.D. dissertation, University of Chicago, 1974.

———. "Sacred Kingship in Early Japan: A Historical Introduction." *History of Religions*, Vol. XV, No. 4 (May 1976), pp. 319–342.

———. "Symbolism of 'Descent' in Tibetan Sacred Kingship and Some East Asian Parallels." *Numen*, Vol. XX (April 1973), pp. 60–78.

Wales, H. G. *The Mountain of God: A Study in Early Religion and Kingship*. London: Bernard Quaritch, 1953.

Wilson, John A. *The Culture of Ancient Egypt*. Chicago: University of Chicago Press, 1956. Originally published as *The Burden of Egypt*.

Zuidema, R. Tom. "The Lion in the City: Royal Symbols of Transition in Cuzco." *Journal of Latin American Lore*, Vol. IX:1 (Summer 1983), pp. 39–100.

4. Literature

Aeschylus. *Agamemnon*. In *Greek Literature in Translation*, ed. W. J. Oates and C. T. Murphy. New York: David McKay, 1944.

Blake, William. *The Complete Poetry and Prose*, ed. David Erdman, rev. ed. Berkeley: University of California Press, 1981.

Euripides. *The Bacchae*. In *Euripides V*, ed. David Grene and Richmond Lattimore. New York: Washington Square Press, 1968.

Herbert, Frank. *Dune*. New York: Putnam, 1984.

Hesse, Hermann. *The Journey to the East*, tr. Hilda Rosner. New York: Farrar, Straus and Giroux, 1988.

Lacy, Norris J., ed. *The Arthurian Encyclopedia*. New York: Garland, 1986.

Lewis, C. S. *'Til We Have Faces*. New York: Harcourt Brace Jovanovich, 1956.

Sophocles. In *Sophocles I*, ed. David Grene and Richmond Lattimore. Chicago: University of Chicago Press, 1954.

Tennyson, Alfred. *Idylls of the King*, ed. Gray. New Haven: Yale University Press, 1983.

Tolkien, J.R.R. *The Lord of the Rings*. New York: Ballantine Books, 1965.

White, T. H. *The Once and Future King*. London: Collins, 1958.

5. Mythology and Religion

Albright, William F. *Yahweh and the Gods of Canaan: A Historical Analysis of Two Contrasting Faiths*. New York: Doubleday, 1968.

Barnstone, Willis, ed. *The Other Bible*. San Francisco: Harper and Row, 1984.

Breasted, James H. *The Dawn of Conscience: The Sources of Our Moral Heritage in the Ancient World*. New York: Charles Scribner's Sons, 1933.

Campbell, Joseph. *The Hero with a Thousand Faces*. Princeton: Princeton University Press, 1949.

————. *The Masks of God: Creative Mythology*. New York: Viking Press 1968.

————. *The Masks of God: Occidental Mythology*. New York: Viking Press, 1964.

————. *The Power of Myth*. New York: Doubleday, 1988.

Carrasco, David. *Quetzalcoatl and the Irony of Empire: Myths and Prophecies in the Aztec Tradition*. Chicago: University of Chicago Press, 1982.

Cohn-Haft, Louis. *Source Readings in Ancient History: The Ancient Near East*. New York: Thomas Y. Crowell, 1965.

Cumont, Franz. *The Mysteries of Mithra*. New York: Dover Publications, 1956. First published by Open Court, 1903.

Dodds, E. R. *Pagan and Christian in an Age of Anxiety: Some Aspects of Religious Experience from Marcus Aurelius to Constantine*. New York: W. W. Norton, 1965.

Eliade, Mircea. *Cosmos and History: The Myth of the Eternal Return*. New York: Harper and Row, 1959; Bollingen Foundation, 1954.

————. *Patterns in Comparative Religion*. New York: World Publishing, 1963. Originally published as *Traite d'histoire des religions*. Paris: Editions Payot.

————. *Rites and Symbols of Initiation: The Mysteries of Birth and Rebirth*. New York: Harper and Row, 1958.

————. *The Sacred and the Profane: The Nature of Religion: The Significance of Religious Myth, Symbolism, and Ritual Within Life and Culture*. New York: Harcourt Brace Jovanovich, 1959. Originally published in German by Rowohlt Taschenbuch Verlag, 1957.

Forsyth, Neil. *The Old Enemy: Satan and the Combat Myth*. Princeton: Princeton University Press, 1987.

Frankfort, Henri. *Ancient Egyptian Religion.* New York: Harper and Row, 1961; New York: Columbia University Press, 1948.

Frazer, James G. *The Golden Bough: A Study in Magic and Religion,* 12 vols., 3d ed., London, 1915; New York: Macmillan, 1922; paperback, 1963.

Gaer Joseph. *How the Great Religions Began.* New York: New American Library, Signet Books, 1954. Originally published 1929.

Godwin, Joscelyn. *Mystery Religions in the Ancient World.* San Francisco: Harper and Row, 1981; London: Thames and Hudson, 1981.

Graves, Robert. *The Greek Myths,* 2 vols. Harmondsworth, Middlesex, England: Penguin Books, 1955.

Hadas, Moses. *The Apocrypha: An American Translation.* New York: Alfred A. Knopf and Random House, 1959.

Hamilton, Edith. *Mythology: Timeless Tales of Gods and Heroes.* New York: New American Library, 1940.

Henderson, Joseph L. *Thresholds of Initiation.* Middletown, Conn.: Wesleyan University Press, 1967.

Hooke, S. H. *Middle Eastern Mythology.* New York: Penguin Books, 1963.

James, William. *The Varieties of Religious Experience.* New York: New American Library, 1958.

Jobes, Gertrude. *Dictionary of Mythology, Folklore, and Symbols.* Metuchen, N.J.: Scarecrow Press, 1962.

Moody, Raymond. *Life After Life.* New York: Bantam Books, 1975.

Mylonas, George E. *Eleusis and the Eleusinian Mysteries.* Princeton: Princeton University Press, 1961.

Otto, Rudolf. *The Idea of the Holy.* New York: Oxford University Press, 1923.

Pagels, Elaine. *The Gnostic Gospels.* New York: Vintage Books, Random House, 1979.

Perry, John Weir. *Lord of the Four Quarters: Myths of the Royal Father.* New York: G. Braziller, 1966; New York: Collier Books, Macmillan, 1970.

Pritchard, James. B., ed. *The Ancient Near East,* Volume I: *An Anthology of Texts and Pictures.* Princeton: Princeton University Press, 1958.

Reichel-Dolmatoff, Gerardo. *Amazonian Cosmos: The Sexual and Religious Symbolism of the Tukano Indians,* trans. from Spanish. Chicago: University of Chicago Press, 1971.

Robinson, James M., ed. *The Nag Hammadi Library*. San Francisco: Harper and Row, 1977.

Scholem, Gershom. *Major Trends in Jewish Mysticism*. New York: Schocken Books, 1946.

————. *Origins of the Kaballah*, ed. R. J. Werblowsky and trans. Allan Arkush. Princeton: Princeton University Press, for the Jewish Publication Society, 1987. Originally published as *Ursprung und Anfänge der Kabbala*. Berlin: Walter de Gruyter, 1962.

Seltman, Charles T. *The Twelve Olympians*. New York: Thomas Y. Crowell, 1960.

Smith, Huston. *The Religions of Man*. New York: Harper and Row, 1965.

Smith, Morton. *Jesus the Magician*. San Francisco: Harper and Row, 1978.

Sullivan, Lawrence, ed. *Healing and Restoring: Health and Medicine in the World's Religious Traditions*. New York: Macmillan, 1988.

Thomas, D. Winton, ed. *Documents from Old Testament Times*. New York: Harper and Brothers, 1961.

Underhill, Evelyn. *Mysticism*. New York: E. P. Dutton, 1911.

Walker, J.B.R. *The Comprehensive Concordance to the Holy Scriptures*. New York: Macmillan, 1948. First published by S. A. Weston, 1929.

Watts, Alan, and Eliot Elisofon. *Erotic Spirituality: The Vision of Konarak*. New York: Collier Books, Macmillan, 1971.

Weston, Jesse L. *From Ritual to Romance: An Account of the Holy Grail from Ancient Ritual to Christian Symbol*. New York: Doubleday, 1957. First published by Cambridge University Press, 1920.

Wheatley, Paul. *The Pivot of the Four Quarters*. Aldine Publishing, 1971.

6. Other Psychologies

Beahrs, John. *Unity and Multiplicity: Multilevel Consciousness of Self in Hypnosis, Psychiatric Disorder and Mental Health*. New York: Brunner/Mazel, 1982.

Bettleheim, Bruno. *Freud and Man's Soul*. New York: Alfred A. Knopf, 1983.

Browning, Don. *Generative Man: Psychoanalytic Perspectives*. New York: Dell, 1975; Phildelphia: Westminster Press, 1973.

Freud, Sigmund. *Moses and Monotheism*. New York: Alfred A. Knopf, 1939.

———. *Totem and Taboo*. New York: W. W. Norton, 1950; London: Routledge and Kegan Paul, 1950.

Hendrix, Harville. *Getting the Love You Want*. New York: Henry Holt, 1988.

Keen, Sam. *Fire in the Belly: On Being a Man*. New York: Bantam, 1991.

Lauzun, Gérard. *Sigmund Freud: The Man and His Theories*. Greenwich, Conn.: Fawcett, 1962; Paris: Pierre Seghers, 1962.

Marcuse, Herbert. *Eros and Civilization: A Philosophical Inquiry into Freud*. Boston: Beacon Press, 1955.

Miller, Alice. *The Drama of the Gifted Child: How Narcissistic Parents Form and Deform the Emotional Lives of their Talented Children*. New York: Basic Books, 1981. Originally published in German as *Das Drama des begabten Kindes*. Frankfurt am Main: Suhrkamp, 1979.

———. *For Your Own Good: Hidden Cruelty in Child-Rearing and the Roots of Violence*. New York: Farrar, Straus and Giroux, 1984. Originally published in German as *Am Anfang war Erziehung*. Frankfurt am Main: Suhrkamp, 1980.

———. *Thou Shalt Not Be Aware: Society's Betrayal of the Child*. Farrar, Straus and Giroux, 1984. Originally published in German as *Du sollst nicht merken*. Frankfurt am Main: Suhrkamp, 1981.

Millon, Theodore. *Disorders of Personality: DSM-III: Axis II*. New York: John Wiley and Sons, 1981.

———. *Modern Psychopathology: A Biosocial Approach to Maladaptive Learning and Functioning*. Prospect Heights, Ill.: Waveland Press, 1983.

Rizzuto, Ana-Maria. *The Birth of the Living God: A Psychoanalytic Study*. Chicago: University of Chicago Press, 1979.

Shapiro, David. *Neurotic Styles*. New York: Basic Books, 1965.

Storr, Anthony. *Human Aggression*. New York: Bantam Books, 1968.

Ulanov, Ann and Barry. *Cinderella and Her Sisters: The Envied and the Envying*. Philadelphia: Westminster Press, 1983.

Winnicott, D. W. *Home Is Where We Start From*. New York: W. W. Norton, 1986.

7. Physics and Cosmology

Editors of Time-Life Books. *Voyage Through the Universe: The Cosmos.* Alexandria, Va.: Time-Life Books.

Ferris, Timothy. *The Red Limit: The Search for the Edge of the Universe.* New York: Bantam Books, 1977. Originally published, New York: William Morrow, 1977.

Morris, Richard. *Time's Arrows: Scientific Attitudes Toward Time.* New York: Simon and Schuster, 1984.

8. Primate Ethology, Anthropology, and Ancient History

Albright, William F. *The Archeology of Palestine.* New York: Penguin Books, 1949.

Aldred, Cyril. *Akhenaten, Pharoah of Egypt: A New Study.* London: Sphere Books, Abacus edition, 1972. First published, Thames and Hudson, 1968.

"Andean Civilization." *Encyclopedia Britannica.* Chicago: 1967. Vol I, pp. 889–891.

Ardrey, Robert. *African Genesis: A Personal Investigation into the Animal Origins and Nature of Man.* New York: Dell, 1963.

————. *The Social Contract: A Personal Inquiry into the Evolutionary Sources of Order and Disorder.* New York: Dell, 1971.

Barnett, R. D., and W. Forman. *Assyrian Palace Reliefs and Their Influence on the Sculptures of Babylon and Persia.* Batchworth Press.

Barr, Stringfellow. *The Will of Zeus: A History of Greece.* New York: Dell, 1965.

Berger, Peter. *Facing Up to Modernity: Excursions in Society, Politics, and Religions.* New York: Basic Books, 1977.

Bourne, Geoffrey H. *Primate Odyssey.* New York: G. P. Putnam's Sons, 1974.

Desmond, Adrian J. *The Ape's Reflection.* New York: Dial Press/James Wade, 1979.

de Waal, Frans. *Chimpanzee Politics: Power and Sex Among Apes.* New York: Harper and Row, 1982.

————. *Peacemaking Among Primates.* Cambridge: Harvard University Press, 1989.

323

Editors of Time. *The Epic of Man*. New York: Time, 1961. Especially Chapter 7.

Editors of Time-Life Books. *The Age of the God-Kings, 3000–1500 B.C.* New York: Time-Life Books.

Edwards, I.E.S. *The Pyramids of Egypt*. Harmondsworth, Middlesex, England: Penguin Books, 1947.

Eisler, Riane. *The Chalice and the Blade: Our History, Our Future*. San Francisco: Harper and Row, 1988.

Fisher, Helen E. *The Sex Contract: The Evolution of Human Behavior*. New York: Quill, 1983.

Fossy, Dian. *Gorillas in the Mist*. Boston: Houghton Mifflin, 1983.

Gernet, Jacques. *A History of Chinese Civilization*. New York: Cambridge University Press, 1982. Originally published in French as *Le Monde chinois*. Paris: Librairie Armand Colin, 1972.

Gillette, Douglas. "Men and Intimacy." *Wingspan: A Journal of the Male Spirit*, September 1990.

———. Review of Gilmore, *Manhood in the Making*. In *Wingspan: A Journal of the Male Spirit*, Spring 1991.

Gilmore, David. *Manhood in the Making: Cultural Concepts of Masculinity*. New Haven: Yale University Press, 1990.

Goodall, Jane. *In the Shadow of Man*. Boston: Houghton Mifflin, 1971.

———. *Through a Window: My Thirty Years with the Chimpanzees of Gombe*. Boston: Houghton Mifflin, 1990.

Gurney, O. R. *The Hittites*. New York: Penguin Books, 1952.

MacKinnon, Michael. *The Ape Within Us*. New York: Holt, Rinehart and Winston, 1978.

Morley, Sylvanus G., George W. Brainerd, and Robert J. Sharer. *The Ancient Maya*, 4th ed. Stanford, Calif.: Stanford University Press, 1983.

Morris, Desmond. *Intimate Behavior*. New York: Random House, 1971.

Morris, Desmond. *The Naked Ape: A Zoologist's Study of the Human Animal*. New York: McGraw-Hill, 1967.

Peterson, Frederick. *Ancient Mexico: An Introduction to the Pre-Hispanic Cultures*. Toms River, N.J.: Capricorn Books, 1962. First published 1959.

Steindorff, George, and Keith C. Seele. *When Egypt Ruled the East*. Chicago: University of Chicago Press, 1942.

Thompson, J. Eric S. *The Rise and Fall of Maya Civilization*. Norman: University of Oklahoma Press, 1954. Especially Chapter 2.

Turnbull, Stephen R. *The Book of the Samurai: The Warrior Class of Japan.* New York: W. H. Smith Publishers.

Turner, Victor. *The Ritual Process: Structure and Anti-Structure.* Ithaca, N.Y.: Cornell University Press, 1969.

Webster, Hutton. *Primitive Secret Societies.* New York: Macmillan, 1932.

Wilson, E. O. *On Human Nature.* Cambridge: Harvard University Press, 1978.

9. Theology and Philosophy

Castaeñeda, Carlos. *Journey to Ixtlan: The Lessons of Don Juan.* New York: Pocket Books, 1974. First published, New York: Simon and Schuster, 1972.

Daley, Mary. *Beyond God the Father: Toward a Philosophy of Women's Liberation.* Boston: Beacon Press, 1973.

————. *Gyn/Ecology: The Metaethics of Radical Feminism.* Boston: Beacon Press, 1979.

Evans-Wentz, W. Y., ed. *The Tibetan Book of the Dead*, 3rd ed. New York: Oxford University Press, 1960.

Goldin, Judah. *The Living Talmud.* New York: New American Library, 1957; New Haven: Yale University Press, 1955.

Greenleaf, Robert. *Servant: Retrospect and Prospect.* Indianapolis: The Robert Greenleaf Center, 1980.

————. *Servant Leadership: A Journey into the Nature of Legitimate Power and Greatness.* New York: Paulist Press, 1977.

Kelly, J. N. *Early Christian Doctrines.* New York: Harper and Row, 1960.

Kelly, Sean. *Individuation and the Absolute: Hegel, Jung, and the Path Toward Wholeness.* New York: Paulist Press, forthcoming.

Kirk, G. F., J. E. Raven. *The Presocratic Philosophers.* New York: Cambridge University Press, 1957.

Loye, David. *The Sphynx and the Rainbow: Brain, Mind, and Future Vision.* Boston: Shambhala, 1983.

Nicholas of Cusa. *The Vision of God*, trans. Gurney, ed. Underhill. New York: Ungar, 1960.

Niebuhr, Reinhold. *The Nature and Destiny of Man*, Vol. I. New York: Charles Scribner's Sons, 1964.

Nikhilananda, Swami. *The Upanishads.* New York: Ramakrishna-Vivekananda Center, 1949.

Nilsson, Martin P. *Greek Piety*. New York: W. W. Norton, 1969.

Norris, Richard A., Jr., and William G. Rusch, eds. *The Christological Controversy*, trans. Richard A. Norris. Philadelphia: Fortress Press, 1980.

Plato. "Apology," "Phaedo," and "Republic." In *Plato*, ed. Jowett and Loomis. Roslyn, N.Y.: Walter J. Black, 1942.

Prabhupada. *Bhagavad-Gita As It Is*. Los Angeles: Bhaktivedanta Book Trust, 1968.

Ruether, Rosemary R. *Sexism and God-Talk: Toward a Feminist Theology*. Boston: Beacon Press, 1973.

Teilhard de Chardin, Pierre. *The Phenomenon of Man*. New York: Harper and Row, 1959.

Tillich, Paul. *The Courage to Be*. New Haven: Yale University Press, 1952.

———. *Systematic Theology*, Vol. III. Chicago: University of Chicago Press, 1963. Especially Chapter 1, and "The Kingdom of God as the End of History."

Wei, Henry. *The Guiding Light of Lao Tze*. Wheaton, Ill.: Theosophical Publishing House, 1982.

Whitehead, Alfred North. *Adventures of Ideas*. New York: Macmillan, 1933; New York: Free Press, 1967.

For information about workshops, seminars, and lectures by Robert Moore and Douglas Gillette, other books by the authors or recommended by them, and audiotapes of Robert Moore's and Douglas Gillette's lectures, send your name and address to:

EarthMen Resources
P.O. Box 1034
Evanston, Ill. 60204

INDEX

abdication syndrome, 159–160, 170,
    171, 178, 182–184
    see also Weakling Abdicator
Abraham, 98–99
active imagination, 210–233, 235
    "as if" technique in, 230–233
    effects of, 222–224
    examples of, 219–223, 232–233
    imaging process in, 203, 214–218,
        219–222
    music for, 217, 219
    prayer in, 224–230
    pyramid icon in, 215–217, 219–221
Adler, Alfred, 25, 39–40, 264
admiration, 152, 229, 233–234
Africa, 67–71, 124, 185

Ahura-Mazda, 77, 99, 100, 101
Akhenaten, 130, 171–173, 288n
Akkad, 96–97
Allah, 101, 108
alpha males, 53–56, 109, 251
androgyny, 274
    radical, 19–20, 283n
Anglo-Saxons, 79–80, 173–174
Anima, 23, 105, 110, 117, 121, 155,
        203, 206, 266, 273–281
Animus, 23, 266, 273, 274–275
ankh, 129
Antigone (Sophocles), 161–162, 163
archetypes, 27, 38–56, 125, 149, 190,
        195, 204–205, 213, 253, 310n
    Anima and, 273–281

archetypes (*cont.*)
  bipolarity of, 39
  brain and, *see* brain
  convergence of, 52–53
  cross-cultural correspondence of,
    59–60
  definition of, 33–36
  identification with, 35–36, 208
  mature masculine, 10, 38–43, 44–48,
    49, 51–53, 191, 206–207, 233,
    234
  in psychotherapy, 206–207
  symbolic nature of, 52, 226–227
  triangular structure of, 38–48
  see also specific archetypes
Archetypes: A Natural History of the Self
  (Stevens), 49
Arjuna, 123, 209
Arthur, King, 172, 173–174
"as if" technique, 230–233
Assyria, 94–95, 97–98, 107, 214
Athens, Greece, 185, 186, 187
atomic energy, 123, 192–194, 307n
autonomous complexes, 31–33, 36–37
axis mundi, 52, 107, 155, 213, 224,
  252, 253
  in sacred kingship, 63–68, 83, 88,
    103, 110, 114, 116, 127, 231,
    234, 235, 295n
Aztecs, 89–90, 135

Ba'al, 98, 99, 100, 304n, 312n
Babylonia, 66, 97, 99, 142, 145, 196
beholding, 124, 129–133, 151, 230
Bible, 29–30, 117, 142, 161, 162, 168,
  248, 250, 304n, 307n
Big Bang, 194, 196, 198, 199
biology, postmodern, 195
Black Elk Speaks, 238–239
Blake, William, 10
blessing, 10, 129–130, 151, 230, 254
Blessing, The (Smalley and Trent), 129–
  130
bliss, Campbell's concept of, 167
body language, 53
Bolen, Jean, 285n–286n
borderline personality, 192
boys, 20, 145, 169, 204–205, 207,
  284n
Bradshaw, John, 245
Brahma, 76, 140, 196, 199

brain, 234, 274
  feminine vs. masculine, 20, 143–144
  limbic system of, 51, 268–272, 287n
  structure of, 49–52, 56, 60, 188,
    196, 217
Browning, Don, 149–150, 240–241
Buddhism, 9, 76, 80, 82, 140, 230
Bultmann, Rudolf, 307n

Campbell, Joseph, 167, 239
Carter, Jimmy, 173
Celtic Quest, A (Layard), 260
Celts, 79, 260
Center, 113, 114–121, 123, 145, 151,
  155, 252, 253
  in sacred kingship, 55, 63–64, 74,
    82, 83, 87–88, 94, 101, 102,
    114, 123, 237
Chamberlain, Neville, 173
chaos, 9, 116, 117–118, 136–140, 153
Charcot, Jean Martin, 33
Child, 203, 206, 309n
children, 21, 168–170, 204, 240, 253,
  302n
  family tyrants and, 166–167
  parental mirroring of, 129, 152,
    301n
  parents idealized by, 204–205
  traumas of, 32, 37, 201–202, 205
chimpanzees, 53–56, 233
China, 83–86, 87, 102, 117–118, 164,
  182, 214, 300n
Christianity, 9, 73, 76, 141–142, 196,
  199, 210–211, 237, 242, 307n
  sacred kingship in, 101–103, 105–
    107, 174, 186–187
  see also Jesus
cities, sacred, 63, 65, 83, 88, 91, 97,
  101, 114
Cody, Buffalo Bill, 168
collective unconscious, 32, 33, 34, 44,
  183, 192, 195
  archetypes in, *see* archetypes
Combat Myth, 96, 97, 142, 145, 196
complexes, 30–33, 37, 49, 161, 206,
  286n, 310n
  autonomous, 31–33, 36–37
confession, prayer of, 228
consciousness, 31, 140–146, 252
  brain and, 49, 143–144
  definition of, 32–33

Ego, 32, 45, 51, 114, 140–141, 143, 153
  feminine, 143–144
  language and, 30
  masculine, 140, 141–146
corporate world, 234, 247
  tyrants in, 166, 168
  weaklings in, 174–176, 177
cosmology, 198–200
  cyclic, 199
  postmodern, 194, 196, 198
creation myths, 29–30, 63, 67, 74, 91, 102, 119, 141–142, 196–197, 198–199
Creon, 161–162, 163, 166
cultural diffusion, 109

Dances with Wolves, 239
dancing the four quarters, 236–240, 250
David, King, 61, 101, 236, 237, 288n
David, the King, 236, 288n
Delphi, Greece, 201
democracy, 91, 96, 185–187
demons, 161, 185, 230
depth psychology, 23, 28–38, 59, 60, 86, 102, 115, 185, 195, 199–200, 207, 242, 306n
  terminology of, 29–38
  see also archetypes
Dharma, 76, 82, 83, 100, 114, 133, 140, 196, 252
dialogue, prayer of, 203, 218, 229–230
dictators, 108–109, 168, 189–190
disidentification, 36, 110, 186
  of sacred kingship, 94–101, 102–103, 110, 133
divine order, 62–68, 71, 74–75, 84–85, 86, 88–89, 91–92, 100, 102, 103, 105–107, 110, 133, 140, 199, 218, 232
  sacred vs. profane dimensions of, 62–63, 77, 83, 114, 118, 195–196
  see also axis mundi
dreams, 34, 49, 195, 200, 203–204, 207, 210, 226–227
Dreams: God's Forgotten Language (Sanford), 227
Dune (Herbert), 8

ecology, 36, 153, 168, 239, 243, 244
Edinger, Edward, 288n

Ego, 26, 30–45, 94, 99, 125–126, 142, 151, 159–161, 168–170, 174, 181, 186, 200, 206, 209, 245, 252, 273
  abdication syndrome in, 159–160, 170, 171, 178, 182–184
  active imagination and, 210, 211, 213
  archetypes and, 33, 35, 36, 38–45, 52
  brain and, 49, 51, 271
  consciousness of, 32, 45, 51, 114, 140–141, 143, 153
  definition of, 30–32
  development of, 169–170
  inflation of, 27, 44, 60, 152, 160, 163, 164, 168, 190–193, 228, 302n, 304n–305n
  male, 161, 189
  optimal functioning of, 160–161
  rationalism and, 188
  Shadow vs., 36–37, 38–39, 118
  splitting of, 32–33, 38–39, 170
  usurpation syndrome in, 159, 170
Ego-archetype axis, 60–61, 62, 102, 103, 107, 114, 115–117, 125–126, 150, 186, 192, 200, 228, 229, 231
Egypt, 77, 142–143, 183, 196
  creative vs. static culture of, 182, 184
  Gods and Goddesses of, 73, 74–75, 101–102, 118–121, 130, 141, 184, 254
  sacred kingship in, 60, 61–62, 70, 71–75, 95–96, 98, 100, 101–102, 107, 118–119, 129, 130, 143, 163, 171–173, 182, 183, 184, 214, 219–223, 253–254, 300n
Einstein, Albert, 188, 193, 307n
Eisler, Riane, 283n, 284n
elders, 25, 27, 70, 148, 224, 234
El Elyon, 98, 100, 293n
Eliade, Mircea, 62–63, 182
England, 107, 138–140
Enlightenment, 187–188
entropy, 198–199
Erikson, Erik, 24, 28, 34, 149–150, 240–241
Everly, George S., Jr., 271, 312n
evil, 117, 118, 303n

Eye of Horus, 130
Ezekiel, 209

family, tyrants in, 166–167, 201, 202
fathers, 201–203, 204–205, 309n
feminine energies, 20–24, 38, 72, 82,
110–111, 246–247, 253, 260–
263
Anima, 23, 105, 110, 117, 121, 155,
203, 206, 266, 273–281
of brain structure, 20, 143–144
patriarchy vs., 20–21, 25
Queen, 9, 105, 117, 169, 204, 205,
246, 260, 274, 275–277, 279,
280–281
of sacred queens, 53, 71, 75, 101,
119–121, 129, 173
feminists, 20, 246, 283n
Forsyth, Neil, 8–9
Frazer, Sir James, 62
free will, 31, 36, 161
French Revolution, 189
Freud, Sigmund, 28, 33–34, 35, 39,
201, 230, 240, 241, 264, 308n–
309n

Gabriel, Peter, 217
Gandhi, Mohandas K., 111, 240, 241
Geb, 119–121
gender identity, 19–25
gender differences and, 19–20, 23–
24, 25, 301n
generative man, 24, 35, 105, 109, 126,
145, 147–156, 167, 178, 183,
184, 192, 204, 218, 224, 234,
240, 243, 254
ideal vision of, 151–156, 237
procreative, 127–128
genetic factors, 9, 10, 24, 33, 53, 109,
234, 254, 287n
Gere, Richard, 236
Germany, 192
Gilmore, David, 24, 55, 147–149, 150,
301n
gnosis, 141, 254
Gnosticism, 185–186, 187, 196, 295n
Gods, Goddesses, 34, 63, 67, 72, 77,
86, 91–92, 96, 137, 185–186,
192, 214, 285n–286n
Egyptian, 73, 74–75, 101–102, 118–
121, 130, 141, 184, 254

Hindu, 76, 123, 140, 196, 199, 209,
237, 238
hubris vs., 161–163
King-, 74, 76, 79, 95, 97, 100, 101,
102, 112, 114, 117, 126, 129,
130, 133, 136, 183, 185, 186,
189, 211
procreativity of, 119–121, 126, 136
as projections, 185
Semitic, 30, 95, 97, 98, 99–101,
117, 123, 126, 135, 142, 293n,
294n, 297n, 304n, 312n
sun, 87, 97, 143, 300n
Golden Bough, The (Frazer), 62
Golding, William, 20
grandiosity, 20–21, 60, 152, 154, 177,
228, 302n
childhood, 168–170
hubris in, 161–163
Greeks, ancient, 62, 73, 76, 79, 101,
161–162, 163, 185, 186, 187,
201, 277, 278, 307n
Greenleaf, Robert, 247–250

Hammurabi, 97, 135, 300n
healing energy, 102, 105, 110
Hebrews, 30, 123–124, 129, 162, 217,
307n
sacred kingship of, 61, 62, 97, 98–
101, 102, 110, 142, 185, 237
heb sed festival, 75
Hegel, G.W.F., 43
heirs, 75, 129, 173
Heisenberg, Werner, 189, 307n
Herbert, Frank, 8
Hermeticism, 101, 185–186, 295n
Hero, 169, 207
Hesse, Hermann, 247–248
Hinduism, 117, 126, 230
Gods of, 76, 123, 140, 196, 199,
209, 237, 238
Hitler, Adolf, 163, 173, 183
Hittites, 98
Horus, 73, 74, 75, 118–119, 130, 254
Huang-Ti, 83–86
hubris, 161–163
humility, 151, 207, 224–225, 245
Hussein, Saddam, 163–164

Id, 34
idealization, 204–205

identification, 35–36, 208
   in sacred kingships, 60–61, 74–93,
      94–97, 98, 99–100, 101–
      102, 103, 105, 109–110, 133,
      142
idolatry, 211, 213
Incas, 92–93
India, 76–77, 79, 124, 237
Indians, North American, 10, 64, 185,
      215, 238–239, 244
Indo-Aryan diffusion, 75–76, 79, 98
inflation, Ego, 27, 44, 60, 152, 160,
      163, 164, 168, 190–193, 228,
      302n, 304n–305n
initiation rituals, 25–27, 105, 123–124,
      150, 184, 234, 279, 284n
   global, 239
inner voices, 200, 229–230
intercession, prayer of, 226
introjects, 204, 230, 309n
Iran, 77, 79, 108, 123, 163
   hostage crisis in, 173
Iraq, 163–164
Ireland, 246
Isis, 73
Islam, 9, 210, 211
Israel, ancient, 99–100
Israel, kibbutzim of, 23–24

Jacobi, Jolande, 196, 286n
James I, king of England, 138–140
Japan, 87–88
Jesus, 122, 151, 211, 237, 306n
   sacred kingship of, 101–105, 127,
      133, 142, 186–187, 199, 250,
      295n, 298n
Jonson, Ben, 138
Journey to the East (Hesse), 247–248
Judaism, 9, 186, 196–197, 210, 211
   see also Hebrews
Jung, Carl Gustav, 23, 28–29, 31–39,
      43, 45, 49, 51, 62, 115, 149,
      189, 190, 192, 195, 210, 227,
      246, 259–267

ka, 74, 129, 130
Kant, Immanuel, 188, 307n
Kennedy, John F., 10, 173
Khomeini, Ayatollah Ruhollah, 108,
      163
kibbutzim, 23–24

King, 10, 38, 40, 42, 44, 45, 52, 60,
      112–146, 148, 149, 163, 169,
      177, 264, 271, 275
   accessing, 104–105, 117, 178, 181–
      250
   as Center, 113, 114–121, 123, 145,
      151, 155, 252, 253
   extroverted vs. introverted energy of,
      113
   fathers as, 202
   inner, 151, 185–192, 235
   poles of, see Tyrant Usurper; Weakling
      Abdicator
   as Procreator, 113, 116, 126–133,
      145, 151, 156, 230, 252, 253
   projection of, 104, 160, 171, 178,
      190, 204, 211–213
   qualities of, 94, 103, 214, 217–218,
      230, 254
   return of, 8–10, 251–256
   as Structurer, 113, 116, 133–146,
      151, 156, 252, 253
   as Transforming Vessel, 113, 116,
      122–126, 151, 156, 252, 253
   see also sacred kingship
King, Martin Luther, Jr., 111
King-Gods, 74, 76, 79, 95, 97, 100,
      101, 102, 112, 114, 117, 126,
      129, 130, 133, 136, 183, 185,
      186, 189, 211
King's Two Bodies, 107
Knights Templars, 244
Kohut, Heinz, 28, 296n, 301n, 302n
Korea, 86–87, 102
Krishna, 76, 123, 209

language, 30, 49, 53, 133
Last Temptation of Christ, The, 103,
      217
laws, 97, 115, 116, 133, 135–136, 142,
      153
Layard, John, 260
Libido, 35, 36, 61, 114, 122, 126, 132,
      189, 191, 200, 206, 214, 228,
      252, 253
Long, Huey, 187
Lord of the Flies (Golding), 20
Lord of the Four Quarters, 55, 61, 76,
      96–97
Lord of the Four Quarters (Perry), 62
Louis XIV, king of France, 105

Lover, 10, 38, 44, 110, 112, 126, 146, 148, 214, 239, 242, 260, 264, 266, 271, 274–275, 277, 278–279, 301n
  brain structure and, 51–52
  poles of, 41, 42, 45, 278, 280
  in sacred kingship, 60, 71, 75, 80, 93, 94
Loyola, Ignatius, 105
Luther, Martin, 240, 241

Ma'at, 74, 83, 100, 114, 118, 133, 137, 140, 184, 196
MacLean, Paul, 49, 268, 269–270
magic, 71, 83, 93, 99, 100, 102, 105, 136, 299n
Magician, 10, 38, 44, 51, 52, 110, 112, 146, 148, 239, 241, 260, 264, 266, 271, 274–275, 277, 279
  poles of, 41, 42, 45, 278, 280
  in sacred kingship, 60, 71–72, 74, 76, 80, 84–85, 94, 97, 100
male bonding, 150, 233–234, 235, 244
male Ego, 161, 189
mandalas, 82, 291n
manhood, cultural definitions of, 24, 55, 147–149, 150, 151, 184, 202, 203, 234
Manhood in the Making (Gilmore), 24, 147
manic-depressive disorder, 39
Marduk, 97, 142, 145, 196
marriages, 200, 202, 227
  in sacred kingship, 68, 71, 119–121, 124, 173
  of tyrants, 166–167
  of weaklings, 176–178
masques, courtly, 138–140
materialistic reductionism, 188, 189, 192, 201
maturity, 148, 169, 183, 190, 229, 254, 303n, 306n
  archetypes and, 10, 38–43, 44–48, 49, 51–53, 191, 206–207, 233, 234
  definition of, 38
  immaturity vs., 20–21, 38
  initiation rituals in, 25–27, 105, 123–124, 150, 184, 234, 239, 279, 284n
Maya, 88–91, 109, 182

men, 9–10, 19–27, 60–61, 148, 150–151, 200, 214, 237–238, 246–247, 253
  admiration of, 152, 229, 233–234
  caring by, 110–111, 121
  gender identity and, 19–25
  psychotherapy and, 201–209
  responsibility in, 103–104
men's movement, 10
merging, 274, 301n
Mesopotamia, 55, 77, 94–99, 142, 183
Middle Ages, 62, 105, 174, 187
Miller, Alice, 21, 28, 312n
Millon, Theodore, 39
mirroring, 129, 152, 301n
modernity, 25–27, 183, 187–197, 201
  Ego inflation in, 190–193
  postmodernity vs., see postmodernity
Modern Psychopathology (Millon), 39
Mohammed, 108, 217
Moses, 123, 135, 142
mothers, 21, 145, 203, 204–205, 280–281, 309n, 312n
mountain, sacred, 52, 63, 74, 83, 86, 97, 114, 123, 142–143, 254
  see also pyramids
Moyers, Bill, 239
multiple-personality disorder, 32
mysticism, 118, 194, 195, 199
myth, 28, 34, 35, 44, 59, 62, 101, 102, 103, 141–143, 196, 213–214, 254, 260, 266, 277, 312n
  Combat, 96, 97, 142, 145, 196
  cosmological, 198–199
  creation, 29–30, 63, 67, 74, 91, 102, 119, 141–142, 196–197, 198–199
  definition of, 29–30
  demythologization of, 188, 307n
  tyrants in, 161–163
  world, 239
  see also Gods, Goddesses

naming, 30, 102, 141–142
narcissitic personality disorder, 170
Navajo, 10, 64
Nazism, 192, 244
Neferrohu, 136–137, 184
Nicholas of Cusa, 196
Niebuhr, Reinhold, 9, 25, 284n
Nixon, Richard, 107

nuclear power plants, 123
Nut, 119–121

Old Enemy, The (Forsyth), 8–9
Osiris, 73, 74, 75, 101–102

Pak Hyŏkkŏse, 86, 102
Palestine, 98, 99–101, 173
paranoia, 167–168, 170, 302n, 304n–305n
parental introjects, 204, 230, 309n
patriarchy, 20–21, 25
Paul, Saint, 117, 122, 133, 295n
Perry, John Weir, 62, 206–207
Persia, 77, 79, 80, 101, 108, 123
persona, false, 231
personality disorders, 39–40, 170, 231
personal unconscious, 32, 33, 49
petition, prayer of, 224–228
Planck, Max, 194, 196
Plato, 185
play, 237, 240–241, 252
pleroma, 186, 196
Portmann, Adolf, 195
postmodernity, 9, 193–197, 198, 213–214, 215, 217
  sacred and profane in, 195–197
power, 105, 110, 125, 152, 204, 281
  abuse of, 9–10, 20–21, 24–25, 27, 284n
  disempowerment vs., 104, 177, 178, 190
  stewardship of, 24–25, 103, 111, 153, 156, 243–250, 254
  see also Tyrant Usurper; Weakling Abdicator
prayer, 203, 218, 224–230
presidents, U.S., 10, 104, 107, 173, 191
priests, 63, 67, 70, 79–80, 96, 97, 123–124
Primordial Hill, 74, 114, 142, 254
Procreator, 113, 116, 126–133, 145, 151, 156, 230, 252, 253
  Gods and Goddesses as, 119–121, 126, 136
  sacred kings as, 53, 60, 71, 75, 93, 94, 121, 126–127, 129, 173
projection, 37–38, 39, 185
  of King, 104, 160, 171, 178, 190, 204, 211–213

onto parents, 204–205
onto sacred kingships, 60–61, 109, 182, 183, 184, 190
Protestantism, 187, 210–211, 242
psychotherapy, 131, 154, 201–209, 227, 230, 242
Ptah, 102, 141
pyramids, 52, 88, 89, 114, 251, 253–254
  in active imagination, 215–217, 219–221
  symbolism of, 44–48, 142–143, 266

Queen, 9, 105, 117, 169, 204, 205, 246, 260, 274, 275–277, 279, 280–281
queens, sacred, 53, 71, 75, 101, 119–121, 129, 173
Quetzalcoatl, 91–92, 135

Ra, 74–75
radical androgyny, 19–20, 283n
rage, 32, 170, 176, 177–178, 231–232
rain kings, 52, 70–71, 185
rationalism, 187–189, 192, 193, 201
regicide, 189–191
Renaissance, 62, 105
repetition compulsion, 37, 201–202
repression, 32, 33, 39, 187–192, 202, 204, 231, 252
Return of the King, The (Tolkien), 8
return of the repressed, 192
Roosevelt, Franklin, 107, 108
Roots of Renewal in Myth and Madness (Perry), 62, 206–207
Russia, 79, 183, 189

sacred kingship, 52–56, 59–111, 117, 140, 151, 154, 175, 218, 251
  abdicated populace and, 182–184
  in Africa, 69–71, 124, 185
  alpha males vs., 53–56, 109, 251
  of Anglo-Saxons, 79–80, 173–174
  axis mundi constellated by, 63–68, 83, 88, 103, 110, 114, 116, 127, 231, 234, 235, 295n
  of Aztecs, 89–90
  beholding by, 124, 129–133, 151, 230
  blessing by, 10, 129–130, 151, 230, 254

sacred kingship (*cont.*)
breakdowns of, 184
as center, 55, 63–64, 74, 82, 83, 87–88, 94, 101, 102, 114, 123, 237
chaos averted by, 9, 116, 117–118, 136–140, 153
in China, 83–86, 87, 102, 182, 214
Christian, 101–103, 105–107, 174, 186–187
cities of, 63, 65, 83, 88, 91, 97, 101, 114
containment of, 123–125
creative vs. static culture of, 73, 181–184
dancing the four quarters in, 236–237
of dictators, 108–109
disidentified with King, 94–101, 102–103, 110, 133
divine order evoked by, *see* divine order
early phases of, 181–182
in Egypt, 60, 61–62, 70, 71–75, 95–96, 98, 100, 101–102, 107, 118–119, 129, 130, 143, 163, 171–173, 182, 183, 184, 214, 219–223, 253–254, 300*n*
healing energy of, 102, 105, 110
of Hebrews, 61, 62, 97, 98–101, 102, 110, 142, 185, 237
of Hittites, 98
identified with King, 60–61, 74–93, 94–97, 98, 99–100, 101–102, 103, 105, 109–110, 133, 142
of Incas, 92–93
in India, 76–77, 79, 124
individual's projection onto, 60–61, 109, 182, 183, 184, 190
in Iran, 108
in Japan, 87–88
of Jesus, 101–105, 127, 133, 142, 186–187, 199, 250, 295*n*, 298*n*
in Korea, 86–87, 102
laws given by, 97, 115, 116, 133, 135–136, 142, 153
Lover in, 60, 71, 75, 80, 93, 94
Magician in, 60, 71–72, 74, 76, 80, 84–85, 94, 97, 100
marriages in, 68, 71, 119–121, 124, 173
of Maya, 88–91, 109, 182

in Mesopotamia, 55, 94–99, 142, 183
modern, 105–111
in Palestine, 98, 99–101, 173
in Persia, 77, 79, 80, 101, 108, 123
procreation in, 53, 60, 71, 75, 93, 94, 121, 126–127, 129, 173
of rain kings, 52, 70–71, 185
ritual sacrifice of, 71, 75, 80, 82, 83, 117, 132, 298*n*
rituals of, 63, 64, 68, 83, 87, 97, 99
as servant leaders, 61, 94–101, 105, 133, 250
study of, 62
taboos imposed on, 70, 77, 123, 124, 129
in Tibet, 82, 107, 124
of Toltecs, 89, 91–92
as Transforming Vessel, 122–123
Warrior in, 60, 71, 74–75, 76, 79, 80, 90–91, 94, 96–98
world building by, 67–68, 94, 96, 110, 145, 154, 237, 252
sacrifice, 103, 132–133, 154
ritual, of sacred king, 71, 75, 80, 82, 83, 117, 132, 298*n*
willing, 103
Sanford, John, 227
Sargon of Akkad, 96–97
Satan, 101–102, 162–163
science, 28, 30, 59, 188, 189, 198
postmodern, 193–195
Scorsese, Martin, 103
Self, 32, 52, 115–117, 145, 150, 182, 259–267, 281, 302*n*
collective, 192–193, 196
masculine, 44–48, 56, 60, 117, 143–144, 189, 204, 211, 213, 215, 217
"Servant as Leader, The" (Greenleaf), 248
servant leadership, 243–250, 254
of sacred kingship, 61, 94–101, 105, 133, 250
skills needed by, 249–250
Set, 73, 75, 118–119, 184
sexual harassment, 164, 174, 177
Shadow, 38–44, 45, 203, 204, 206, 244, 266, 273–274, 283*n*, 297*n*, 303*n*
bipolar, 38–39, 44, 160, 170
collective, 118
definition of, 36–38

Shadow King, 159–178, 191–192, 201, 207–209, 228, 251–252
  see also Tyrant Usurper; Weakling Abdicator
shamans, 63, 64, 67, 70, 238–239, 279
Shamash, 97, 135, 142
shame, 244–245
Shiva, 76, 237, 238
Siegel, Bernie, 131–132
Smalley, Gary, 129–130
Socrates, 185, 186
Solomon, King, 61, 100, 101, 141, 288n
Sophocles, 161–162, 163
space, sacred vs. profane, 63, 74, 77, 83, 195–196
Stalin, Joseph, 163
Stevens, Anthony, 49, 56
stewardship, 24–25, 103, 111, 153, 156, 243–250, 254
"Structural Forms of the Feminine Psyche" (Wolff), 263, 275–279
Structurer, 113, 116, 133–146, 151, 156, 252, 253
Sumeria, 96
sword of gnosis, 141–142
synchronistic events, 227, 243
synthesis, 240–241

taboos, 70, 77, 123, 124, 129
Tao, 86, 102, 114, 117–118, 133, 140, 196, 252
teh, 83, 86
Teutonic tribes, 76, 79, 192
thanksgiving, prayer of, 228–229
Tiamat, 97, 142, 145, 196
Tibet, 82, 107, 124
Tillich, Paul, 43
time, 88, 196, 198
  sacred vs. profane, 63, 74, 77, 83, 195–196
Tolkien, J.R.R., 8
Toltecs, 89, 91–92
Torah, 97, 100, 114, 124, 133, 140, 186, 196, 295n, 297n, 306n
Transforming Vessel, 113, 116, 122–126, 151, 156, 252, 253
Transpersonal Other, 26–27, 61, 150, 169, 192, 209, 279, 303n, 305n
traumas, childhood, 32, 37, 201–202, 205
tree, sacred, 52, 63, 88, 98, 107, 114, 127, 231

Trent, John, 129–130
Tyrant Holdfast, 167
Tyrant Usurper, 40, 42, 45, 159–170, 173, 177–178, 182, 183, 201, 202, 252, 280–281
  grandiosity in, 20–21, 60, 152, 154, 161–163, 168–170, 177, 228
  historical examples of, 163–164
  modern examples of, 163–168, 248–249
  mythological examples of, 161–163
  in psychotherapy, 208–209

unconscious, 33–38, 114, 143, 153, 186, 200, 210, 213, 229
  collective, 32, 33, 34, 44, 183, 192, 195
  personal, 32, 33, 49
  psychotherapy and, 201–209
  see also Shadow
usurpation syndrome, 159–170

Vikings, 79

Warrior, 10, 38, 44, 51, 52, 80, 110, 112, 125, 145–146, 148, 152, 239, 241, 244, 260, 264, 271, 274–275, 277–279, 281, 302n
  poles of, 39, 40, 42, 45, 278–279, 280
  in sacred kingship, 60, 71, 74–75, 76, 79, 80, 90–91, 94, 96–98
Washington, George, 107
Waters of Life, 127
Weakling Abdicator, 40, 42, 45, 159–160, 171–178, 201, 252
  characteristics of, 174–176, 177, 228
  historical examples of, 171–174
  marriages of, 176–178
  modern examples of, 173, 174–178
  in psychotherapy, 209
Whitehead, Alfred North, 43
Winnicott, D. W., 28
Wolf, Ernest, 302n
Wolff, Toni, 260–263, 275–279
women, 9, 19–27, 56, 105, 110–111, 121, 246–247, 275, 280–281, 283n, 284n
  see also feminine energies
women's movement, 246
words, 30, 102, 105, 107, 142–143

workplace, 245–246
   tyrants in, 164–166, 167–168, 248–249
world building, 67–68, 94, 96, 110, 145, 154, 237, 252
World Tree, 88, 114, 231, 295n
Wotan (Odin), 79, 192

Yahweh, 30, 99–101, 117, 123, 126, 142, 294n, 297n
Yeats, William Butler, 52

ziggurats, 97, 142–143, 215
Zoroastrianism, 9, 77, 101